The Voyage of the 'Frolic'

PERSIA

HINDU KUSH
Kabul

AFGHANISTAN

PUNJAB

TIBET

ARABIA

Indus R.

SIND

Delhi

Ganges R.

H I N D U S T A N

Chambal

MALWA

Ahmadabad

Indore

Ghazipur

Patna

Ganges R.

BENGAL

Calcutta

Damaun

Arabian

Sea

Bombay

INDIA

Goa

Bay
of
Bengal

10

Madras

Malwa opium
bound for China

CEYLON

0

0   100   200   300   400   500

Sea miles

Indian   Ocea

60   70   80

Map of South and East Asia, showing the route of the *Frolic* in the opium trade, 1845–50. Drawn by S. F. Manning.

The Voyage

New England Merchants
and the Opium Trade

Thomas N. Layton

STANFORD UNIVERSITY PRESS, STANFORD, CALIFORNIA

Stanford University Press
Stanford, California
© 1997 by Thomas N. Layton
Printed in the United States of America

CIP data appear at the end of the book

Published with the assistance of
the Edward M. Kahn Memorial Fund

To my father,
Laurence Laird Layton, Ph.D.,
for his encouragement and support

Acknowledgments

This book was researched and written during a 1989–90 sabbatical year granted by San Jose State University. Additional funding for research was supplied by a grant from the California Department of Parks and Recreation and by donations from my father, Dr. Laurence L. Layton, my sister, Deborah Layton, and Michael Cartmell.

I have drawn heavily on the Augustine Heard Papers curated by the Special Collections Department, Baker Library, Harvard Business School. I thank Florence Lathrop, Director of Special Collections, and Elise Thal Calvi for helping to make my two-month visit there both pleasant and productive. My work at Harvard was additionally facilitated by Dr. Stephen Williams, Professor of Anthropology at the Peabody Museum. During my two-week stay in Baltimore, Catherine Chandler and James A. Knowles helped me explore Fells Point, while Mace and Bobbie Miyasaki supplied a bedroom, hot meals, and a lively family life.

The original illustrations scattered throughout this volume are the work of Samuel F. Manning of Camden, Maine. I thank Sam for persevering with me throughout the many discussions and sketches leading to illustrations that are as historically correct as we could make them.

Colleagues at a number of institutions supplied important information and useful leads, helping me bring this book to completion. They include Dr. H. A. Crosby Forbes, Curator of Asian Export Art, John Koza, Librarian, and Carl Crossman at the Peabody Essex Museum of

Salem; Karl Kortum, Founder, Richard O. Everett, Curator of Exhibits, and Irene Stachura, Reference Librarian, National Maritime Museum; Katherine Griffin, Reference Librarian, and Chris Steele, Curator of Photographs, Massachusetts Historical Society; Michael Raines, Harvard University Archives; Dr. Jacques Downs, University of New England; Gary Boyd Roberts, Massachusetts Historical Genealogical Society; Thomas Hollowak and Thomas Cotter, Baltimore City Division of Archives; Mary Markey, Reference Librarian, Baltimore City Life Museums; Mike Chalk, Baltimore City Registry of Wills; Stanleigh Bry, Librarian, Society for California Pioneers; Dr. Stephen Kwan, Karl Lueck, Dr. Jan English-Lueck, and Patricia Dunning, San Jose State University; Drs. Adrian and Mary Praetzellis, Sonoma State University; Daniel Foster, California Department of Forestry; Dr. Peter Schultz, Dr. Glenn Farris, John W. Foster, and Robert Orlins, California Department of Parks and Recreation; Mark Rawitsch, Director, Mendocino College Willits Center; Daniel Taylor, Director, Mendocino County Museum; Suzanne Abel-Vidor, Director, and Keith Whitewolf James, Pomo Cultural Consultant, Grace Hudson Museum; Kate Magruder, Ukiah Players Theatre; Linda Noel, independent poet; L. Thomas Frye, Curator of History, Oakland Museum; Dr. Victoria Patterson, Mendocino County Office of Education; Dorothy Bear and Megan Coddington, Mendocino Historical Research, Inc.; Lila Lee, Mendocino County Historical Society; Dr. Julia Costello, Foothill Resources Ltd.; Dr. Peter Fay, California Institute of Technology; Kevin Foster, Maritime Historian, National Park Service; and James Delgado, Executive Director, Vancouver Maritime Museum.

I also acknowledge the following independent scholars who shared information derived from decades of research: John G. Earle of Easton, Maryland; James A. Knowles of Baltimore, Maryland; Richard Tooker of San Francisco, California; Amelie Elkinton of Carmel, California; Virginia Steele Wood of Washington, D.C.; and Helen Pierce of Swansea, Massachusetts.

Early drafts of this manuscript were read and commented upon by a number of friends and colleagues: Karl Kortum, Dr. H. A. Crosby Forbes, James Delgado, Samuel F. Manning, Dr. Jacques Downs, Dr. James Freeman, Dwight D. Simons, Richard Carlson, Edith Smith, Dr. Laurence L. Layton, and D. A. Weaver. The final draft was professionally edited and substantially improved by Ruhama Veltfort.

At Stanford University Press I thank Muriel Bell, Senior Editor, for nominating this book for publication and for shepherding it through production. Laura Bloch, Associate Editor, made important suggestions regarding content and organization.

Fifteen California wreck divers generously allowed me to study their collections from the *Frolic* shipwreck, and most of them have since donated those collections to the *Frolic* Repository at the Mendocino County Museum: David Buller, Steven Buller, Cliff Craft, Louie Fratis, Patrick Gibson, Dale Hartesveldt, James Kennon, Vilho Kosonen, Vic LaFountaine, Bruce Lanham, Richard Lanham, Patrick Philpott, Larry Pierson, Dr. Kenneth Prewitt, and Dr. Paul Selchau.

Finally, I thank the descendants of the historical characters in this book who shared information and photographs: Francis D. Everett, Jr., Richard O. Everett, Marion Everett Gallagher, Morris Earle, Cecily M. Johnson, Bazil S. Dixwell, Douglas Dixwell Morrison, Eleanor Dixwell Morrison, Stephanie Dixwell Quigley, and Arnold W. Knauth.

Contents

Figures

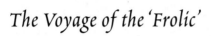

The Voyage of the 'Frolic'

Point Cabrillo, 1850

Keetana pulled the otter skin cape closely around his shoulders and gazed at the sailing vessel wedged in the rocks. With each wave she rolled, her great masts arcing across the sky, her sails snapping in the wind. Now and then her creaking moans were punctuated by the sharp crack of breaking timber. Keetana remembered a whale he had found washed up on the beach three winters ago. Its long black carcass, too, had rolled with each wave.

Keetana had followed the bearded men across the bluff from the sand bar at Big River, just as he had followed the cloud of screaming seagulls to the dead whale. He had watched as they opened the vessel's hatch and floated scores of boxes and barrels to the beach. The men had remained for three days, cutting packs from the canvas sails and loading them with treasures. The first night they had huddled on the beach without a fire, but on the morning of the second day Keetana had called to them from the bluff and presented their leader with a small hollowed-out log filled with hot coals.

The men were darker than Mexicanos—like Indians—and their language was a little different too, just as his mother's Yokaya speech had been different from his father's Mitom. They had seemed appreciative, but Keetana knew that men without women could be dangerous, and he had not revealed the location of Buldam village in the redwood grove overlooking Big River. Instead, he had directed them to the trail over the mountains to the valley where they would find Juan Parker, the nearest white man.

Now a pile of smoldering ashes lay where the sailors had built their driftwood fire. Hundreds of broken long-

Figure 1. Keetana's band of Mitom Pomo salvage some of the *Frolic*'s cargo of China trade goods, early August 1850. Original illustration by S. F. Manning.

necked bottles surrounded the fire pit, and flies were sucking the last sweetness from the sticky blue and white ceramic jars.

This year had been particularly good for the people. The burden baskets were almost filled with dried abalone, mussel, and chiton meats, and the young people had already made three trips carrying these delicacies over the ridge trail to Tsaka, the winter village in the Valley of the Gnats, two days distant. On their last return, they had reported that the tanoaks surrounding Three Chop Village—the midway point on the trail—were heavy with green acorns. In a moon, maybe a bit longer, Keetana would urge the people to leave the coast and travel to the redwood bark houses at Three Chop Village to begin acorn gathering. From there, they would carry many loads to fill the granaries at Tsaka.

After the harvest, there would be time for visiting and ceremony. The mornings would reverberate with the thud of women's pestles as they smashed acorns into meal. Later they would add dried shellfish meats to flavor the steaming baskets of stone-boiled mush.

Now, turning away from the ship, Keetana looked south toward the bluff where the women had scraped this year's accumulation of coyote salt—evaporated sea spray—from Coyote's salt hole. His mouth watered as he thought of nibbling a fist-size salt cake between bites of roasted meat. Horny old Coyote had taken the first salt to buy the favors of an Eastern woman, and even in Keetana's youth the old people still remembered trading coyote salt to the Yokaya for glassy black obsidian. The Yokaya brought obsidian over the mountains from the quarries at Clear Lake, but the people had not had any since the Mexicanos had begun stealing young men and women from there and taking them south to the mission at Sonoma.

Keetana glanced at the pile of broken green bottles the sailors had left. They could be flaked into arrow tips every bit as sharp as obsidian, and the sticky blue and white porcelain jars could be used to make clamshell bead money—for the Mexicanos had also interrupted the trade in clamshells from the south.

A loud clanging noise shattered Keetana's reflection. Two youngsters were beating the ship's bell with rocks. He turned to view the treasures carried up from the beach. His wife had a fringed cape over her shoulders like a Russian woman. Granddaughter pointed at the green beast embroidered across it and shrieked in excitement. Eldest daughter was taking yellow fruit from a porcelain jar. She placed a small piece into her baby's mouth and licked the syrup dripping from her hand. Her husband opened a brass-bound wooden box and found another smaller one inside. Keetana's younger daughter folded soggy rolls of colored

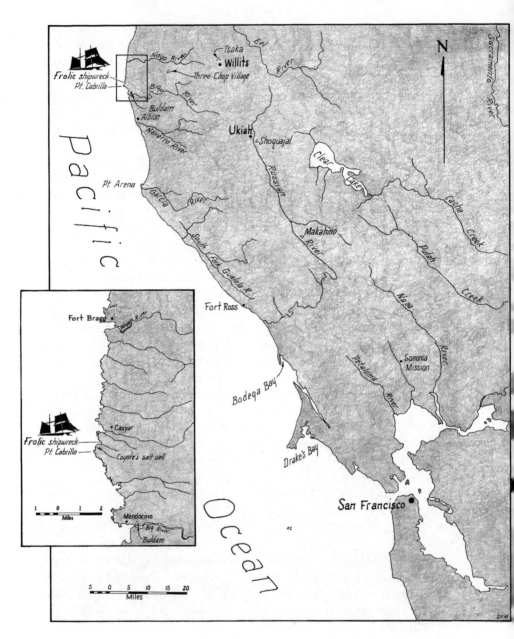

Figure 2. Map of northern California and the *Frolic* wreck site. Drawn by
S. F. Manning.

cloth into her basket, her hands stained red and blue from the dripping dyes. This fall, after the acorn harvest, but before the rains brought salmon up the streams from the ocean, he would work some of this colorful material into his dance costume. He imagined his feather skirt edged in purple cloth, the fringe of abalone pendants clacking in rhythm with the boom of the foot drum.

Keetana decided to host a trade feast in the fall. It was good to share bounty with the other villages. You could never tell when you might need something from them.

⚜

Keetana is, of course, a fictional character, but he knows the kinds of things that a 37-year-old leader of a Mitom Pomo community might reasonably have known in 1850. Pomo people were inveterate travelers, making regular trips to the coast to gather shellfish and to distant villages to participate in trade feasts and to exchange news.

Keetana would have had knowledge of both the Russians, who occupied Fort Ross from 1811 to 1841, and the Mexicans, who established the Sonoma Mission in 1823. The Russians conducted an active trade with neighboring Pomo tribelets, their Aleut otter hunters living with Pomo women just outside the fort's palisade.

Pomo contacts with Mexicans were more intense. Pomo people were often captured and brought to the Sonoma Mission by force. Following secularization in 1833, mission lands were distributed to private ranchers, and many Pomo returned to their home villages, bringing detailed information about the Mexicans and a knowledge of Spanish vocabulary.

Tsaka village was located about two miles northwest of present-day Willits, at the edge of what the local Mitom people called the "Valley of the Gnats." Buldam, their summer home, was located near present-day Mendocino. Archaeological excavations at Three Chop Village, midway between Tsaka and the coast, have yielded fragments of arrow tips flaked from bottle glass and beads ground from blue and white porcelain ginger jars, salvaged by Mitom Pomo people from the *Frolic* shipwreck in 1850. The dark-skinned sailors from the *Frolic* (Lascars from western India and Malays from modern Indonesia) spoke Portuguese, the trade language employed from Bombay to Macao. The story of "coyote salt" comes from John Hudson's ethnographic manuscript No. 20097, courtesy of the Grace Hudson Museum, Ukiah, California.

The traditional lifeway of Keetana's people would not last long after the *Frolic* shipwreck. In 1852 a lumber mill began operations at the mouth of Big River near Buldam. By 1857 Keetana and his people were scattered, some driven onto the Mendocino Indian Reservation near Fort Bragg and the remainder to the reservation at Round Valley.

$\mathcal{I}$ntroduction

Three Chop Village

THE PREVIOUS SPRING, each bounce of a bulldozer blade had left a washboard gouge in the moist clay of Road 200. Now, in late summer 1984, the gouges had dried to concrete hardness. Driving slowly to Three Chop Village, we bounced from ridge to ridge. When we accelerated, the bumps merged into machine gun chatter, amplified to a roar under the steel roof of the university carryall. Forty minutes on this road carried us up steep slopes from the heat of the canyon bottom to a long, sinuous redwood-forested divide known as Three Chop Ridge.

Just below the crest of that ridge, my archaeology students were excavating Pomo Indian house depressions. Each of these had once served as the foundation for a conical hut made of broad slabs of redwood bark. The students had found the expected stone tools flaked from obsidian and chert, but they had also found fingernail-size fragments of Chinese porcelain. I had not expected this. The subsequent chapters of this book were researched and written in an effort to trace the connections that brought blue and white Chinese potsherds to Pomo Indian houses on a remote ridge in Mendocino County, California.

Scholarly research often leads one down unexpected paths. In its broadest frame, this volume is about mid-nineteenth-century commerce. It is the story of New England merchants, Baltimore clippers, opium traders, and finally, a rich cargo of Chinese goods bound for Gold Rush San Francisco. The story begins and ends in the territory of the Mitom Pomo Indians on the rugged Mendocino County coast of northern California, but the interconnecting trail of events leads virtually around the world. Since I began intending merely to describe the prehistory of the Northern Pomo, it is only fair to explain how this story has taken me so far afield.

Archaeologists choose research areas for many reasons, some of which are purely expedient. When I was hired by San Jose State University in 1978, my prior research had been in the deserts of northwestern Nevada and southeastern Iran. Continuing research in either of these areas seemed impractical at a commuter school where most students held jobs and were supporting families. I needed to develop an archaeological program that would be more accessible to them.

During my first semester at San Jose State I was urged to teach a field class in archaeology. This was at a time of rapid residential and industrial growth in San Jose and its environs, popularly known as Silicon Valley. This had led to conflict among commercial archaeologists, land developers, and the local American Indian community, with each group attempting to protect, exploit, control, or ignore archaeological resources. In this politicized environment the only possible site for an archaeological field class would have to be one that was being destroyed by development. Consequently, the first field class I offered involved a seemingly endless succession of Saturdays spent screening bulldozed tailings from a prehistoric midden destroyed during construction of a swimming pool in East San Jose.

Privately, I felt we were wasting our time, and at least one of my students must have guessed my sentiments. One hot afternoon, Tony Musladin, a semi-retired physician, told me he had collected a pestle and an obsidian projectile point from his property near Albion on the central Mendocino County coast of northern California. Tony asked if I would like to plan an archaeological project there. I jumped at the opportunity, for while the prehistory of the central Mendocino County coast was virtually unknown, there was an extensive published literature describing the late-nineteenth- and early-twentieth-century lifeways of the Northern Pomo who had lived in this region.

At the time of first contact, Northern Pomo tribelets occupied winter villages in interior valleys of the North Coast Range, well inland of the coastal redwood strip. Apparently, the narrow strip of coastal prairie and the adjacent redwood forest provided too little year-round food and too much inclement weather to attract permanent occupation. Northern Pomo groups made seasonal expeditions to the coast to hunt and to gather shellfish and other coastal foods. Archaeological sites along the coast would thus reveal evidence of short occupations by Indian people engaged in a narrow range of specialized economic activities.

The sharp-edged tools the Northern Pomo used were "flaked" from hard, glassy stone such as obsidian or chert. Because there was no such stone suitable for flaking tools anywhere along this section of coast, Indian people would need to bring previously manufactured tools with them. If this was indeed true, these discontinuous seasonal occupations, specialized activities, and carefully curated premanufactured tools would simplify the archaeological record and make it easier to define discrete archaeological components, the basic building blocks of cultural chronologies.

During four summer field seasons (1980–83) my students excavated three culturally stratified sites, and we were able to develop a chronology of seven cultural assemblages dating from circa 3500 B.C. to late prehistoric times. Although these components appeared to represent occupations by both Pomoan and earlier Yukian-speaking groups, we would need to apply the "direct historical approach"[1] to determine their specific ethnolinguistic identity. This approach required that we identify distinctive tools or artifacts from early historic sites of known ethnographic affiliation. These tools or artifacts would serve as cultural markers, which could then be traced back through earlier deposits to form a continuous chain of evidence leading into the remote past.

One morning in late July 1983, Dan Foster, an archaeologist with the California Department of Forestry, visited our Albion excavations. Dan was responsible for management and protection of archaeological sites throughout the vast logging region extending inland from Albion, and during our conversation he encouraged me to expand my research in that direction. I asked Dan to find me two mid-nineteenth-century archaeological sites, one clearly within Northern Pomo territory, and the other in Coast Yuki territory. I wanted village sites where circular house depressions were still visible. The contents of observably discrete houses would be minimally mixed with earlier deposits and would thus provide a reliable baseline for applying the direct historical approach.

Dan suggested we visit four possible sites. A week later, we drove north from Albion along mist-shrouded Highway 1. We turned inland just south of Fort Bragg, and, ascending a series of wave-cut beach terraces of Pleistocene age, we entered a conifer forest. Unfortunately, a century and a half of commercial logging, road building, and construction had taken their toll. The first site lay beneath a baseball diamond at a state conservation camp, the second was under the intersection of two rutted logging roads, and the third had been leveled in the late nineteenth century for a logging camp.

It was early afternoon when Dan parked the car near a deep road cut and led me into a tanoak grove on a level bench just below the crest of Three Chop Ridge. As my eyes adjusted to the subdued light, I began to comprehend the unnatural undulation of the ground surface, and during the next hour I counted seventeen distinct circular house depressions and nine fainter ones. These depressions, ranging from ten to twelve feet in diameter, were quite shallow, none more than ten inches deep. Several had large tanoak trees growing within them. Scraping away the thickly matted duff of rotting leaves I found obsidian and chert flakes—unmistakable signs of stone tool manufacture.

This site appeared to be an undisturbed late prehistoric village containing distinct house depressions. It was clearly within the territory of the Northern Pomo and thus would be an ideal place to apply the direct historical approach to Northern Pomo prehistory. Moreover, its location—close to the midway point of a major ridge system linking the Mitom Pomo home territory, near present-day Willits, with the coast—would make it an ideal spot to document interior-to-coast traffic. The village had been recorded in 1970 by a public-spirited avocational archaeologist, and it bore the unmemorable California site designation CA-MEN-790.[2] That fall, my father insisted our site needed "a real name," and so we named it Three Chop Village.

In June 1984, I returned to Three Chop Village for a one-day test excavation with a crew of three undergraduate students. We chose a single house depression near the outside edge of the bench, designated it House 1, and with stakes and string divided it into four quadrants. We scraped away the leaf duff from the northeast quadrant of the house and troweled down through six inches of rich black archaeological deposit. Passing this deposit through a one-eighth-inch mesh screen, we recovered a small handful of chert and obsidian flakes, a chert arrow tip, a small fragment of porcelain, and two slivers of green bottle glass.

At the time I suspected that the house deposit predated European contact and thought the fragments of porcelain and bottle glass, all smaller than thumbnail size, might have been dumped recently by loggers.

A month later, we began our final summer field season at Albion and I assigned three undergraduate veterans of earlier field classes to complete the excavation of House 1. Since the camp at Three Chop Village was a two-hour drive from our Albion base camp, I tried to visit my students every other day. On the first day they found four more pieces of porcelain and another fragment of green bottle glass. On my next visit, they showed me more fragments of coarse white porcelain, some bearing bits of oriental design in blue.

A few days later, while driving to Three Chop Village, my colleague Dwight Simons and I were discussing Chinese ceramics. Dwight described Ming period porcelains recovered from Coast Miwok sites along Drakes Bay, 70 miles south.[3] Some, he noted, could be attributed to the landing of Sir Francis Drake in 1579, and others to Cermeño's visit in 1595. Perhaps the sherds we had found had been collected from the wreck of a sixteenth-century Manila galleon. I was doubtful, and argued for a "more reasonable" explanation. I suggested the sherds might have been discarded in the late nineteenth or early twentieth century by a Chinese cook or work crew employed in a nearby logging camp. After all, we had found a trash pit from the 1920s filled with bottles and tin cans less than a hundred feet from Three Chop Village.

By mid-afternoon of that day I had changed my mind. The students had excavated a piece of bottle glass, clearly flaked along one edge, and a piece of porcelain that appeared to have been deliberately flaked and ground. It now seemed clear that Northern Pomo Indians living at Three Chop Village had possessed Asian ceramics, and we would have to explain that.

Part of our answer arrived a few days later from an unexpected source. In order to precisely date the occupation of the village, we needed to determine the ages of the trees growing within the house depressions. Obviously, the houses had been occupied and abandoned before the trees had grown there. Dana Cole, a forester with Jackson State Forest, kindly agreed to core the tanoaks and calculate their ages by counting annual growth rings. Unfortunately, the trees were only 60 years old—information that was not very useful to us, since we already knew the houses to be much older. Over a lunch of dry sandwiches, the crew showed Dana the artifacts they had recovered and recounted our theories about the Asian porcelain sherds they were finding.

Dana had seen similar sherds on the "pottery beach," in a small cove near Caspar, ten miles west. There, he said, pottery was washing in from a wrecked "sampan," sunk a little over a hundred feet from shore. A friend of his who lived just above the cove had collected pottery from the wreck while diving for abalone. Dana brought his friend, Dale Hartesveldt, up to Three Chop Village the following week. Dale brought with him eight large pieces of coarse blue and white porcelaneous stoneware he had collected from the wreck. We saw immediately that the glaze and blue designs on some of Dale's sherds closely matched sherds we had excavated at Three Chop Village. By the end of our two-and-a-half-week field season at Three Chop Village we had completely excavated three house depressions, each of which contained porcelain sherds and green bottle glass. The 50 fragments of porcelain we recovered included one carefully ground disk which appeared to be a bead, lacking only a central perforation. The 150 fragments of green bottle glass included three unfinished arrow tips.

I was excited by an apparent connection between the Mitom Pomo and a historic shipwreck for three reasons. First, the location of the wreck would tell us exactly what part of the coast the people of Three Chop Village had visited. Second, identification of the wreck would provide an exact date for at least one occupation of the houses. Finally, just as a physician could inject a radioactive tracer into a vein to view the entire circulatory system, these distinctive porcelain sherds in various Mendocino County archaeological sites would "trace" the entire settlement system of a Mitom Pomo tribelet.

As our field season drew to a close, I asked Dana Cole to take me to the "pottery beach." He led me to a wave-cut bluff, 65 feet above a small rocky cove. I could see the Point Cabrillo lighthouse beacon six-tenths of a mile south. Dana pointed out into the waves and foam about a hundred feet from the base of the bluff. "There," he said, "just beyond that jagged rock," was the wreck.

That fall I began to research the wreck's identity. Dorothy Bear, one of the founders of the Kelley House Museum in Mendocino, told me that a sport diver had collected a shoe and several large sherds of Chinese pottery from a nearby wreck and had donated them anonymously to the Kelley House. The diver was David Buller. In 1979, he had heard rumors about a wreck with a cargo of Chinese porcelains located near Caspar on the central Mendocino coast. The wreck was then being worked by divers from Los Angeles and San Diego who would not reveal its location. Researching shipwrecks in the Bancroft Library in Berkeley, David found a citation for a news article in the *Daily Alta California* of August 5, 1850, describing the wreck of the brig *Frolic*. David knew the southern California divers had launched from Caspar Cove, so he explored the ocean floor extending south from the cove with a portable magnetometer. On the first day he "magged" the *Frolic*'s ballast pile, hundreds of cast-iron blocks.

David made six dives between 1980 and 1982 and acquired an extensive collection from the wreck. He presented me with two cardboard boxes containing a selection of retrieved artifacts, some waterlogged and preserved in jars of fresh water. His collection included several almost whole porcelain bowls, some flatware with ivory and mother-of-pearl handles, brass trunk handles, an ivory fan, and a selection of ship's fittings, including bolts, hinges, spikes, and screws. David also showed me several pieces of fine gold filigree jewelry he had taken from the wreck.

I learned from the *Daily Alta* article that the Boston-owned brig *Frolic* had left China for San Francisco under the command of Captain E. H. Faucon on June 16, 1850, with a valuable cargo of Chinese goods. She had been wrecked and totally lost on the Mendocino County coast during the night of July 25, 1850. A library search of nineteenth-century maritime literature produced two references to the *Frolic*: Basil Lubbock's volume *The Opium Clippers* and William Fairburn's *Merchant Trade*. From Lubbock's work I learned that the *Frolic* had begun transporting opium from India to China about 1845,[4] and from Fairburn's book I discovered she was extremely fast. On her second 1845 run from Hong Kong to Bombay, she had covered the distance in 35 days, the fastest run by any vessel in that year.[5]

Now I had identified the vessel, discovered the date of its wreck, and verified that the porcelains on board were part of a cargo from China. Dorothy Bear provided two additional bits of information linking local Indians to the wreck. Jerome B. Ford[6] had traveled up the Mendocino coast in the spring of 1851, hoping to salvage the cargo from a recently wrecked vessel. In his diary, Ford described Indian women wearing silk shawls taken from the wreck, but by the time he arrived, there was nothing left to salvage. And from an oral history transcript[7] at the Kelley House Museum I learned that Mrs. Kelley, whose restored house now serves as the museum, had made clothing from three bolts of silk traded to her by Indians who had taken them from the wreck. I now had enough information to supply a date and provide an explanation for the Chinese porcelains we had recovered from Three Chop Village, and during 1985 and 1986 I wrote up the site as a chapter of a volume titled *Western Pomo Prehistory*.[8]

This, I thought, was sufficient investigation into the brig *Frolic*. But I still wanted to use her Chinese ceramics to trace the settlement pattern of the Mitom Pomo, and in order to do this, I would need to document all the different ceramic forms the *Frolic* had carried. Shifting my research focus to these ceramics, I sought out additional wreck-diver collections in order to develop a ceramic typology. By the time I had examined several collections, I realized the *Frolic* had carried a veritable emporium of mid-nineteenth-century Chinese export items, of which ceramics were only a small part.

The process of identifying these items led me to a network of archaeologists excavating nineteenth-century Chinese communities throughout the western United States. From the 1850s until the exclusion acts of the 1880s and 1890s, large numbers of Chinese had immigrated into California. Current archaeologists, many of whom were principally trained as American Indian specialists, were now struggling to identify and describe Chinese materials excavated from mining communities scattered throughout the Sierra foothills, and from the "Chinatowns" that were once an integral part of such California cities as Riverside, Ventura, San Jose, and Sacramento.

The published literature revealed that considerable academic attention had been given to top-of-the-line nineteenth-century Chinese export ceramics, manufactured in well-known, prestigious kilns and purchased by prominent New England families. These elegant items, however, were virtually never found in sites occupied by overseas Chinese. Relatively little research had been conducted on the far more plentiful and less expensive Ch'ing dynasty domestic wares that were now being recovered from excavations at numerous nineteenth-century overseas Chinese communities from New Zealand to California. There was a critical need for definition of well-dated assemblages of these more humble Chinese export ceramics, and the cargo of the brig *Frolic* was a time capsule. She had contained not only a selection of ceramic vessels, but also a diverse array of additional export items available for purchase in Canton in 1850. Thus, the cargo of the *Frolic* could provide a well-dated collection that would facilitate cross-dating of other nineteenth-century assemblages recovered from less controlled archaeological contexts in both Asia and the Americas.

In addition to cargo items manufactured in China, the wreck-diver collections from the *Frolic* contained many non-cargo items, including weapons, supplies, personal possessions of the officers and crew, and pieces of the vessel itself. In order to distinguish the *Frolic*'s cargo from the other items carried aboard, and from pieces of the vessel, it would be useful to find out when and where the *Frolic* had been built.

According to Basil Lubbock,[9] the brig *Frolic* was American-built and owned by Russell & Co., a firm of American commission merchants operating out of Canton and New England. But historians studying Russell & Co. papers at the National Archives found no record of the *Frolic*. A list of Russell & Co. vessels prepared over a century ago by Captain Forbes, senior partner of the firm,[10] did not list the *Frolic* either. Nor did her name appear in Lloyd's Register, the British insurance consortium's listing and evaluation of commercial vessels published annually during the 1830s and 1840s.

At the National Park Service in San Francisco, marine historian James Delgado noted that *Frolic* was a common name for British naval vessels over several centuries. Such vessels usually carried a permanent ballast of kentledge—cast-iron blocks such as those that had led the diver David Buller to the Caspar wreck. Commercial vessels, which would be filled with cargo on both outgoing and return voyages, generally did not require a permanent—and expensive—source of stabilizing weight. The *Frolic* might thus have been a British naval vessel, later sold to a private party. But though British naval records from the nineteenth century are virtually complete, a search of them revealed no mention of our *Frolic*. It was possible, I thought, that the cast-iron blocks had been cargo items destined for the blacksmiths of iron-poor California.

The *Daily Alta* article attributed the *Frolic* to Boston, but an alphabetical listing of vessels registered at the Port of Boston did not include her.[11] There remained only one tedious and time-consuming possibility. I would need to examine the tables of ships' arrivals and departures in various nineteenth-century commercial newspapers. With luck, I could trace the *Frolic* back, voyage by voyage, to her birthplace.

Most nineteenth-century newspapers published in port cities featured commercial columns listing the name of each vessel arriving and sailing, her national affiliation, her registered tonnage, the name of her captain, the company to which the cargo was consigned, and finally, either her port of origin or port of destination. The *Daily Alta* article reported the *Frolic* had departed China on June 16, 1850. So I began with the *China Mail*, a weekly English-language newspaper published in Canton. There, I learned the *Frolic* had arrived at Canton from Bombay on May 25, 1850, had proceeded to Hong Kong on May 30, and was cleared for passage to San Francisco on June 7.

As I worked my way backwards in time, month by month, through thick volumes of the *China Mail*, I could follow the winding holes of ancient bookworms that often passed through the entire seven-inch thickness of a volume. Slowly, the rhythm of the *Frolic*'s life began to emerge as I recorded arrivals and departures. Through the listings of dates and places, the pattern of her existence was revealed as a simple one. Sometimes her cargo would be characterized in a single word. Three times a year the *Frolic* would arrive in China from India with a cargo of opium, usually from Bombay but rarely from Calcutta. From China she would return to India with a cargo of "specie" (coinage) or "treasure."

The earliest record of the *Frolic* in the *China Mail* was her arrival at Macao on June 13, 1845, having departed Bombay on May 8. I obtained the *Bombay Times and Journal of Commerce* and quickly found a listing of the *Frolic*'s May 8, 1845, departure from Bombay to China. Then, with growing excitement, I slowly rolled the reel of microfilm backwards. The *Bombay Times* had published two hefty issues per week. The shipping lists were long, the print small, the microfilm faint, and it seemed the *Frolic* had sat in Bombay harbor forever during the spring of 1845.

Suddenly, I saw the crucial entry. The brig *Frolic* had arrived at Bombay on March 29, 1845, having departed Baltimore December 8, 1844. Acting on intuition, I rolled the film forward, scanning entire newspapers for some additional mention of the *Frolic*. In the April 30 issue, I hit the jackpot—the ultimate key unlocking the *Frolic*'s identity. A brief advertisement in the classified section said it all: "FOR CHINA, to sail

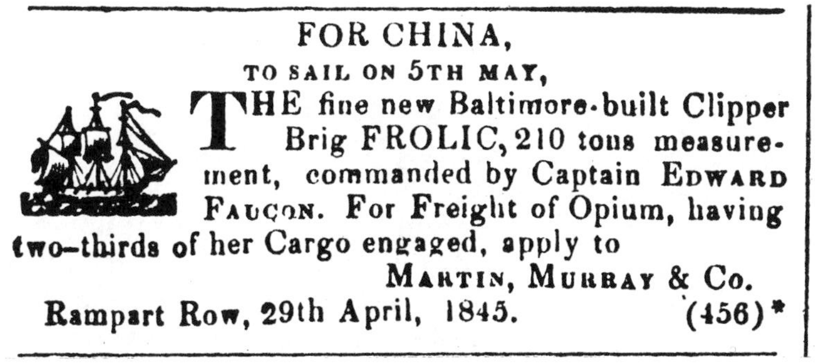

FOR CHINA,
TO SAIL ON 5TH MAY,

THE fine new Baltimore-built Clipper Brig FROLIC, 210 tons measurement, commanded by Captain EDWARD FAUCON. For Freight of Opium, having two-thirds of her Cargo engaged, apply to

MARTIN, MURRAY & Co.

Rampart Row, 29th April, 1845.   (456) *

Figure 3. *Bombay Times* advertisement soliciting an opium cargo for the *Frolic*, April 30, 1845.

on 5th May, The fine new Baltimore-built Clipper Brig FROLIC, 210 tons measurement, commanded by Captain Edward Faucon. For freight of opium, having two-thirds of her cargo engaged, apply to Martin, Murray & Co."

So the *Frolic* had been built in Baltimore! A short article in the *Baltimore Sun* published the day before her departure for Bombay announced her completion and identified the Gardner brothers of Fells Point as her builders.[12] The Baltimore listings in the National Archives contained both her Federal Registry and the master carpenter's report.[13] The *Frolic* was a brig of $212^{30}/_{95}$ tons burthen, with a hull 99 feet 2 inches long. She was 24 feet wide and 9 feet 11 inches tall, sharp-built, with a square stern, no galleries, and a billet head.

During the previous century, Baltimore builders had perfected what came to be known as the "Baltimore clipper." These vessels were usually lightly built schooners and brigs, 75 to 100 feet in length, less than 200 tons burthen, and sharp-prowed, with two tall, raked masts, rigged to carry vast amounts of sail. Their sharp bows and dead-rise sacrificed carrying capacity for speed. These vessels had gained fame as privateers in the American Revolution and the War of 1812. In times of peace they hauled fast-ripening fruit up the Atlantic coast from the Caribbean islands. They were later used as slavers to penetrate the British blockade of West African slave ports.

The *Frolic* was a highly refined Baltimore clipper, built during the final years of the evolution of that vessel form, specifically for the opium

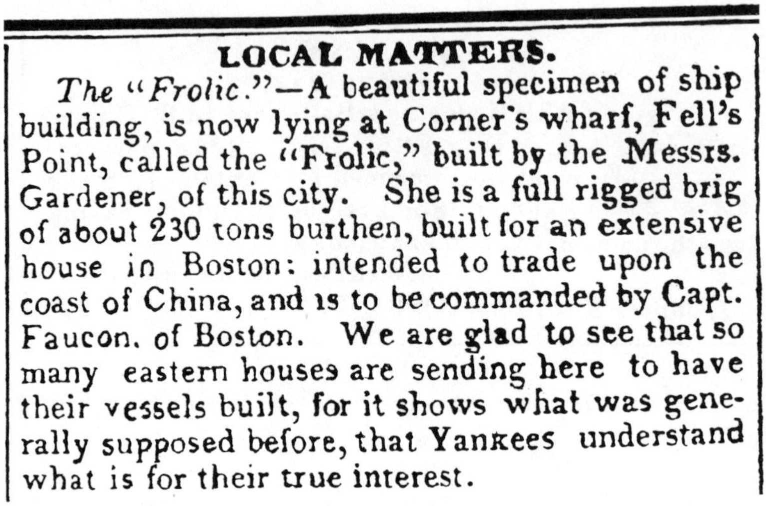

LOCAL MATTERS.

The "Frolic."—A beautiful specimen of ship building, is now lying at Corner's wharf, Fell's Point, called the "Frolic," built by the Messrs. Gardener, of this city. She is a full rigged brig of about 230 tons burthen, built for an extensive house in Boston: intended to trade upon the coast of China, and is to be commanded by Capt. Faucon, of Boston. We are glad to see that so many eastern houses are sending here to have their vessels built, for it shows what was generally supposed before, that Yankees understand what is for their true interest.

Figure 4. *Baltimore Sun* article announcing completion of the *Frolic*, December 7, 1844.

trade. Very little was known, however, about the construction of Baltimore clippers. Their hulls had been built almost exclusively from models rather than from plans; no complete vessels and few models had survived into modern times. This gave new significance to the *Frolic*. Not only did she appear to be the only known remains of an American-built opium clipper, but she was also a classic example of the Baltimore style. While the primary focus of my research up to now had been the *Frolic*'s cargo, now the vessel herself was discovered to be an important source of information for maritime historians.

The *Frolic*'s Federal Registry revealed an additional bit of useful information—the final clue to her commercial life. Her owner was listed as John James Dixwell of Boston. John Dixwell was well known. He had been associated with Augustine Heard & Co., one of the four major firms of commission agents active in China during the 1840s and 1850s. I had already read a great deal about Augustine Heard & Co., and several economic historians had cited the company papers held in the Baker Library at Harvard University's Graduate School of Business Administration.

I telephoned Harvard, and Elise Thall, a manuscript librarian who had prepared the collection to be microfilmed, told me of one archival

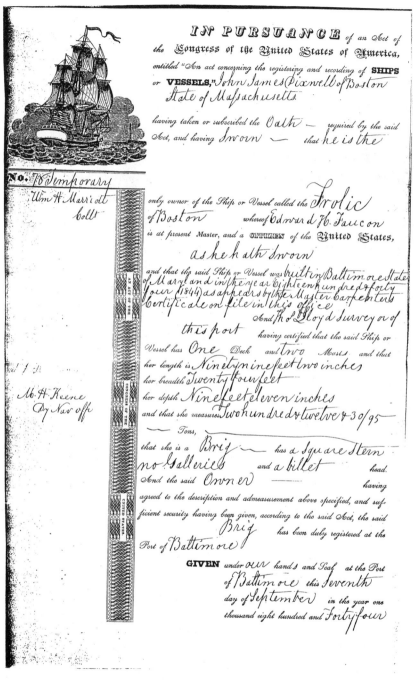

Figure 5. The *Frolic*'s Federal Registry, September 7, 1844. Courtesy National Archives.

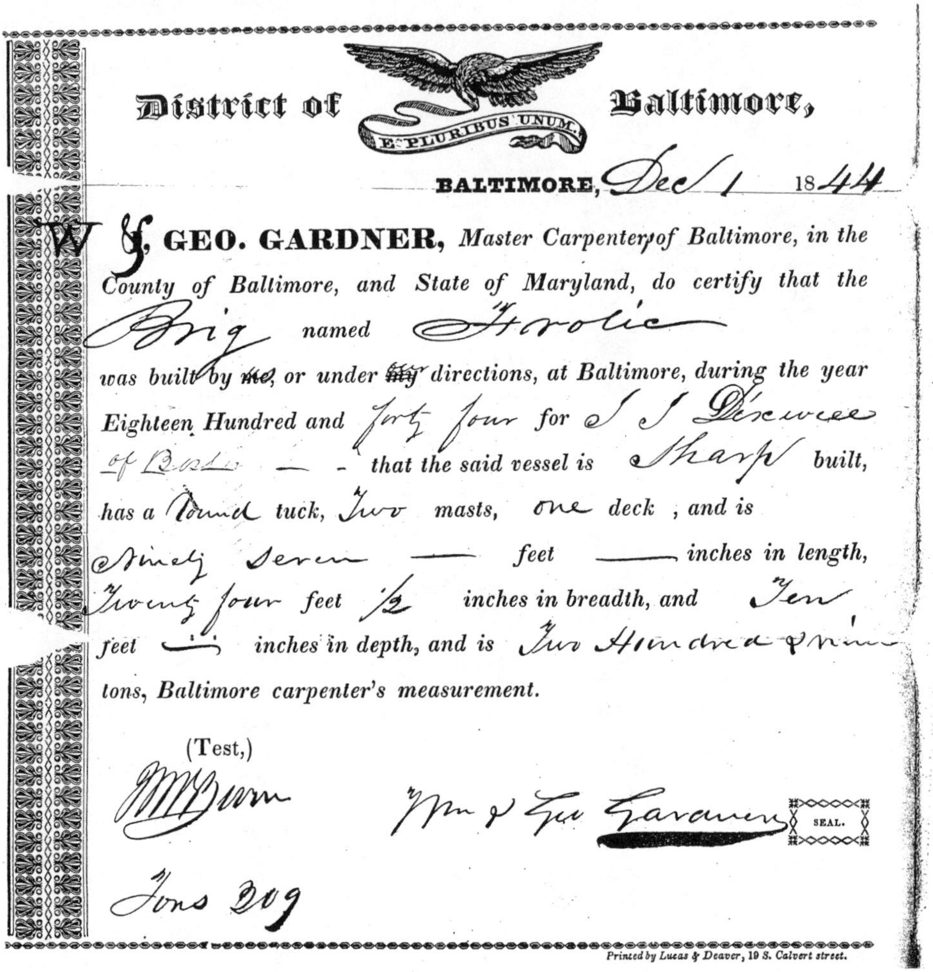

District of Baltimore,

E PLURIBUS UNUM

BALTIMORE, Dec 1 1844

W & GEO. GARDNER, *Master Carpenter of Baltimore, in the County of Baltimore, and State of Maryland, do certify that the* Brig *named* Frolic *was built by ~~me~~, or under ~~my~~ directions, at Baltimore, during the year Eighteen Hundred and* Forty four *for* [illegible] *that the said vessel is* Sharp *built, has a* round *tuck,* Two *masts,* one *deck, and is* Ninety seven — *feet* — *inches in length,* Twenty four *feet* ½ *inches in breadth, and* Ten *feet* — *inches in depth, and is* Two Hundred & nine *tons, Baltimore carpenter's measurement.*

(Test,)

[illegible]

Wm & Geo Gardner SEAL.

Tons 209

Printed by Lucas & Deaver, 19 S. Calvert street.

Figure 6. The *Frolic*'s master carpenter's certificate, December 1, 1844. Courtesy National Archives.

box containing seven inches of documents relating specifically to the *Frolic*. These documents, she said, included invoices, receipts, insurance policies, account statements, and an extensive correspondence concerning the vessel's activities. In June of 1989 I traveled to Harvard intending to spend two weeks studying that seven-inch stack of documents. On my arrival, I discovered that the Heard collection occupied

261 shelf feet, and was Harvard's largest collection of business papers for a nineteenth-century firm.

Packed in scores of archival boxes, these papers told the story of an American firm's entry into the opium trade. Correspondence from Canton, Bombay, and Boston, as well as from Captain Faucon aboard the *Frolic*, provided not only a history of the vessel but also a detailed account of how the opium trade was conducted. The six-year life of the *Frolic* was clearly traceable—from the earliest descriptions of her speed and grace in 1844 to her sudden obsolescence when steamers arrived in 1847 and her death on the Mendocino coast of California in the summer of 1850.

Two months in the Baker Library archives forced me yet again to reframe my research. I had begun hoping to explain why Chinese ceramics were found in a Pomo Indian village in California. I had then turned my attention to the *Frolic*'s ceramics and expanded it to her entire cargo of China export goods. Then, when the *Frolic* was revealed to be a classic example of the Baltimore clipper vessel form, it became important to collect and document her physical remains. Finally, discovery of the vast Augustine Heard & Co. archive at the Baker Library demanded that I examine the opium trade itself and its place in the American economy of the mid-nineteenth century. In the chapters that follow, I tell the story of the *Frolic* and of the merchants in Boston, Baltimore, Bombay, and Canton who built and managed her during the six years of her life. It is a story inspired by artifacts, some professionally excavated from the houses of Pomo Indians, some privately collected by sport divers from a shipwreck.

Generally, when our excavations are successful, we archaeologists are both rewarded and burdened with thousands of fragments to analyze and describe. As a consequence, our reports often bog down in detailed descriptions of cultural minutiae. Although we have a professional obligation to describe what we dig up, the sheer number of artifacts often leads us to focus our analysis on them rather than on their broader cultural context. The interested reader will find my painfully detailed description of the artifacts from Three Chop Village in *Western Pomo Prehistory*.[14] The artifacts recovered from the *Frolic* shipwreck will be reported elsewhere.

This story, however, looks beyond the artifacts recovered at Three Chop Village and the *Frolic* wreck site. It is, instead, a story of connections. I have tried to describe a world system that ultimately linked Pomo Indians with Boston businessmen, Baltimore shipbuilders, Bombay opium merchants, smugglers on the coast of China, and newly rich consumers in Gold Rush California.

What follows, then, is a tale about a little known and awkward chapter in American history: a story of American participation in the opium trade.

$\mathcal{T}$he China Trade

EARLY IN THE SPRING of 1844, George Basil Dixwell wrote from Canton, China, to his brother, John James Dixwell, in Boston, asking him to have two fast vessels built for use on the China coast. George had been in China since the fall of 1841, when, at age 27, he joined Augustine Heard & Co., a newly established partnership of American commission merchants. The Dixwell brothers and Augustine Heard already had extensive commercial experience in India and China. Now George Dixwell, the company's opium specialist, wanted fast ships to give his firm a competitive edge in the drug trade. If the company had its own fleet to transport opium from India to China and to distribution points along the China coast, the increased drug consignments from native dealers in India would yield large profits from both transport fees and commissions on sales.

While the opium trade was prohibited by the Chinese government, it did not contravene any United States law of that time. Indeed, medicinal preparations containing opiates were legal and routinely consumed in nineteenth-century America by much of the population. In any case, American shippers were accustomed to walking a fine line between legal and illegal ventures. They had, after all, already been active in the slave trade, blockade running, and privateering. Further, as we shall see, by the second quarter of the nineteenth century opium had become the primary commodity by which the Western world balanced its trade with China.

The Augustine Heard firm had begun with Augustine Heard himself, born in 1785 to a prominent Ipswich, Massachusetts, commercial family.[1] His father, John Heard, owned half interest in a distillery and was active in shipping—importing molasses for the distillery from the West Indies, along with sugar, coffee, and other luxury items. The Revolutionary War had exerted a long-term salutary effect on American commerce. It spurred shipbuilding, taught aggressive seamanship, and rewarded innovative entrepreneurs. It also produced a generation of merchants with a taste for international commerce and a workforce of skilled mariners for a growing merchant fleet.

John Heard was an adept businessman and quickly recognized this opportunity. He invested heavily in New England privateers—heavily armed merchant vessels commissioned to prey upon British shipping—and advanced money to Ipswich sailors for their shares of captured booty. This piracy was strongly encouraged by the fledgling Continental Congress, which issued over six hundred letters of marque in Massachusetts, while the Massachusetts General Court issued yet another thousand.[2] These documents authorized the holders to seize British merchant vessels and their cargoes.

By the beginning of the nineteenth century, the Heard family interests had expanded to include the China trade. Direct trade between the United States and China had existed since August 23, 1784, when the *Empress of China*, from New York, arrived at Macao. Over the next 45 years, Americans purchased Chinese teas, silks, and porcelain. Even as early as the late 1790s, American trade with China surpassed that of all other nations except Britain.[3] In 1801, Augustine Heard's older brother, Daniel, sailed to India and China carrying $4,260 in Spanish dollars invested by family members. This first Heard family venture into the China trade was unsuccessful. Daniel died at the youthful age of 22 and was buried at Whampoa anchorage in China.

Augustine Heard completed his studies at Phillips Academy, Exeter, New Hampshire, in 1803, and he began his business training in Boston as a clerk in the countinghouse of Ebenezer Francis. Two years later, Mr. Francis sent the twenty-year-old Heard on his first trip abroad as supercargo aboard a Boston vessel to India. The supercargo managed the sale of outgoing cargo and attempted to purchase a suitable return cargo with the proceeds; thus he was responsible for the venture's commercial success. Heard proved himself both shrewd and reliable on his

Figure 7. Augustine Heard (1785–1868), founder of Augustine Heard & Co., photograph circa 1860. Courtesy Peabody Essex Museum of Salem, Massachusetts.

first voyage, and thereafter he was regularly employed as supercargo on voyages to the Mediterranean, the West Indies, and the Far East.

The first decade of the nineteenth century was a time of high risks and high profits for the developing American merchant marine, and Augustine Heard's career mirrored this growth. The French republic declared war on Great Britain in 1793, and New England merchants profited well from this conflict. From the beginning, opportunistic American carriers continued to trade with both sides, disguising the national origins and destinations of their cargoes in order to avoid capture and confiscation by either side. Although this commerce was initially profitable, by 1806 it had become too risky, as American vessels were stopped and confiscated by both warring powers, as well as threatened by privateers of all nations. Early in 1807, when Augustine Heard sailed for Smyrna, Turkey, as supercargo on the schooner *Betsy*, the vessel was stopped six times on the Mediterranean: twice by British naval vessels, once by an English privateer, and three times by Spanish privateers.

To avoid entanglement in the ongoing European wars, Congress passed the Embargo Act of 1807, which prohibited American vessels sailing to foreign ports. This, of course, devastated American shipping. Two years later the blanket prohibition was superseded by the Non-Intercourse Act, which forbade the importation of French and British goods into the United States and prohibited the departure of American vessels for French and British ports. Though now technically illegal, voyages to British-controlled Calcutta remained immensely profitable, and, in defiance of federal law, Augustine Heard was fully employed on voyages throughout this period—to Calcutta in 1807, Canton in 1809, and Calcutta again in 1810. Heard used his sea time well, mastering navigation and learning how to pilot a sailing vessel. In 1812, his firm appointed him both captain and supercargo of the brig *Caravan* on a voyage to Calcutta.

The War of 1812 brought what was left of American merchant trade to a virtual standstill. In 1811, the British prohibited direct voyages between India and the United States, and Heard, returning from Calcutta, was forced to sell the *Caravan* and her cargo at Bahia on the Brazilian coast to prevent the vessel's seizure by British warships. He remained stranded in South America for over a year, until 1815, when he finally found passage to the United States.

The Peace of Ghent, signed December 24, 1814, had ended hostilities between the United States and Britain, and the second Peace of Paris, November 20, 1815, concluded the Napoleonic Wars between Britain and France. Thus Augustine Heard was able to return to sea in 1816. A New England captain or supercargo of that time was generally allowed free transport for a specified amount of goods he might purchase on his own account, and during his thirteen years of commerce, Heard had invested well. Thus in May 1816 he sailed for Calcutta as both supercargo and one-quarter owner of the brig *Hindu*, carrying $131,000 in silver supplied by Boston merchants. Five years later, when Heard sailed again for Calcutta (as captain and supercargo of the brig *Governor Endicott*), he not only represented the most prominent Boston merchants but carried $20,000 in goods on his own account as well.

Augustine Heard sailed to the Far East nearly every year until 1830, when, at the age of 45, he retired from the sea. During the preceding 25 years he had made ten passages to Calcutta, two to Canton, and many others to Mediterranean, West Indian, and South American ports. He had not only amassed capital and experience but also established strong ties with other Boston merchants, which would serve him well during his career on land. Nineteenth-century business connections were built on such personal relationships, in an age without wire services or telecommunications.

From the earliest days of trade between the United States and China, the major obstacle to this commerce had been the lack of American commodities that could be sold in China. American merchants exported silver coinage in order to pay for the Chinese goods that American consumers wanted.

Initially, America had exported ginseng to China, but the market for this reputed aphrodisiac was too small to contribute much to balancing trade. Animal skins were slightly more significant; America exported sea otter from the coast of the Pacific Northwest and seal, hunted from the Falklands to the Aleutians. In 1801 fourteen Boston vessels on the Northwest Coast traded New England manufactured goods to Indians for furs,[4] and in September 1803 the *Pilgrim*, out of Boston, sold a cargo of twelve thousand seal skins in Canton.[5]

Yet American imports from China far outstripped exports. In 1805–6 American merchant vessels carried ten million pounds of tea from Canton. In exchange, American exports to Canton totalled five million dollars, only a fifth of which came from commodities. The remainder was silver coinage.[6] Americans needed a commodity to sell in China, but they produced very little that the Chinese wanted to buy. Although New England merchants were aggressive in seeking out new export commodities such as sandalwood from Hawaii, between 1805 and 1818 70 million dollars in specie was shipped from America to China.[7] During the early 1820s the Chinese market for furs began to diminish while American demand for Chinese goods continued to rise. Thus, although the China trade was a relatively small part of total American foreign trade,[8] the American economy was already suffering from a growing trade deficit.

The British, who imported vast quantities of tea from China, had handled a similar trade deficit during the eighteenth century by producing opium in India and selling it in China to reverse the imbalance. India's Moghul emperors had maintained a monopoly over production and sale of opium in Bengal. This monopoly passed to the British East India Company when the British conquered this portion of India in 1793,[9] and by the end of the eighteenth century the Company was reaping huge profits from the sale of opium in China.

In 1799, the emperor of China responded to the burgeoning trade in Indian opium by issuing an imperial decree prohibiting its import. Since opium was the only commodity for which Chinese merchants paid silver, the East India Company ceased using company-owned ships to transport their opium to China, instead selling the drug to British and Parsee merchants. These private merchants, licensed by the Company, transported the drug to China aboard their own vessels. By this subterfuge the Company disclaimed responsibility for the sale of opium in China, without losing profits from it.[10]

The economic benefit was immediate. By 1804 Britain had reversed its trade deficit with China, and between 1806 and 1809 seven million dollars in silver were exported from China to India.[11] The British East India Company maintained its monopoly by restricting opium sales in India to British subjects. But opium could be purchased elsewhere, and Americans entered the trade in 1811 when the brig *Sylph*, of Philadelphia, arrived in Macao with a cargo of opium from Smyrna, Turkey. Americans soon developed a regular trade in Turkish opium, but by 1817 they controlled only 10 percent of the drug trade at Canton.[12]

Sales of Indian opium in China increased almost geometrically. In 1820–21, a total of 4,244 chests, each containing 140 pounds of opium, were shipped to China. By 1830–31, a total of 18,956 chests were exported. After the British Parliament terminated the British East India Company's monopoly in 1834, the amount of opium shipped to China grew even more dramatically, reaching over 30,000 chests in 1836.[13]

In 1838, the British finally allowed American-owned vessels to carry opium from India to China.[14] The Turkish opium previously carried by American vessels was considered inferior, both in flavor and potency, by Chinese customers. This had limited the American share of the opium market. Once high-quality Indian opium was available to them,

American carriers abandoned Turkey for Bombay and Calcutta and began large-scale traffic in the Indian drug. At last, American merchants enjoyed free access to a product the Chinese were eager to buy.

Russell & Co. was one of three Boston firms maintaining agencies, or branch houses, in China. In 1830, Philip Ammidon, one of the firm's partners, chose not to return for his term of service in China and convinced Augustine Heard to go in his place. Heard had just retired from his 25 years at sea and was ready to begin a new career, so he accepted Ammidon's offer and sailed for China. Shortly after his arrival in Canton, Heard was made a full partner and assumed a three-sixteenth interest in the company.

Augustine Heard remained in China four years. As his associates succumbed one by one to illness and returned to the United States, he came to assume overall management responsibility for the house. During his term at Russell & Co. the firm's legitimate commerce in teas, silks, and New England cottons, as well as its illegal traffic in Turkish opium, brought Heard large commissions. Before Heard returned to Boston in 1834, he brought three young Americans into the Russell firm as working partners: John Forbes, John Green, and Joseph Coolidge. Conflict between Green and Coolidge eventually led to Coolidge being forced out of Russell & Co., and Heard authorized him to establish a new firm. On January 1, 1840, Coolidge announced the founding of a new commercial house, Augustine Heard & Co.[15]

But even as the Heard firm was being established, the rapid expansion of the opium trade was precipitating a crisis in China. By 1837, opium constituted 57 percent of all imports into the country, and between 1828 and 1836 38 million dollars in silver had been exported.[16] This outflow of silver for opium caused domestic problems for the emperor.

Chinese peasant cultivators of that time accumulated copper currency in numerous small transactions throughout the year, and then used the copper cash to purchase the silver required for payment of land taxes. When silver was diverted into the opium trade, its value inflated against copper currency, producing widespread hardship and consequent social unrest in rural areas.[17] The crisis was exacerbated by the wholesale corruption of Chinese officials, bribed into complicity by opium smugglers. The Chinese government's authority weakened as bonds between emperor and subject were undermined.[18]

The Opium War of 1840–42 permanently altered Western commercial relations with China. Prior to 1840, foreign merchants had been restricted to a small enclosed area of warehouses and residences at Canton, called "factories." Moreover, by law all commerce required the services of government-appointed Chinese intermediaries known as Hong merchants. But in 1839 the Chinese government determined that traffic in opium was the primary cause of lawlessness within the country and concluded that harmony could be reestablished only by permanently terminating the opium trade. A statute of 39 articles was enacted, detailing severe penalties for trading or consuming opium, and the emperor dispatched a special commissioner to Canton to enforce this law. Commissioner Lin's crackdown first resulted in sixteen hundred arrests, primarily of Chinese. But Lin then acted against foreign merchants, confiscating twenty thousand chests of opium and closing Canton to foreign trade.[19] Britain retaliated by seizing several Chinese ports, beginning the formal hostilities known as the Opium War.

The Treaty of Nanking, signed August 29, 1842, ended the war and forced the Chinese to open five "treaty ports" to foreign merchants. The island of Hong Kong was ceded to Britain and an indemnity paid for loss of property. The principle of extraterritoriality was established, wherein Westerners were placed under the legal jurisdiction of consuls appointed by their own countries. Perhaps the most important provision of the treaty abolished the so-called Hong system and instituted free trade.[20] While the treaty made no mention of opium, imports of the still-illegal drug into China continued without serious interference.

The United States had remained neutral during the Opium War. Thus while British firms were temporarily forced to suspend their operations, American firms such as the newly established Augustine Heard & Co. received an immediate deluge of business. Throughout 1840, the fledgling Heard firm acted as opium and tea agents for the gigantic British house of Jardine, Matheson & Co.[21] And as the volume of business steadily swelled, an overwhelmed Joseph Coolidge asked Augustine Heard to return to China.

In May 1841, Augustine Heard sailed from Boston aboard the *Mary Ellen*. Heard, who had a reputation as a driving captain, wrote Coolidge: "To be certain that she is not sailed by a drone, I shall take the management of her into my own hands."[22] Heard brought two young men to serve as clerks while learning the business. But the firm

Figure 8. George Basil Dixwell (1814–85), architect of Augustine Heard & Co.'s opium commerce. Photograph probably taken in China circa 1870. Courtesy Massachusetts Historical Society.

needed experienced help as well, and Augustine Heard invited a brilliant young merchant, George Basil Dixwell, to join him in Canton. George Dixwell was to become the principal architect of the Heard firm's immensely profitable commerce in opium.

George Basil Dixwell was one of three brothers, all distinguished members of an old New England family notable for academic as well as commercial success. They were descended from one of the three seventeenth-century judges who had condemned King Charles I to death. In America, the family included physicians and schoolmasters as well as businessmen. The middle brother, Epes, after a short career in business, became headmaster of the famed Boston Latin School from 1836 to 1851 and subsequently opened his own preparatory school in Cambridge.

John James Dixwell, George's oldest brother, completed his studies at Boston Latin in 1821 and began work as a clerk in the counting-house of Thomas Wigglesworth, a Boston merchant with offices on India Wharf. He spent nine years learning to keep accounts, calculate commissions and exchange rates, and analyze market conditions affecting imports from the West Indies, India, and China. In 1830, Mr. Wigglesworth sent him on his first trade voyage to Calcutta, the start of a ten-year career as a supercargo. John Dixwell's voyages during this period reflect the extraordinary efforts of New England merchants to find new trade items to sell in India and the Far East, in order to reduce the need to export hard currency. In 1833, for example, Mr. Wigglesworth dispatched John Dixwell as supercargo on the brig *Tuscany* with 180 tons of Massachusetts ice[23]—for which Dixwell found an equally creative return cargo: monkeys![24]

As this experience was preparing John, the eldest Dixwell brother, for a career as an independent businessman, John was also preparing his younger brother George for the East Asia trade. George had made his first trip to Calcutta in 1835, at the age of twenty, and while there had begun studying the Bengali language. To assist George in this pursuit, John brought a Calcutta native with him on his return voyage to Boston in 1836. George was both enthusiastic and proficient in his study of language, and he later became one of the few Westerners of his generation to speak and write Chinese.

When John Dixwell returned to Boston in 1836, he began to expand his career in trade and finance, and George Dixwell took his turn representing the Dixwell and Wigglesworth interests in the bazaars of Calcutta. Two years later, when John traveled to London, Geneva, and Paris to become personally acquainted with European merchants and banking houses, George was making his first voyage as supercargo. Despite the recession in America caused by the Panic of 1837, George did well. Brother Epes Dixwell wrote to John in London on April 22, 1838: "George sailed last Tuesday for Calcutta on the Barque Brighton with a stock of about $160,000—which in these hard times & considering it is his first voyage as super, is a very good stock."[25] Epes and John Dixwell were meanwhile establishing other important business con-

Figure 9. John J. Dixwell (1806–76). Photograph circa 1873. Courtesy Massachusetts Historical Society.

nections. In 1839 Epes married Mary Ingersol Bowditch, the daughter of Nathaniel Bowditch, and seven years later John married her sister Elizabeth.[26] A self-trained astronomer and mathematician, Nathaniel Bowditch was an American intellectual giant in the first third of the nineteenth century. His *American Practical Navigator* taught Augustine Heard and subsequent generations of American seamen to navigate, and it remains even today, after almost two hundred years and numerous revised editions, a classic instructional text for marine navigation.[27]

By 1839 John Dixwell had his own office and import warehouse on India Wharf. That same year he was appointed one of twelve directors of the Suffolk Insurance Company,[28] and in 1841 he was designated one of six directors of the Massachusetts Bank.[29] The Dixwell brothers had "arrived," having a store of experience, capital, social connections, and youthful energy. In the spring of 1841, when Augustine

Heard desperately needed a reliable and energetic partner in his new firm in Canton, he consulted John Dixwell, whom he had known for twenty years, and John suggested George, who by then had accumulated six years of experience as clerk and then supercargo in the India trade. George Dixwell would bring to the Heard firm not only his services and talents, but all of John Dixwell's massive orders for teas and silks as well. Only a month after Augustine Heard departed, George Dixwell sailed for China.

In those days, young men from Boston went to China to become rich. But although the Protestant ethic lauded mercantile endeavor, the unbridled pursuit of profit could easily turn to rapacious greed. George Dixwell's aunt Henrietta Sargent, an ardent abolitionist, recognized this danger, and as George sailed toward Canton, she wrote him a cautionary letter: "Dear Nephew, . . . I pray you not be over anxious about lucre, 'Man wants but little, nor wants that little long.' Do not have an Eldorado the object of your pursuit, of your toil by day, and the disturber of your sleep by night. It is unphilosophical, it is unchristian."[30]

❧

In 1839, on the eve of the Opium War, British subjects had been ordered to leave their "factories" at Canton. Americans and other foreign nationals had continued to represent the interests of their departed English colleagues. These few remaining firms were shipping over a half million pounds of tea daily,[31] and the crush of business now demanded every waking moment. Augustine Heard & Co., represented by Joseph Coolidge, handled a large share of this business. Although commissions were small, the volume was immense, and as Heard sailed for China, Coolidge was inundated with paperwork.

In the early morning hours of May 21, 1841, as British warships lay anchored just downriver from Canton, the Chinese launched a surprise attack. Opening with cannon fire from batteries hidden along the riverbanks, the Chinese then dispatched three deadly waves of fireboats, paired incendiary hulks loaded with oil-soaked bales of raw cotton, tied together with long chains. Set to drift on the last of the ebb tide, they would embrace and incinerate the British vessels.[32] By sunrise virtually all of the Western merchants had abandoned their Canton establishments.

Joseph Coolidge was working late, and by the time he finally attempted to escape, it was too late. Captured outside the factory by a mob of angry Chinese, he was saved from death only when loyal Chinese employees shouted out he was "a flowery flag [American] devil, not an English one."[33] Coolidge spent the next two nights in a Chinese prison. Later, from the safety of a British warship, Coolidge wrote, "I cannot tell you with what feelings of good will we looked on every one of those redcoats."[34]

The Chinese attack failed, and within a week the people of Canton had paid the British a ransom of six million dollars in silver to save their city from retaliatory siege. The mob had pillaged and then burned the building, and destruction at the Augustine Heard factory was complete. Except for one ledger, all company documents were lost. Coolidge submitted a claim listing excessively high values for his losses and doubled the amount to cover his pain and suffering. The innocent Hong merchants were forced to pay Coolidge this inflated amount by the Chinese government, and many members of the European community in Canton were disgusted by his greed.[35]

When Augustine Heard arrived in Canton near the end of September 1841, he brought with him two young men, his nephew John Heard and Joseph Roberts, to clerk in the new firm.[36] George Dixwell had joined them by early December, and in January 1842 a new copartnership was announced, with Augustine Heard, Joseph Coolidge, and George Dixwell each holding a one-third interest in the firm.[37] The workload for the partners and their two young clerks was formidable throughout 1842. As they laboriously reconstructed the firm's financial records from documents provided by vendors and customers, the volume of business was growing dramatically. The firm continued to act as agent for the outlawed British firm Jardine, Matheson & Co., whose Canton business totaled nearly ten million dollars annually.[38]

The Americans divided up the work. John Heard handled the firm's extensive correspondence, Joseph Roberts worked on the company books, Augustine Heard managed the export of teas, and George Dixwell began to focus on the opium business. Soon the firm, now occupying the old "Dutch Hong," was operating efficiently and turning a hefty profit with as much business as it could manage.

Relations between foreign nationals and the Cantonese remained tense, ready to erupt into violence at the least provocation, and the behavior of undisciplined foreign sailors on shore leave was a continual

Figure 10. John Heard
(1825–94) in China circa
1850. Watercolor on
ivory. Courtesy Carl L.
Crossman.

irritation. In early December 1842, as John Heard described it in a letter to his parents,[39] some indiscretion by Lascar (Indian) and Malay
seamen attracted a crowd of Chinese outside the factories. George
Dixwell, speaking the "Indian language" and braving a barrage of
stones, barricaded the sailors safely in a vacant warehouse, while the
belligerent crowd of Chinese, now grown to a mob, stoned, pillaged,
and set fire to adjacent European residences.

The Heard firm had nearly a half million dollars in silver in its vaults,
and all of its reconstructed ledgers were in the building. Defending the
front door with muskets, company personnel and Chinese laborers attempted to transfer some of the treasure to a tea boat. Although they
were able to transfer only a few thousand dollars, this diversion enabled the staff to send the company ledgers and papers through a pas-
sageway to the safety of a nearby hong. When the mob forced entry

into the Heards' building, George Dixwell fired into their midst, and an ingenious laborer, seeing that most of the intruders were barefoot, "caused all the old bottles in the establishment to be brought and broken . . . strewing the whole passage with glass."

Low on ammunition after defending the house for eight hours, Augustine Heard led the besieged Americans to safety from their burning headquarters. Brandishing pistols and muskets, the Americans marched warily through narrow streets, defended by ten loyal Chinese workers who held the menacing mob at bay by threatening impalement upon leveled wooden pikes. Enraged, the mob then descended on the Heard headquarters, carrying away everything that could be moved. Fortunately, the burning building delayed their assault on the vaults. The following morning, accompanied by armed reinforcements from Whampoa, Augustine Heard returned to his burned-out factory. The looters had broken into one of the vaults and, standing inside the smoking ruins of the building, were fighting one another for the money.

Ultimately, the Heard firm recovered over $200,000 from the remaining vaults, and the Chinese government was forced to reimburse the firm for both company and personal losses. The Chinese authorities punished several of the rioters by yoking them together on the steps of a municipal building where they died slowly and publicly of thirst and starvation.[40]

Augustine Heard & Co. recovered rapidly from the second burning of its headquarters, but the market was changing. The Opium War had ended, and Jardine, Matheson was able to reestablish its own operations at Canton. Representing this large British company had nevertheless provided the Heard firm with a good start, and more important, George Dixwell had used the association to analyze the older company's China operations. Throughout the war Jardine, Matheson & Co. had paid for its massive cargoes of teas with silver gained from opium sales along China's north coast. Jardine, Matheson was, in fact, one of the largest firms engaging in this illicit traffic. The hub of the opium trade was Lintin Island, about 60 miles below Canton. Here, out of sight of Chinese authorities, Jardine, Matheson and other foreign merchants anchored heavily armed hulks to serve as floating warehouses for shipments of Indian opium.[41]

The opium market in the Canton estuary was highly competitive, and profits were diminished both by the collusion of Chinese dealers and by the large bribes and fees extracted by Chinese officials. Jardine, Matheson & Co. had found a way to bypass the Canton market, developing its own delivery and distribution system along the China coast, where the firm could charge considerably higher prices than those paid in Canton. At the same time, they could undersell local dealers who received their opium supplies overland or by junk from Canton.[42] This plan required a small armada of vessels—fast clippers to carry opium from India to China, stationary hulks to receive opium at Lintin Island and other coastal distribution points, and a fleet of maneuverable, shallow-draft schooners to outrun pirates and deliver opium to Chinese merchants in coastal towns.

In 1838, Jardine, Matheson & Co. already employed twelve vessels in the opium trade.[43] Thus when the Indian opium market crashed in the fall of 1839, the firm was poised to profit from this opportunity. When the news reached India that all British merchants had been expelled from Canton, the Indian opium dealers panicked and the price of Malwa opium collapsed. Since Jardine, Matheson & Co. possessed its own fleet and an established delivery network, it was able to profit from the depressed prices. The firm's Singapore agents quietly bought up much of the 1839 crop of Malwa opium at only $200 per chest. Most of this opium they later sold in China for $800 a chest.[44] Jardine, Matheson used some of these windfall profits to expand its opium fleet, purchasing ten additional vessels between 1840 and 1842.[45] Almost all of these were small, selected for speed and maneuverability rather than cargo capacity.

From the experiences of Jardine, Matheson, George Dixwell learned that to compete successfully in the opium trade, the Heards would need to purchase swift vessels and develop their own distribution system. In 1843, George convinced his brother John, as well as Augustine Heard, to order such a vessel built to bring opium from India to the coast of China. He felt the need for a new vessel all the more urgently, for in that year Robert Bennet Forbes had sent the newly built, 370-ton clipper brig *Antelope* from Boston to China to transport opium for Russell & Co., the Heards' major American competitor. Early in 1844 John Dixwell dispatched the brand-new, 319-ton, Boston-built bark *Sappho* to Canton.[46]

The Treaty of Wanghia between China and the United States was signed July 3, 1844, giving Americans most of the rights and privileges the British had won in the Treaty of Nanking. A major difference, of course, was the British acquisition of Hong Kong. But there was another significant difference between the two treaties. While the Treaty of Nanking omitted any reference to the opium trade, the American treaty specifically prohibited it.[47] But the prospect of trading illegally did not dampen Augustine Heard & Co.'s enthusiasm for acquiring an opium fleet. The new bark *Sappho* arrived in China shortly before the signing of the Treaty of Wanghia, and under George Dixwell's orders two more vessels, the *Frolic* and the *Dart*, were already under construction in Baltimore. John Dixwell's February 5, 1844, letter to Augustine Heard in Canton clearly revealed a man attempting to drown the voice of his conscience with bluster. "I hope the Sappho will prove a favorite in China, and make us some money," he wrote. "How, I dont care, so it is made."[48]

By the spring of 1844, George Dixwell had become the dominant member of Augustine Heard & Co. Old Mr. Heard, now 59, was preparing to return to the United States, and Joseph Coolidge, after a conflict with Dixwell, left the firm at the end of May. The new articles of copartnership listed Augustine Heard and George Dixwell each with a third of the firm, the remaining third being divided between young John Heard and Joseph Roberts.[49]

George Dixwell had ordered the *Sappho* to fill his immediate need for a maneuverable vessel to transport opium to delivery points along the coast. Opium dealers would prefer to consign cargoes to a firm with a reputation for delivery ahead of other houses. Fast transport was essential to sell consignments at higher prices, before the slower bulk carriers arrived to glut the market. Although the *Sappho* had been built to compete with Russell & Co.'s *Antelope* on the India-to-China run, she was too large for that purpose.

The unsuitability of the *Sappho* to make coastal deliveries was a short-lived disappointment for George Dixwell. Before the end of August he had chartered the four-year-old, 123-ton, Baltimore-built schooner *Don Juan* for $1,000 per month,[50] and within three months he had purchased a three-quarters interest in her.[51] Dixwell found a cargo for the *Sappho* and dispatched her to Boston with Augustine Heard as her most prominent passenger. On Heard's departure from China, John Dixwell estimated the old man's personal wealth to exceed $200,000.[52] In addition, George Dixwell had ordered two more vessels crafted to his specifications from the Gardner Brothers at Fells Point on the Baltimore waterfront. The *Frolic* and the *Dart*, together with the *Don Juan*, would soon form the nucleus of the Augustine Heard & Co. opium fleet.

George Dixwell believed the *Don Juan*'s Baltimore ancestry would attract customers, for among maritime men, that city's very name had been synonymous with speed since before the American Revolution. Several days after the *Sappho*'s departure from Canton, a droll George Dixwell, confident the *Sappho* would be soon overtaken, wrote to Augustine Heard via the *Eliza*. "The Captain of the Eliza says his vessel has a Baltimore bottom and that he means she shall beat the Sappho."[53] The letter would remind the cautious Mr. Heard that George Dixwell was decisively preparing the firm to enter the opium trade with a fleet of Baltimore-built vessels—reputedly the fastest in the world.

CHAPTER 2

Baltimore

BALTIMORE SHIPBUILDERS had produced some of the most successful privateers used in the American Revolution and the War of 1812. William and George Gardner of Fells Point were the preeminent heirs of this tradition, so they were the obvious choice when George and John Dixwell wanted two fast opium clippers built. The Gardner Brothers had achieved international recognition in 1838 with construction of the 465-ton ship *Venus*. Probably the most notorious slave ship ever built in the United States, the *Venus* was widely discussed in the newspapers of the time.

On July 4, 1838, as the *Venus* reached completion at Fells Point, the *Baltimore American* reported: "A noble corvette ship, the Venus, Captain Wallace, pierced for 18 guns, built in this city on foreign account, is . . . ready for sea. She is, we learn, the sharpest clipper-built vessel ever constructed here, and according to opinion of nautical men, must outsail anything that floats."[1]

Not to be outdone, the *Baltimore Sun* reported a week later, "We understand the sloop of war Venus, built for the Mexican government, by one of our Fells Point ship builders, yesterday sailed for her place of destination. She is modelled in the peculiar 'clipper' style, which makes Baltimore vessels so celebrated as fast sailers, and it is thought she will prove, perhaps, the fastest sailer which has ever been launched from our ship yards. She goes out unarmed, but completely rigged."[2] However, on July 14, the *Sun* had to publish a correction: "We are requested to say that the information we gave on Thursday relative to this vessel [the *Venus*] is incorrect. She was built by Messrs. Wm. & Geo. Gardner, for Lambert Giddings, Esq. for a merchantman, and has sailed for the West Indies."[3]

In fact, the *Venus* was neither a warship nor a merchantman, but a slave ship in disguise. Indeed, like the merchant traders of New England, Baltimore shipbuilders had a long tradition of employing ruses to conduct their craft in defiance of the law. Since 1794, it had been illegal for an American citizen to "build, fit, equip, or load" a vessel for procuring slaves from a foreign country. Initially the penalty was forfeiture of the vessel and a fine of $2,000. Then in 1818, additional penalties of imprisonment for three to five years and a fine of up to $5,000 were enacted. Finally, by an act of May 15, 1820, the offense was declared to be piracy, punishable by death.[4] Thus the Gardners had to foster ambiguity about the *Venus*'s purpose during her construction to provide their firm with plausible deniability and protection from prosecution, although her real purpose had never been in doubt. The Gardners were careful to protect themselves by selling the slave ships they built to foreign buyers. These transactions through intermediaries, though contrived and transparent, sufficed to enable the Gardners and other Baltimore builders to construct the world's most profitable slavers while remaining officially and legally ignorant.

As soon as the *Venus* was ready to be launched, Lambert Giddings, Esq., signed a document appointing Charles Drake & Co. in Havana as agents for transfer of the vessel to Jose Mazorra, a notorious slave trader.[5] Commanded by Captain Wallace, the *Venus* cleared Baltimore the following day, July 10, with a crew of nineteen and a cargo of "flour and bricks."[6] She arrived at Havana August 4, and on August 23, after taking on a cargo of "merchandise," she ostensibly sailed for Bahia, Brazil, where she was to be transferred to the Portuguese flag.[7] As the *Venus* left Havana "with equipment for the slave trade,"[8] we may assume that during her nineteen-day layover in Cuba carpenters were busy fitting her out with platforms in her hold and tons of iron shackles and chains.

On November 5, the *Venus*, still under the American flag, arrived at Lagos on the West African coast—without ever stopping at her official destination, Bahia. Three weeks later she departed Lagos with a cargo of about 1,150 slaves. The American flag and papers had provided protection for the vessel until the slaves were driven aboard,[9] whereupon the vessel was given over to an agent of Jose Mazorra who carried papers from a defunct Bahia slaver, the *Duqueza de Braganza*.[10] With these fraudulent papers, and her name painted out, the *Venus* sailed from Lagos disguised as a wholly different vessel.

The following day, about a hundred miles south of Lagos, the *Venus/Duqueza* was sighted and pursued by Her Majesty's sloop *Pelican*. The *Pelican*'s commander reported that while he had gained on her at first, "she was lightened by throwing her deck cargo and spars overboard, and sailed away from us with ease, although every effort was made to come up with her."[11] A slightly different version of the race was recounted by the crew of the *Venus/Duqueza* in whiskey shops along the Baltimore waterfront: "On seeing the 'Pelican' they lowered the royal yards out of sheer bravado, and allowed the 'Pelican' to gain for a time, but finally hoisted the sails again and soon left her out of sight."[12]

On January 7, 1839, the so-called *Duqueza de Braganza* arrived at Havana, in ballast. She had already secretly discharged "no less than 860 slaves in the immediate neighborhood of Havana."[13] Although several hundred of the original 1,150 had perished during transit, the venture still yielded an immense profit. The original cost of the *Venus* had been about $30,000. Her fitting-out expenses, including the cargo of slaves, were estimated at $60,000 more, for a total investment of less than $100,000. In Cuba the 860 slaves brought $340 each, for a total of nearly $300,000—two-thirds of which was net profit.[14] The *Venus* made three more slaving voyages.[15] Her ultimate fate is unknown. Many slavers were deliberately burned, after discharging their shackled cargo, in order to destroy evidence of their activities, and the *Venus* probably fared the same.

In 1841, the role of the *Venus* in the illegal transport of slaves from West Africa to Cuba became the focus of a report by President Martin Van Buren to the United States House of Representatives. Ironically, this well-publicized document provided the Gardner Brothers firm with unprecedented advertising. Quoting from many sources, the president's message described the *Venus* as "one of the fastest sailing vessels ever built" and "likely to outsail anything that floats."[16] The document was widely distributed among Americans engaged in maritime commerce, and we can be virtually certain it was read by the Dixwells just as they were seeking the fastest possible vessels for the opium trade.

⚜

In 1844, when the Dixwells chose William and George Gardner to build their fleet, the firm was already 31 years old. However, as the successor firm to Baltimore's most famous shipbuilder, Thomas Kemp, their roots went far deeper.[17] Kemp had specialized in building swift, sharp-lined vessels described as "pilot boat-schooners." The term "Baltimore-built" appeared during the War of 1812; the designation used today, "Baltimore clipper," was not commonly used until the late 1830s.[18]

Baltimore shipbuilders had a history of building swift vessels for adventurous pursuits in times of conflict. During the American Revolution 248 privateers with letters of marque and reprisal sailed from Baltimore to wreak havoc on British shipping,[19] and Baltimore merchants seeking easy money soon developed a lasting taste for plunder.

Baltimore grew rapidly after the Revolutionary War, her population doubling from 13,503 in 1790 to 26,614 in 1800.[20] Much of this growth was the direct result of the high-risk, high-stakes maritime commerce generated by the Anglo-French conflict that began in 1793. From the moment France declared war against Britain, Citizen Genet, the French minister to the United States, acted to gain American support for France, issuing nearly 50 letters of marque to Baltimore vessels, which entitled them to prey upon the British merchant fleet.[21] The Anglo-French war, which lasted until 1815, had a salutary effect on Chesapeake Bay shipbuilding. Between 1792 and 1797, the number of Baltimore ship registries increased four and one-half times.[22]

Warfare, and its consequent disruption of normal maritime commerce, ensured a strong demand for fast vessels to evade British and French warships and sneak cargo into blockaded ports. The needs of Baltimore privateers, engaged in legalized piracy, also stimulated refinements in hull design and rigging. Clearly, "trouble and unrest were the Baltimore clipper's foster parents."[23] During the War of 1812, a total of 126 privately armed vessels operated out of Baltimore, and altogether they captured and plundered some 500 British vessels.[24] The most successful of these Baltimore-based raiders, the schooners *Comet* and *Chasseur*, under Captain Thomas Boyle, were designed and built by Thomas Kemp, one of the most prominent of the Baltimore ship-builders. The *Chasseur*, Kemp's masterpiece,[25] was renowned for capturing 80 vessels in the year 1814 alone, three of which were appraised at a total of $400,000.[26]

The Treaty of Ghent ended the war in 1815, and the *Chasseur* returned to Baltimore, laden with spoils, on February 20. Passing Fort McHenry, where Francis Scott Key had recently penned some memorable verses, Boyle fired a broadside salute, answered by the cheers of a crowd of thousands.[27] A few months later Kemp, planning to retire from shipbuilding, began a new partnership with George Gardner, who had worked for him for some years as a carpenter. The new firm, Kemp and Gardner, allowed Kemp to transfer his shipbuilding obligations to George Gardner, his chosen successor.

George Gardner's 1815 partnership with Thomas Kemp lasted only a year before Kemp retired to his Talbot County estate on the eastern shore of the Chesapeake. But Kemp's influence was critically important for Gardner's career. During the early nineteenth century most Baltimore business ventures were carried on among friends with long histories of cooperation, and much of George Gardner's subsequent success as a shipbuilder was owed to repeated purchases of his vessels by a circle of Baltimore businessmen with strong bonds to each other and to Thomas Kemp.

In 1816, Joseph Robson, formerly a master carpenter for Thomas Kemp,[28] took Kemp's place in the firm, and the partnership became known as Gardner and Robson. As the anointed successors of Thomas Kemp, Gardner and Robson enjoyed great success even during the postwar slump. The first Gardner and Robson vessel, the 151-ton *Ammande*, was completed in 1816. The following year they built two sharp-hulled schooners and a sloop, and in 1818 they completed six more schooners ranging from 43 to 146 tons burthen, all but one designated as sharp. The Gardner and Robson partnership specialized in small, sharp schooners until 1820, launching fourteen altogether, none exceeding 133 tons. One brig, the comparatively mammoth 344-ton *Hyperion*, was completed in 1819 and remained the largest Gardner-built vessel until 1831. Joseph Robson left the partnership in 1821, and George Gardner became the sole owner. Over the next decade, three of his four sons joined him in the firm.

George Gardner and his sons continued the specialization in "sharp" vessels begun during the Gardner and Robson partnership. Of 32 vessels completed between 1820 and 1831, 25 were sharp schooners and brigs with "pilot boat" hulls. These sharp schooners and brigs were highly specialized for speed and maneuverability. We do not know how Gardner found a lasting market for his vessels, nor do we know for certain how they were used by their owners. Circumstantial evidence, however, suggests that many may have been employed in South America and Mexico.

The termination of Anglo-American and Anglo-French warfare might have brought an end to the demand for sharp-built Baltimore schooners by 1816. But such a slump in the local economy was averted by the Spanish-American wars of liberation. The United States took little interest when these wars first began in 1810. But early in 1816, Thomas Taylor, an American bearing six blank privateer's licenses, arrived in Baltimore as the official representative of the Spanish colony of Buenos Aires.[29] The appeal to patriotism and the lure of plunder proved irresistible to Baltimore merchants, who quickly built and dispatched scores of sharp-built vessels to South America with such names as the *Fourth of July*, the *Patriota*, and the *Enemy of Tyrants*.[30] Over 50 vessels from the Chesapeake, each with 90 to 100 officers and men, received privateer's licenses from the colonies of Artigas (now Uruguay), Buenos Aires (now a province of Argentina), and Venezuela over the next few years.[31]

These vessels swiftly drove Spanish and Portuguese commerce from the Atlantic and Caribbean, and even successfully blockaded harbors on the coasts of Spain and Portugal. But when independence was won in 1821, the last of the South American privateer licenses was revoked,[32] and demand for sharp-built vessels declined precipitously. Nevertheless, Mexico and the new South American nations, now building their own navies, continued to purchase a few vessels, and between 1826 and 1829 George Gardner built six brigs and schooners with "pilot boat" hulls bearing the Hispanic names *Chimboraza*, *Celino*, *Rosa*, *El Ora*, *La Zona*, and *Count Villanueba*. The Gardners probably received these contracts through old business associates who may have acted as purchasing agents for the navies of Mexico and other emergent South American republics. By the mid-1830s the Gardners were building formal naval vessels for Mexico.

While sharp schooners and brigs were George Gardner's specialty, he also built other vessel types. Between 1821 and 1832, he built seven vessels described as "full," including two schooners, two brigs, two ships, and a steamboat. Although Gardner vessels were usually built with simple billet heads, two of his "full"-bodied vessels carried carved figurehead busts beneath their bowsprits. These were the 281-ton brig *George and Henry*, built in 1823 and named for his old friends, the Pattersons, and the 302-ton brig *George Gardner*, completed in 1824. Proud of his success, Gardner bolted his own oaken likeness to the prow of the vessel that bore his name.

Five years later, the patriarch George Gardner honored his eldest son, now 26, by naming a 149-ton pilot boat *Wm. Gardner*. But he had not long to live. The following year he suffered what was probably a stroke, and by the end of 1830, when he was 55 years old, this former master carpenter was only able to mark an "X" in place of a signature on his will.[33] George Gardner died three years later, at the age of 58, on December 20, 1833.[34] Throughout George Gardner's final illness, work continued at the shipyard, albeit mainly for repairs. At the time of his death, the firm employed 25 carpenters, 19 caulkers, and 12 oakum pickers. The names of these men are listed in probate documents, which provide evidence of the racial composition of the Gardner labor force. In the 1833 Baltimore City Directory,[35] "free colored" persons were listed in a separate section at the end of the volume. All of Gardner's carpenters whose names appeared in the directory were white. Six of his nineteen caulkers appeared in the directory, and four of these were "colored." Of the five oakum pickers listed, one was "colored."

Work at the Gardner shipyard must have been somewhat disrupted during George Gardner's final illness and the subsequent settlement of his estate, for no new Gardner-built vessels were completed between 1833 and 1835. Gardner's two eldest sons apparently purchased most of their father's shipyard equipment and remained at the Lancaster Street location. In 1836 the firm, now known as Wm. & Geo. Gardner, completed three new vessels.

A unique perspective on the Gardner shipyard in 1836 was provided by an eighteen-year-old slave named Fred Bailey, whose master, Hugh Auld, Jr., had placed him with the Gardners as an apprentice caulker. Bailey later achieved international renown as the abolitionist writer, or-

Figure 11. A daguerreotype showing Frederick Douglass (1818–95) in his late twenties. He received the scar over his left eyebrow, extending down to his cheek, in 1836 during an attack by white apprentices at the Gardner Brothers' shipyard. Courtesy National Portrait Gallery, Smithsonian Institution, Washington, D.C.

ator, and editor Frederick Douglass, the most prominent African-American of the nineteenth century. When Hugh Auld's brother Thomas married Lucretia Anthony in 1823, her father had given five-year-old Freddy Bailey to them to be raised as a house slave.[36] Three years later, the Aulds sent Freddy to Baltimore to become a companion for Hugh's infant son. As later recounted in his autobiography,[37] Frederick Douglass lived with the Aulds in Fells Point from 1826 to 1833 and again from 1836 to 1838. Hugh Auld sent young Fred to the Gardners' firm largely as a result of the ties he and the Gardners had to the Kemp family.[38] Frederick Douglass spent eight months at the Gardners' shipyard. It was during a period of frenzied activity, as the Gardners rushed to meet a contract deadline. It was also a time of labor unrest, and the environment proved a difficult one for Douglass to learn a trade in. As he later described it:

Mr. Gardner was engaged that spring in building two large man-of-war brigs, professedly for the Mexican government. The vessels were to be launched in the July of that year, and in failure thereof, Mr. Gardner was to loose a considerable sum; so that when I entered, all was hurry. There was no time to learn anything. Every man had to do that which he knew how to do. In entering the ship-yard, my orders from Mr. Gardner were to do whatever the carpenters commanded me to do. This was placing me at the beck and call of about seventy-five men. I was to regard all these as masters. Their word was to be my law. My situation was a most trying one. At times I needed a dozen pair of hands. I was called a dozen ways in the space of a single minute. Three or four voices would strike my ear at the same moment. It was—"Fred., come help me to cant this timber here."—"Fred., come carry this timber yonder."—"Fred., bring that roller here."—"Fred., go get a fresh can of water."—"Fred., come help saw off the end of this timber."—"Fred., go quick and get the crowbar."—"Fred., hold on the end of this fall."—"Fred., go to the blacksmith's shop, and get a new punch."—"Hurra, Fred.! run and bring me a cold chisel."—"I say Fred., bear a hand, and get up a fire as quick as lightning under that steambox."—"Halloo, nigger! come, turn this grindstone."—"Come, come! move, move! and bowse this timber forward."—"I say, darky, blast your eyes, why don't you heat up some pitch?"—"Halloo! halloo! halloo!" (Three voices at the same time.) "Come here!—Go there!—Hold on where you are! Damn you if you move, I'll knock your brains out!"[39]

In 1830, Baltimore had a large population of free blacks. One of every six black men held a skilled job,[40] and the shipyards were one of the few areas where the employment of blacks was tolerated. Douglass wrote that until shortly before he had gone to work for the Gardners, "black and white ship-carpenters worked side-by-side . . . and many of the black carpenters were free men."[41] This tolerance was undermined during the early 1830s, when massive numbers of young immigrants from England and Ireland arrived at the port of Baltimore.[42] The resulting competition for jobs was intense. Abruptly one day in 1836, knowing the Gardners had a deadline, the white carpenters struck, saying "that if free colored carpenters were encouraged, they would soon take the trade into their own hands, and poor white men would be thrown out of employment."

Anti-black sentiment spread to the apprentices,[43] who, encouraged by journeymen, "began to put on airs and talk about the 'niggers taking the country.'" Several incidents followed in which Douglass nearly lost his life. Once, he was driving bolts through the keelson, deep in the hold of a vessel, with an apprentice named Hayes. A bolt bent, and Hayes accused Douglass, saying it was his blow. When Douglass denied it, Hayes attacked him with an adze. Douglass parried the blow with a maul and survived. A group of apprentices, "armed with sticks, stones and heavy hand spikes," then attacked Douglass as 50 white carpenters looked on, some shouting, "Kill the damned nigger!" Douglass was viciously beaten and almost lost an eye. When his master, Hugh Auld, attempted to file charges, the magistrate replied, "Sir, I am sorry, but I cannot move in this matter except on the oath of white witnesses." Not one of the 50 whites who had witnessed the beating of Douglass in the Gardner shipyard was willing to testify. By this time Hugh Auld had become foreman of the neighboring Price shipyard, and Douglass finished his apprenticeship there during 1836 and 1837.

⁂

The sharp brigs and schooners of the Baltimore shipyards found another market in the 1830s and 1840s. Slavery in British colonies had been officially ended by an act of Parliament in 1833. But while the Royal Navy patrolled the west coast of Africa to intercept slavers, the demand for slaves was increasing dramatically. Since import of African slaves into the United States was illegal, much of the American demand was met by slave breeders in Virginia and other East Coast states, who sold the children south to the cotton plantations in the lower Mississippi Valley. The demand for labor on the rapidly expanding sugar plantations of Cuba and Brazil, however, was supplied by large-scale importation of slaves from West Africa, and fast slave ships were needed to penetrate the British blockade. Unknown to Frederick Douglass, at Price's shipyard he helped to complete the slavers *Delorez*, *Teayer*, and *Eagle* in 1836 and 1837. In the spring of 1838, as a young journeyman, he worked on the slaver *Laura* at the nearby Butler & Lamdin yard.[44]

Continued "foreign" orders for slavers during 1838 and 1839 helped the Gardners' business survive the financial panic of 1837. In July 1838, William Gardner launched the 465-ton *Venus*. Frederick Douglass probably watched this launch from the Price shipyard, only three hundred yards away. Less than two months later, carrying papers borrowed from a free black seaman, Douglass fled north to begin his life as a free man in New York City. Yet even as he traveled north, the *Venus* sailed for Africa, where her exploits as a slaver would bring international recognition to the Gardners—and, ultimately, an order for two opium clippers from John and George Dixwell of Augustine Heard & Co.

$\mathcal{T}$he 'Frolic'

BY APRIL 1844, John Dixwell had negotiated a contract in Baltimore with William Gardner to build two vessels. When he returned to Boston he wrote his brother George that he had "just contracted for two clipper vessels—one a schr. of 140 tons, and the other a herm. brig of 200, to be built at Baltimore and dispatched for China about 1st Sept."[1] The larger of the two, the *Frolic*, was to be run between India and China. The smaller schooner *Dart* was to be used for deliveries along the China coast.[2] Constructing and outfitting the ships would take about six months and require payments to numerous suppliers, so Dixwell contracted with the Baltimore commission house of Birckhead & Pearce to represent him for a fee of 2 percent of the total building and outfitting costs. Dixwell's personal fee for overall management of the project was to be 2.5 percent.[3]

George Dixwell was ready to move the Heard firm into large-scale opium commerce. While the Heards had acted as Jardine, Matheson's agent, he had learned that the larger firm had maximized its profits by using its own fleet to bring opium from India and distribute it along the China coast. But the Dixwells had to consider what type of ships would best suit their purpose. He thus grappled with the age-old problem of shipowners, that of finding an optimum compromise between a fast, maneuverable vessel able to outrun the competition and one able at the same time to carry enough freight to generate a profit.

The *Frolic* was originally planned as a hermaphrodite brig, square rigged on the foremast and fore-and-aft rigged on the main mast. However, for the Dixwells and the Gardners the size and shape of the hull was the fundamental design decision. Rigging could always be altered, as indeed the *Frolic*'s was, for she was eventually completed as a standard—not hermaphrodite—brig, square rigged on both masts. The design of the *Frolic* began with George Dixwell's letter from China, in which he generally described the size and hull form he required. John Dixwell then discussed these instructions with William Gardner, who supervised the carving of a half-model of the hull. Like most Baltimore clippers, the *Frolic* was built from a model, rather than from paper plans. The half-model was cut from a block of wood built up from alternating layers of red cedar and pine. These layers, termed lifts, were held together with dowels and clamps while the model was sawed, carved, and sanded into a hull design that met Dixwell's specifications. (For a detailed description of laying out and building the *Frolic*, see Appendix B.)

Generally, the scale of a Baltimore half-model was one-fourth inch to the foot. The master carpenters' certificate,[4] filed December 1, 1844, reveals the *Frolic* to have been 97 feet long, 24 feet ½ inch wide (both measured on deck), and 10 feet deep (measured amidships, from the top of the keelson to the underside of the deck planking). Thus, the finished half-model approved by John Dixwell would have been just over 2 feet in length, 6 inches wide, and 2.5 inches thick.

For the Gardners, the *Frolic*'s design would be but a variation on the sharp pilot-boat hull form that had been the family specialty for 31 years. There would, of course, be refinements appropriate to her intended use, but her general characteristics would follow the traditional pattern. At 209 tons, the *Frolic* would be relatively large for a Baltimore clipper. The Gardners would be paid $24 per ton, Baltimore carpenters' measure, to construct the hull.

The masts of Baltimore clippers were long, light, and set with an extreme rake, often approaching twenty degrees. The mast sections and yards, fashioned from round timbers (tree trunks), were designed to carry massive amounts of sail. In fact, the heavy spars and ponderous sail could render the ship unstable. Standing rigging (the permanently placed stays and shrouds used to support the masts) was as light and sparse as safety would allow. This reduced wind resistance and provided some margin of safety in storm conditions, by ensuring that the

rig "could be removed by the Lord if the crew failed to do so in time."[5]
Over-sparring was indeed a problem for the *Frolic* from the very start.
Following her maiden voyage from Baltimore to Bombay, her captain,
Edward Faucon, had complained: "In squally weather her yards [are]
rather too heavy for her & she requires a stronger crew to handle her
than we had coming out."[6]

Though the classic Baltimore clipper was built with clean lines, her
beam (the maximum width measured on deck) was usually great in re-
lation to her length. The *Frolic*'s length-to-beam ratio was a fairly standard four to one. Most brig-rigged clippers, like the *Frolic*, had their
greatest beam relatively far forward, partly to achieve sufficient forward displacement to support the added weight of their foremast yards,
extended bowsprits, jib booms, and flying jib booms.[7] Yet even this increased forward displacement could not always compensate for the in-
stability engendered by over-sparring, and thus when driven hard by
an inexperienced master these vessels could be forced under—"pitch-
poling" end over end—by the leverage of their masts under press of
sail.

Baltimore clippers were built with low freeboard (distance from deck
to waterline), particularly amidships. The single deck was flush, extending in an unbroken expanse the whole length and breadth of the
vessel. These clear decks provided space for men to work the vessel and,
when necessary, to maneuver cannon. The *Frolic*, like other large vessels employed in dangerous trades, had bulwarks built around the edges
of the deck. These helped to prevent heavy seas from washing aboard
and sweeping crew members away. Even more important for an opium
clipper, they provided the crew some measure of protection against
shots fired by pirates, and a secure platform for swivel-mounted blunderbusses. The *Frolic* would carry a dozen of these unforgiving antipersonnel weapons.

The *Frolic*, like other clippers, was sharp-built at the bow, with extreme dead-rise amidships. Dead-rise is the angle above horizontal from
the top of the keel to the turn of the bilge (where the side of the hull
becomes vertical). Dead-rise on classic Baltimore clippers is believed to
have ranged from 25 to 29 degrees.[8] This produced a V-shaped bottom,
resulting in significant loss of cargo capacity compared to that of standard merchant vessels with U-shaped bottoms. Hulls of Baltimore clippers were built shallow at the bow and much deeper at the stern, pro-

ducing considerable "drag" aft. This increased depth toward the stern enabled the hull to track properly and remain responsive to the helm when pressed under canvas. The *Frolic*, at ten feet deep, was about average for a Baltimore clipper of her size, but her captain, Edward Faucon, who had earned a reputation for driving his vessels hard, later complained, "She is much too shallow to be a powerful vessel in strong breezes."[9]

Most of these attributes of the classic Baltimore clipper were already developed by the end of the War of 1812. Later builders seeking extra speed exaggerated specific features of the type—increasing dead-rise, sharpening bows, over-sparring, and raking stems and sterns with extreme overhangs.[10] Some of these exaggerations were undoubtedly incorporated into the *Frolic*.

Two rare mid-nineteenth-century waterfront views preserve for us the ordered disarray of the traditional Baltimore shipyard. A daguerreotype (Figure 12), taken from Federal Hill in 1851, shows an unnamed shipyard with two small schooners, framed and partially planked, with sterns just above the high tide mark, each surrounded by a lattice of spindly scaffolding. Rough, round timbers are piled at the water's edge, while sawed planking is neatly stacked on a loading dock. At center, providing a date for the picture, lies the Gardner's newly finished 250-ton steamboat *Bertha Harrascowitz*, awaiting delivery to a firm in Caracas, Venezuela.

The second view (Figure 13), probably from the late 1850s, shows Thomas Booz & Bros. shipyard on Harris Creek, about seven blocks east of the Gardner yard. Here we see two merchant vessel hulls under construction. One is already planked, while the other provides a lesson in shipbuilding. Newly placed body frames are propped in position atop an unfinished keel. Underlaid by heavy blocks, the keel slopes upward from the water's edge, ending in a squared scarf. Additional keel timbers lie on the ground below. To the right is the mould loft; in the foreground, stacks of oak knees; and finally, at center, the steam box with its brick chimney. Working from these Baltimore waterfront scenes and from early maps of Fells Point, we have created two views of the Gardners' shipyard circa 1844, with the *Frolic* and the *Dart* in various stages of construction (Figures 14 and 15).

Actual work on the *Frolic* began as soon as John Dixwell had approved the half-model (see Appendix B for more details). She was prob-

Figure 12. An 1851 daguerreotype view of an unidentified Baltimore shipyard below Federal Hill. At center the Gardner Brothers' side-wheel steamer *Bertha Harrascowitz* awaits delivery to a firm in Caracas, Venezuela. Courtesy Peale Museum, Baltimore City Life Museums, Baltimore, Maryland.

ably launched soon after her hull was completed. Launching ways— long paired timber tracks—were placed beneath her hull and extended into the black, filthy water of the harbor. The runners (sliding ways) of a minimal cradle, supporting props braced up against the hull, were then placed atop the well-greased launching ways. When all was ready, a "rally line" of men, driving oak wedges, raised the vessel just far enough to knock out the support blocks. Others jumped in unison on the deck to rock her loose, and as the acrid fragrance of burnt oak and tallow permeated the air, the *Frolic* slid "into her destined element."

Now afloat, the *Frolic* was positioned beneath the sheer legs of the crane mounted on Captain Frazier's wharf, and two lower masts were eased through her deck into hollowed-out mast steps bolted to the keelson. The New England white pine used for the masts was light, as well as strong, and thus helped reduce the top-heavy tendency of the over-sparred vessel.

By the beginning of September the *Dart* was almost ready to sail for China. Her total cost to build and outfit had been $13,431.30.[11] On September 3, John Dixwell traveled to Baltimore, where he remained for ten days looking after the *Dart* and the *Frolic*.[12] There he drafted a letter to be carried aboard the *Dart* to the Heard office in China. "This goes by the Dart," he wrote, "a schooner which I have built at this

Figure 13. Thomas Booz & Bros. shipyard, about seven blocks east of the Gardner Brothers, with two large cargo vessels under construction. Photograph probably late 1850s. Courtesy Peale Museum, Baltimore City Life Museums, Baltimore, Maryland.

Figure 14. The Gardner Brothers shipyard at Fells Point, Baltimore, in July 1844. To the left carpenters shape sections of the *Frolic*'s keel, while at center others piece together and raise the *Frolic*'s frames. To the right, a yellow pine plank is pulled from the steam box while workmen prepare to fasten another to the hull of the *Dart*. Original illustration by S. F. Manning.

place in compliance with orders received from your Mr. [George] Dixwell, and which will get to sea in about a week. She is of the very best materials, and strongly put together altho' not so daintily finished as some of the vessels which have gone from Boston and New York."[13]

John Dixwell was too much a businessman to allow the *Dart* to depart only in ballast. He paid $2,639.04 for a typical Baltimore cargo, comprising 100 barrels of Richmond flour, 110 boxes of tobacco, 50 barrels of pitch, and a total of 50 hogsheads and 50 barrels of Baltimore-baked pilot bread.[14]

In the meantime, the Dixwells had chosen a captain for the *Frolic*— Edward Horatio Faucon. Almost the same age, John Dixwell and Faucon had known each other for 28 years, since their boyhood days at Boston Latin School. Although Faucon had spent most of the previous 22 years at sea, he was still well connected in Boston. His mother, Catherine Waters, was descended from the Dawes family, and on the

Figure 15. The Gardner Brothers shipyard in August 1844. At left, carpenters drinking whiskey from a jug toast the fully coppered *Dart* as she stands ready for launching. At right, a carpenter hammers in treenails fastening yellow pine planks to the *Frolic*'s hull. Original illustration by S. F. Manning.

Figure 16. A pencil sketch of Captain Edward Horatio Faucon (1806–94) in China, circa mid-1840s. Courtesy Massachusetts Historical Society.

night of April 18, 1775, her great-uncle, William Dawes, an associate of Paul Revere, had raced south with the same news that Revere carried north.[15] Faucon's father, Nicolas Michel Faucon, had taught French at Harvard College.[16] Born in Haiti, Nicolas Faucon had grown up in Rouen, France, and had been educated partly in England. In 1804 he was granted a passport from Calcutta to the United States aboard the American brig *Lydia*. During the passage he developed a friendship with John Waters, the *Lydia*'s supercargo. The *Lydia* docked in Boston on July 28, 1804. Fifteen months later, a week before he turned 31, Nicolas Faucon married John Waters's younger sister, Catherine.

Nicolas Faucon first found employment as a private tutor with several "Old Boston" families among whom he quickly established his teaching competence. In 1806, he was appointed instructor of French at

Harvard College, and on November 22 of that year his only child, Edward Horatio, was born. He wanted the best for his son, and in 1816 he enrolled nine-year-old Edward at Boston Latin School. Nicolas Faucon died the following year at the age of 44.

At Boston Latin, Edward Faucon came to know the two older Dixwell brothers. John Dixwell had enrolled in 1815, while Epes entered together with Faucon in 1816. The classes of 1815 and 1816 had only 28 students each, so the boys had ample opportunity to form lasting impressions of each other. These were difficult years of reduced circumstances for Edward and his newly widowed mother, and he began to develop an intense ambition. In the early 1820s, Boston was a rapidly growing port and business center, and a bright Boston boy could become a financial success by going to sea as a captain or supercargo. The virtues of commerce were not only manifest on the streets of Boston but preached from her pulpits as well. For Edward Faucon, the lure proved irresistible, and in 1822, at the age of sixteen, a year short of graduation, he went to sea.

Faucon's uncle, John Waters, was secretary of the New England Marine Insurance Company.[17] He had broad contacts in Boston shipping circles, and it was probably through him that Edward was placed aboard the Boston brig *Ant* to begin his training as a mariner. Faucon made a record of his early maritime career 40 years later, on the inside cover of a ship's log, where he listed every vessel upon which he served, the ports visited, and the number of visits he made to each port.[18] Between 1822 and 1828, Faucon served on five Boston brigs, visiting ports on the Atlantic coast of South America, in the West Indies, and in the Mediterranean. At this time Massachusetts merchants, lacking local products from which to assemble marketable outbound cargoes, engaged in triangular, four-, and even five-cornered trade.[19] Coffee and sugar were imported from Brazil; sugar, molasses, and tobacco from the West Indies; cotton from the southern states; tea and silk from China; and spices from the East Indies. Mixed cargoes composed of these goods along with New England lumber, cotton cloth, and rum were dispatched to the Mediterranean in exchange for wine, lemons, oranges, figs, raisins, olives, nuts, sponges, and carpets. Faucon received his early training on repeated voyages from South America and the West Indies to Boston and then on to the Mediterranean.

This pattern was broken in January 1829 when, at the age of 23, Edward Faucon began the first of three voyages to the coast of California for Bryant & Sturgis. The Bryant & Sturgis firm, established in 1811, had earlier specialized in the fur trade, carrying New England manufactured goods to the Pacific Northwest and trading them to the Indians for furs, especially those of sea otters. These, in turn, were sold in China. After years of overhunting, however, sea otters had become scarce by the early 1820s. Moreover, the market for furs in China had declined. In 1822, seeking new business, Bryant & Sturgis sent a vessel to California to gather hides and tallow for sale in Boston. At first such ventures were not very successful. Most hides came from mission herds, and from 1823 through 1826 the British firm of McCulloch & Hartnell had an exclusive contract to purchase hides from the missions. When McCulloch & Hartnell was dissolved in 1828, Bryant & Sturgis had no other serious rivals, and business began to thrive.[20]

Faucon sailed for California as first mate aboard the firm's 208-ton brig *Plant*. The voyage lasted 26 months, 11 of which were spent collecting hides from ranchos and missions up and down the California coast. Then, on October 14, 1831, three weeks after the death of his mother, Faucon began his second hide-gathering voyage to California as first mate aboard the Bryant & Sturgis brig *Chalcedony*. Faucon's grief was partly assuaged by the warm family life aboard the *Chalcedony*. Captain Joseph Steele had brought his young wife along, and during the two-year voyage she gave birth to a son and a daughter. Also aboard was John H. Everett, who, as clerk of the vessel, recorded the numerous exchanges of manufactured goods for hides. On the voyage, Everett and Faucon developed a close friendship that lasted the remainder of their lives. Sixteen years hence, they would both be fellow employees of Augustine Heard & Co. in China.

A week short of his 28th birthday, in 1833, Edward Horatio Faucon sailed from Boston as captain of the Bryant & Sturgis ship *Alert*. When he arrived in California, following the owners' sealed instructions, he surrendered the *Alert* to Captain Francis A. Thompson and took command of the firm's brig *Pilgrim*. Five months earlier, Richard Henry Dana, Jr., had joined the *Pilgrim* for the voyage to California as a seaman. Dana, a nineteen-year-old Harvard freshman, had dropped out of school to go to sea, hoping to improve his health. Dana had developed a strong dislike for Captain Thompson. His diary portrayed him

Figure 17. John H. Everett (1810–89) in China circa 1850. Watercolor on ivory. Courtesy Francis D. Everett, Jr.

as a cruel and arrogant man, representing all that was wrong with the merchant marine.

In contrast, Dana found the erudite, energetic Faucon the epitome of a good captain. Faucon, like Dana, had been educated at Boston Latin School, and the two men shared a common worldview. In Dana's words, "Faucon was a man of education, literary habits, and good social position," one who "held things at their right value."[21] Their first meeting occurred on the beach at San Diego, where Dana was scraping the meat from a dirty cowhide. As Dana recorded it in his diary, Faucon came up to him quietly and addressed him in Latin, quoting the opening line of Virgil's first eclogue, "*Tityre, tu patulae recubans sub tegmine fagi . . .* " ("Tityrus, lying back beneath wide beechen cover . . . ").[22] Dana was hardly languishing in the shade of a beech tree, but Faucon had skillfully punned on the Latin *tegmine* ("cover"),

Figure 18. Richard Henry Dana, Jr. (1815–82), at age 25, from an 1840 daguerreotype. Courtesy National Park Service, Longfellow National Historic Site.

meaning "hide." From this first encounter, a deep and lasting bond grew between Dana and Faucon.

Dana's opinion of Captains Thompson and Faucon would have had no lasting consequence had he not published his memoir in 1840. *Two Years Before the Mast* was an immediate best-seller, and Edward Faucon's competence and character were immortalized in Dana's words:

Captain Faucon was a sailor, every inch of him; he knew what a ship was, and was as much at home in one, as a cobbler in his stall. I wanted no better proof of this than the opinions of the ship's crew, for they had been six months under his command, and knew what he was; and if sailors allow their captain to be a good seaman, you may be sure he is one, for that is a thing they are not always ready to say.[23]

Edward Faucon returned to Boston with the *Pilgrim* on July 6, 1837. Two weeks earlier John Everett's brother, Oliver, had married Betsy Weld, the daughter of Daniel Weld, a prominent Boston merchant. Since the orphaned Faucon no longer had a family of his own, John Everett included his friend in his extended family's activities. The youngest Weld daughter, Martha, was then thirteen, and fifteen years later Faucon would marry her.[24]

By 1837, Bryant & Sturgis's profits from the hide and tallow trade were declining.[25] Competing firms now plied numerous vessels along

the California coast, and enormous numbers of hides from the grass-
lands of South America were being shipped to Boston at less expense
than California hides.[26] In addition, when Faucon returned to Boston
that summer, the city was suffering a financial crisis. Hard currency was
tight and commerce slow, and it appeared unlikely that Bryant & Sturgis would soon send another vessel to California. After eight years, Faucon knew he would not become rich hauling hides, but Boston men
were making fortunes in China.

The following spring, Faucon began his new career in the China
trade. As he lacked experience, he first signed on as an officer aboard
the *Trenton* out of Boston. The *Trenton* sailed for Canton via the Cape
of Good Hope on March 16, 1838, and again on June 11, 1839. Faucon probably served as first mate on both voyages. Then, in the fall of
1840, having some China experience to his credit, Faucon was appointed captain of the *Florida*, sailing her to China in 1840 and probably again in 1841. Finally, in January 1843, he sailed from Boston to
Canton as an officer aboard the new ship *Paul Jones*.

The *Paul Jones* had been built for Russell & Co. At the time of her
arrival at Canton, Augustine Heard, a former partner in Russell & Co.,
was also in Canton establishing the Heard firm with his younger partners, Joseph Coolidge and George Dixwell. In the busy social scene of
Canton, Russell and Heard employees were in regular contact. The *Paul
Jones* lay anchored at Canton for six weeks while her outbound cargo
was assembled, and during this layover Faucon, now made famous by
Dana's recently published book, met Augustine Heard and George
Dixwell. Faucon was in the right place at the right time. Dixwell was
assembling an opium fleet, and Faucon was looking for an opportunity
to become rich. Dixwell was an aggressive businessman and probably
urged Faucon to discuss possibilities with his brother John—whom Faucon had known in school—in Boston.

By the summer of 1844 Faucon was negotiating with John Dixwell
to become master and part owner of the *Frolic*. He knew that in addition to becoming wealthy by trading on his own account, a captain
might become still richer if he owned a share in his vessel. On September 14, 1844, John Dixwell wrote to the Heard firm in China that Edward Faucon had taken a one-fifth share in the *Frolic*, and he predicted
the vessel would be ready to sail for Bombay in about a month. Dixwell
probably dispatched Faucon to Baltimore at about that time to super-

vise the *Frolic*'s completion. A master mariner would have strong opinions regarding the rigging and outfitting of his ship, and by giving Faucon responsibility for overseeing the job Dixwell hoped to avoid later discord and added expense.

The type of rigging determines the number of men required to sail a vessel, and a smaller crew, of course, results in lower operating costs. Faucon had a reputation for scientifically re-rigging his vessels for efficient operation and maximum speed. In 1837 Dana had noted that the *Alert*, under Faucon, was worked with two fewer men than a much smaller brig anchored nearby—as Faucon "had reeved anew nearly all the running rigging of the ship, getting rid of useless blocks, putting single blocks for double wherever he could, using pendant blocks, and adjusting the purchases scientifically."[27] The *Frolic* did not sail from Baltimore until December 7, and Faucon's attention to detail may have contributed to this delay. Dixwell had planned the *Frolic* as a hermaphrodite brig, square rigged on the foremast and fore-and-aft rigged on the main mast, but most of Faucon's sailing experience had been on full brigs, square rigged on each mast. He now determined to have this rig on the *Frolic*. The many changes Faucon required, including purchasing and installing of yards and tailoring an additional suit of square sails, delayed the date of the *Frolic*'s completion.

During September 1844, the Gardner firm's master carpenters worked below deck completing cabinets for ship's stores and cabins for Faucon and his officers.[28] To cover the companionway—a ladder descending to the cabins below—a low deckhouse was fashioned with portholes let through its sides and skylights let through its roof. Joiners set heavy glass decklights into openings cut through the deck planking at strategic points. On their upper sides these glass blocks lay flat and flush with the deck. Below, they were prismatic, diffusing light laterally. Elsewhere on deck, the joiners built chicken coops and a hog house for the fresh meat the *Frolic* would carry.

The *Frolic* was equipped with the best available mechanical fittings. At her stern, a "steering apparatus" provided mechanical advantage between the wheel and the rudder. In clear view from the wheel was the binnacle, a lamp-lit box containing the *Frolic*'s compasses and "timepiece." Abaft the main mast, in the deepest part of the bilge, mechanics installed a pump to be powered by men working hand levers on deck. Near her bow they bolted down a geared windlass to raise the vessel's anchors.

The *Frolic* had two main "bower" anchors, weighing 943 pounds and 824 pounds, and an auxiliary anchor weighing 275 pounds. Near the stern she carried two stream anchors. To raise these anchors she carried three 90-fathom (540-foot) chains. Since the vessel would be engaged in a dangerous trade and exposed to piracy, two cannons and various small arms were purchased. Mounted on wheeled carriages, the cannons could fire nine-pound balls through hinged gunports placed along the *Frolic*'s bulwarks.

In Baltimore during the 1840s, ships were rigged by itinerant crews who followed the work from shipyard to shipyard. Such a crew first installed the *Frolic*'s standing rigging, the permanently secured ropes, shrouds, stays, and backstays used to support her masts. As they worked upward, they were able to send up first the topmasts and finally the top gallant masts into position. After getting up the standing rigging for these spars, they "rove off" the running rigging, the ropes and blocks used to hoist and lower from the yards—the transverse spars that would establish the *Frolic*'s sail plan.

Once the sail plan had been determined, sail makers working in nearby lofts began to make the *Frolic*'s 27 sails from 101½ bolts of cotton duck. Because the *Frolic* was designed for speed, she carried a large complement of sails to enhance her performance in various wind conditions. Specific references to her sails are found scattered throughout letters and invoices over her six-year life. We know she carried a square course, topsail, topgallant, and royal on each of her two masts. She also carried studding sails that could be rigged beyond the lateral edges of each square sail to form a vast wall of canvas during light weather or when sailing before the wind. Three triangular sails—a staysail, jib, and flying jib—were set from the bowsprit and jib boom extending from her bow. For sailing into the wind, she carried a spencer, suspended from a gaff attached to the after side of the fore mast, and a spanker rigged to the aft side of the main mast.

The accommodations for the captain and officers were made comfortable with cabin furniture, drawer knobs, upholstery, damask curtains, and linens. The quarters were equipped with crockery, glassware, lamps, candles, and a medical chest. A "caboose," or galley (a small, movable deckhouse), was furnished with pots, pans, and utensils. John Dixwell planned the *Frolic*'s staple food stores to last eighteen months, so he included 30 barrels of beef, 15 barrels of pork, and 4,506 pounds of bread. In addition to casks of water and a water filter, he supplied wine, cider, and ale. There were also fresh meats and sausages, and fresher still, live fowl and pigs to be housed in coops and pens on deck. Other food stores included butter, cheese, preserved meats, and lemon syrup, perhaps intended for prevention of scurvy. (See Appendix C for a detailed account of the costs of outfitting the *Frolic*.)

While Faucon scoured Fells Point for competent officers and experienced seamen, the Gardners handled finishing touches. Richly carved and ornamented trailboards were bolted beneath the *Frolic*'s bowsprit, carrying aft the scrollwork on her billet head. An American flag, or ensign, was to be flown from her monkey gaff. The final touch was the Augustine Heard firm's "red white diamond" pennant, to be flown from the top of the main mast.

By the mid-1840s, so many vessels were being built in Baltimore that only the launchings of the most notable were mentioned in the newspapers. The *Frolic* was such a vessel. Unlike many Baltimore clippers, she had been built of the best materials. Not only was she larger than most, but her lines were so extreme as to give the overall look of a giant racing yacht. As she lay at Corner's wharf, Fells Point, ready to depart on her maiden voyage, the *Baltimore Sun* described her as a "beautiful specimen of shipbuilding" and noted she had been built for an "extensive house in Boston, intended to trade upon the coast of China." Unable to restrain his partisan pride for Baltimore shipbuilders, the reporter concluded: "We are glad to see that so many eastern houses are sending here to have their vessels built, for it shows what was generally supposed before, that Yankees understand what is for their true interest."[29]

It rained on and off all day on Saturday, December 7, 1844, as the *Frolic* was prepared for departure. Dixwell's Baltimore agents had not been able to find a cargo suitable for export to Bombay, so 18 tons of iron kentledge and 60 tons of stone and "junk" were placed in her hold to provide ballast. On Sunday, December 8, the weather cleared, and the *Frolic* cast off from Corner's wharf. Faucon hired a pilot to steer the *Frolic* safely out of the Patapsco River and down Chesapeake Bay. The wind blew from the northwest, and the following morning, as they passed the Capes and entered the Atlantic, Faucon dismissed the pilot and took command.

The *Frolic* was a new vessel, with new officers, a new crew, and a deck cluttered with two yawls, a longboat, and a barnyard of caged an-

Figure 19. The *Frolic* under sail, with the "red white diamond" flag of Augustine Heard & Co. flying from her main mast. Original illustration by S. F. Manning.

imals. Within two days of sailing, a severe and unexpected southeast gale put her to her first test. Faucon knew the Dixwells would judge him by his elapsed time from Baltimore to Bombay, and he responded to the storm aggressively. In his own words, "For a portion of the time the Brig laid with her monkey rail almost continually under water." Faucon later reflected, "It was rather earlier than desirable to try her qualities in a strong gale but I was glad to find her so good a sea boat."[30]

The *Frolic* sailed down the coast of South America and around Cape Horn uneventfully. Faucon concluded that the vessel's sailing qualities were good but "by no means extraordinary." The vessel's "best days work," during a 24-hour period, was 202 miles "with royals." During a burst of speed east of the Cape he found her running, per observation, at a rate of 245 miles per day, or just over ten miles an hour. From the equator to the Indian Ocean the vessel experienced "nothing but light winds and calms." Faucon found these light breezes showed the *Frolic* "to the best advantage." Much of her later success as an opium clipper derived from her ability to move forward with dispatch under her massive cloud of studding sails while other vessels sat becalmed. Indeed, only eighteen months after departing Baltimore her studding sails were worn so thin from frequent use that they needed replacement.

In his overall review of the *Frolic*, Faucon listed a number of complaints. "In arranging the cabin," he wrote, "it was found impossible to cut side ports" because the clamp, running fore and aft, had been placed "exactly where the ports are wanted." The resulting absence of cross-ventilation made the cabin insufferably hot in the tropics. Next, he noted that the *Frolic*'s main hatch "had been cut exactly amidships instead of near the mainmast." This required moving the main launch to use the hatchway. Then, "the sails were all made of cotton" when "they should have been made of kyanized stuff to prevent their injury by mildew." Finally, he noted that the vessel was so heavily sparred that in "squally weather" she required a stronger crew than the one he had hired in Baltimore.[31]

On March 28, 1845, the *Frolic* arrived at Bombay, 109 days out of Baltimore. Always conscious of the advancing calendar, Faucon had just fought weeks of calms and must have experienced great stress imagining the anxiety and disappointment of Dixwell's Bombay agent at the *Frolic*'s tardy arrival. Faucon was more than ready to throw open her hatches to receive his first cargo of opium.

But there was no opium to be had. Sir Jamsetjee Jejeebhoy, a rich Parsee opium merchant, had received a shipment of four thousand chests from Malwa in the interior, but he refused to allow local merchants to inspect it. These merchants, in turn, refused to receive the drug until they had examined it. While this deadlock awaited resolution in the courts, Faucon and the *Frolic* would languish almost six weeks in Bombay before taking on their first cargo.

$\mathcal{B}$ombay

IT MAY SEEM STRANGE that a single native merchant could bring the entire opium commerce of Bombay to a halt. But whereas Patna opium, exported from Calcutta, was produced under British East India Company monopoly, the Malwa opium shipped from Bombay was produced by independent princely states in the interior of India, beyond British jurisdiction. The Bombay trade was monopolized by native merchants, mainly Parsees and Hindus, who purchased the drug in the Malwa uplands and then exported it to China. Some of these firms shipped the drug to Canton aboard their own vessels and sold it directly to Chinese opium brokers. Others consigned their opium to British firms, who earned both transport fees and commissions on sales. Sir Jamsetjee Jejeebhoy, one of the three largest opium exporters operating out of Bombay, consigned most of his drug to Jardine, Matheson.[1]

American firms had not found it easy to gain access to the Malwa opium trade. In 1833, while still a partner in Russell & Co., Augustine Heard had dispatched Joseph Coolidge to Bombay to solicit consignments. The native merchants, however, maintained strong loyalties to British firms,[2] and Coolidge had only limited success. George Dixwell began a sustained attempt to secure increased consignments of Malwa opium for the Augustine Heard firm in August 1843, when he chartered the schooner *Don Juan* to transport the narcotic for sale along the China coast.

Figure 20. Sir Jamsetjee Jejeebhoy (1783–1859), the Bombay Parsee opium merchant and philanthropist. Oil portrait attributed to Lamqua circa 1845. Courtesy Patrick Connor, Martyn Gregory, London.

The *Don Juan* opened a new and lucrative market to the Heards. On the China coast they were able to negotiate higher sales prices for their Bombay consignors than could have been obtained in Canton. In November 1844, when the Heards bought a three-fourths interest in the *Don Juan*, George Dixwell boasted of receiving up to $890 per chest on the coast, while their opium would have remained unsold in Canton even as the market slumped to $600. Dixwell felt confident that these "splendid" sales would bring the firm increased consignments. "You see," he wrote Mr. Heard, "how absolutely essential it is to have one or two vessels for the coast trade."[3]

Although Dixwell believed he would receive increased consignments of Malwa opium from Bombay, he did not know whether native merchants would send those shipments aboard the *Frolic*. On December 10, 1844, two days after the *Frolic* sailed from Baltimore, Dixwell wrote to Mr. Heard, "If we have early consignments of the drug we shall keep the Don Juan at Woosung [the port serving Shanghai] as a station vessel, and send supplies up to her by the Dart. The Frolic, I shall sell unless she brings so heavy a freight from Bombay as to promise a profitable business in that direction."[4]

Before the *Frolic* sailed from Baltimore, John Dixwell had contracted with Martin Murray & Co. of Bombay to acquire her first cargo of opium. Meanwhile, the Heard firm, in Canton, wrote to Jehangeer Cursetjee in Bombay, begging him to "exert his influence with our various constituents there to procure her a good freight."[5] Jehangeer Cursetjee, a Parsee opium merchant, had done business with old Mr. Heard during his Russell & Co. days and had broad contacts among native merchants. To insure his active assistance in finding a cargo for the *Frolic*, the firm informed him that if it became profitable through his assistance to run the *Frolic* regularly between Bombay and Canton, he would be given a share of the freight fees she earned.

Jehangeer Cursetjee immediately went to work "influencing shippers of the drug." Unfortunately, both Cursetjee and Martin Murray expected the *Frolic* to have left Baltimore in September, and thus anticipated her arrival in Bombay during December or early January. The *Frolic* was delayed, however, and Martin Murray had to report to the Heards in Canton that Cursetjee "had a considerable quantity ready for her . . . had she arrived as 1st anticipated."[6]

During 1844, the Bombay firm of Kessressung Khooshalchund had consigned several hundred chests of Malwa to the Heard firm. As they had secured high prices for his opium on the coast, the Heards hoped that Huttasung Kessressung, the managing partner of Kessressung Khooshalchund, would "open his heart" and give them a larger consignment the following year.[7] More important, they wanted Mr. Kessressung to purchase a share in the *Don Juan*, the *Dart*, and the *Frolic*. The Heards reasoned that if Kessressung owned a share in the vessels, he would not only ship his opium aboard the *Frolic* but would consign it to them to sell as well. Since Jehangeer Cursetjee was an old friend of Mr. Kessressung, the Heards asked him to influence Kessressung to buy into the company fleet.

Kessressung, an elderly Hindu, resided in Ahmedabad, 290 miles north of Bombay. Each year the firm contracted for opium produced in the Malwa uplands. The Malwa plateau of west central India was bounded to the south by the Vindhya range and drained to the north by three tributaries of the Chambal River: the Spira, the Kali Sindh, and the Parbati. This plateau area was subdivided into small, independent native states, most of which had accepted British "protection" in 1818. The southern portion of this plateau, about 1,500 feet in elevation, possessed a soil and climate ideally suited for opium cultivation.

The principal object of the Kessressung Khooshalchund firm "was to obtain a good interest on the capital of the House, employing it in advances to smaller men."[8] Profits were earned by selling opium to smaller speculators on credit, taking brokerage commissions for purchase of the drug, arranging its transport to Bombay and its export to China, and returning profits to the speculators. To a lesser degree, the principals of the firm engaged in their own speculations, exporting opium on company account.

"Old Jehangeer" must have been successful in his discussions with Huttasung Kessressung, for on March 4, 1845, George Dixwell wrote to Mr. Heard that Kessressung had offered to take a half-interest in the firm's three vessels and looked to "making a good deal of money out of them. This," remarked Dixwell, "was only usual for he is the largest speculator in Bombay after Sir Jamsetjee."[9]

From the beginning, Augustine Heard & Co. had earned its profits from transport fees and commissions. It was company policy not to engage in opium speculation, and in spite of Mr. Kessressung's urging, the Heard firm had not consented "to buy drug in order to give the vessels employment." Even without direct speculation in the cargo, the ships would make $20,000 to $30,000 a year profit if Kessressung made large consignments, and at the worst they would make their expenses. Dixwell noted that all of the consignments they received during the spring and summer of 1845 would be owed to the *Frolic*, the *Dart*, and the *Don Juan*, but pointed out that had the *Don Juan* not been successful on the China coast, the firm would have had "all of last years consignments still on hand."

George Dixwell was optimistic regarding sale of the three vessels to Kessressung Khooshalchund. However, Huttasung Kessressung was a cautious businessman, and negotiations with him broke down in early

July when he learned the Heards had not obtained a good price for the opium he had shipped the previous fall. Mr. Kessressung's practice was to test the competence of the firms to whom he consigned drug by shipping identical consignments aboard the same vessel, but to competing firms. The firm providing the best returns would be favored with larger consignments.

The low proceeds Mr. Kessressung had received from the Heards had largely resulted from George Dixwell's misplaced confidence in Captain Harding of the *Don Juan*. One of Dixwell's reasons for purchasing the *Don Juan* in the first place had been to secure the services of her captain, C. F. Harding. As he put it, "the mistakes of an inexperienced man in the coming year might put an end to our opium business which is, by far, the best we have."[10] But Harding, against Dixwell's "most earnest instructions to sell," had held on to the firm's old stock of Malwa through the winter, hoping for better prices.[11] Mr. Kessressung complained that he and his friends had suffered not only from the low prices but also from the shipment's being found 8 percent short in weight.[12] While the competition had received good returns, the Heards had—as expressed in the Anglo-Indian English of Kessressung's clerk— made one group of consignors "sufferers, whilst the others mirth with joice." Kessressung blamed the low weights on the chicanery of Chinese opium brokers: "We are told here that the Chines Dealers, in opium, goes on board the opium receiving vessel and play many tricks with her Commanders and officers . . . and to make good opium boil white they make boil in water containing alum or saltpeter."

Huttasung Kessressung's reluctance to buy shares in the Heards' opium vessels ultimately turned the negotiations to his advantage. On July 25, he informed the Heards that although he was "not anxious to be interested in any Clipper as part owner," their "mutual friend Jehangeer Cursetjee had often brought the subject" to his attention, and he was now willing to take the shares.[13] He did not, however, want his purchase to become public knowledge, so he asked the Heards not to register a bill of sale in his name. Mr. Kessressung knew he would be influencing speculators to ship aboard the Heard vessels, and he did not wish to reveal his conflict of interest. As he put it, "Such a document could never be kept a secret, and if known in China or here that I have an interest in any of them, it would create a deal of jealousy . . . perhaps injurious to your interest."

Kessressung took a two-fifths share of the *Frolic*, half of the *Dart*, and three-eighths of the *Don Juan*. In a letter marked "private" and dated the following day, Jehangeer Cursetjee told the Heards the rest of the story.[14] "I have at last succeeded . . . in bringing him around," wrote Cursetjee, "but I was obliged to accept half a share in the clippers according to what you allot him to convince him that everything would go well." Cursetjee explained that without his own investment Kessressung would have declined the clippers altogether, and he warned the Heards to pay close attention in all their dealings with the old merchant for "if you loose him once, he will never come to you again."

Cursetjee now gave the Heards the bad news. "Hereafter . . . [they would] be obliged to speculate in opium" to help fill the *Frolic* at such times when sufficient freight was not otherwise obtainable. Having just heard Mr. Kessressung's outrage on discovering that his Malwa consignments were 8 percent underweight, Cursetjee reminded the Heards to send an expert opium inspector to Bombay, suggesting that he might even send the inspector up to Malwa, where he and Kessressung would be contracting for the coming year's crop. The Heard firm needed an opium inspector to represent their interests in India because Malwa opium was always of uncertain quality. Whereas the British East India Company controlled every step of opium production in eastern India, there were no controls over quality among the private producers in the Malwa uplands. Adulteration of the Malwa narcotic was so pervasive that inspection prior to purchase was absolutely essential.

The "opium year" in Malwa began in early October, when "buniahs," native merchants who would later buy the product, entered into agreements with peasant cultivators.[15] Often buniahs advanced cash to the cultivators to pay for draft animals, seed, manure, and living costs while they were producing a crop. Operating in arrears, the cultivator usually became deeply obligated to the buniah and thus was unable to bargain for the highest price. At the same time that the buniahs were contracting with the growers, native firms such as Kessressung Khooshalchund contracted with the buniahs for given quantities of opium to be delivered on certain dates at specific prices. As these agreements were entered into even before seed was sown, they were highly speculative, anticipating market conditions a year or more in the future.

Meanwhile, peasant cultivators began to prepare their fields for planting. Opium was a winter crop, and farmers began cultivation only after they had gathered in their summer, rainy-season crops and rooted out and burned old stalks. The farmers prepared the soil for planting by plowing four times on consecutive days, then harrowing to break up remaining clods, and finally mixing in sixteen to eighteen cartloads of manure per half acre. The farmers then subdivided the cultivated areas into small plots from eight by twelve feet (at the largest) to half that size, surrounding each with a low ridge to hold irrigation water. Seed was hand sown in late October and early November. The first watering was given the day the seed was sown, and the second three days later. Plots were irrigated seven or eight times more at eight-day intervals. Young poppy plants germinated within eight days of planting and were thinned when about six inches tall, leaving a hand-span's distance between the strongest stalks.

In Malwa, the opium poppy reached the desired half-ripe state in three and a half months. Shortly after the flower petals fell, the immature, juicy seed capsule began to approach three and a half inches in length. From late February through March, cultivators bled and tapped the capsules. Each plot was bled three to four times at intervals of three to four days. Lengthwise incisions were made by dragging a three-pronged tool upward along the capsule during the hottest part of the day. Almost immediately, the capsule would begin to exude a white milky sap. This liquid was held in place by the rapid formation of a sticky outer skin, the result of evaporation. Juice continued to ooze out during the night, reaching a thick, gummy consistency by morning.

Beginning at sunrise, harvesters removed this accumulation, termed "cheek," with an iron scraper lubricated with linseed oil. Each day's collection was deposited in an earthen vessel and covered with additional linseed oil—ideally two parts oil to ten parts cheek—to prevent further evaporation. The oil permeated the cheek and became the first of many adulterants. The cheek was sold by weight to the buniah, who would not purchase it if its consistency was thinner than half-dried glue. Half an acre of well-tilled land might yield 20 to 30 pounds of cheek—ultimately, about two-thirds that weight in opium.

The buniah took the fresh cheek to his repository, where it was hung in doubled cloth bags from the ceiling of a darkened room. Within eight days most of the linseed oil had dripped away, but the cheek was allowed to hang 30 to 40 days longer. During this time fermentation began, ultimately imparting a distinctive flavor to the product. The bags of cheek were taken down before the start of the rainy season, which began in June or July. The cheek was then scraped from the bags and thrown into shallow copper vats, each holding about 140 pounds. Workmen kneaded the mass until a homogeneous mixture "resembling thickened treacle" or "strawberry jam" was achieved. This blending was necessary because the bags of cheek had been produced by numerous farmers cultivating a multitude of plots and thus varied significantly in quality.

During the mixing process, the buniah supervised adulteration of the cheek with foreign substances. Cheek was adulterated to augment weight, increase volume, and improve color. To this end, the buniah employed a wide variety of substances, including fruit and vegetable juices; oils, gums, and resins; ground seeds and husks; pulverized steatite, lime, and clay; and, quite commonly, cow dung. When appropriate adulterants had been added and the mixture had reached the desired color and consistency, workers, their hands lubricated with linseed oil, pulled large handfuls from the vats and shaped them into smooth, rounded cakes. These were rolled first in a chaff of finely pulverized poppy capsules and then in a mulch of ground leaves and stalks. The soft cakes were laid to dry on a bed of leaves and stalks. After twenty days they were turned, reshaped, and then exposed on the floor of a well-ventilated room until hard enough to be packed. The resulting product was an uneven, flattened cake about five inches in maximum dimension and weighing eight to ten ounces. The hard exterior was embedded with fragments of leaves, stalks, and chips of capsules, while the soft interior had the consistency of cream cheese and a rich chestnut color.

The official weighing season began on the first of October. By this time the opium cakes were hard enough to be packed, the rainy season had ended, and the roads to Bombay were dry enough to be passable. Kessressung Khooshalchund and other native firms were now ready to receive their first deliveries of the opium contracted for a year earlier.

Up to the time of its transport to Bombay, native cultivators and merchants worked entirely outside British jurisdiction. The British, none-theless, had worked out an effective arrangement to derive huge rev-enues from the Malwa crop while at the same time protecting their Patna opium monopoly in eastern India. Shipments of Malwa opium to China had first attracted British interest in 1813. By 1818, the in-expensive Malwa product had seriously undercut the price of the Com-pany-produced Patna drug.[16] Monopolist Patna could not compete with the cheap Malwa product, and the Company was threatened with loss of its major revenue source. The Company first responded by attempt-ing to purchase the entire 1821–22 Malwa crop, but this was an ex-pensive failure. Later, during the mid-1820s, the British extracted agree-ments from native princes to reduce production and established quo-tas limiting opium exports from Bombay. This policy likewise failed when Malwa producers responded by exporting large quantities of the drug from the Portuguese port of Damaun, a hundred miles north of Bombay.

In 1831, the British finally worked out a lasting resolution to the de-structive competition from cheap Malwa opium. They abandoned ex-port restrictions and levied a transit duty of 175 rupees on each chest of Malwa opium exported from Bombay. Since the route from the Malwa uplands to Bombay was much more direct than that to the Por-tuguese ports of Damaun and Goa, 90 percent of Malwa opium re-turned to Bombay as soon as the restrictions were lifted.[17] The British were able to adjust the duty just high enough to maintain Bombay as the most economical port for export,[18] while at the same time raising the selling price of Malwa in China to a level at which Patna opium was still competitive.

By 1845, a finely tuned British bureaucracy efficiently administered the export of Malwa opium through Bombay. As the contracted deliv-ery date approached, the buniah in Malwa would pack the opium cakes into flimsy wooden chests, each containing about 250 eight-to-ten ounce cakes, padded with poppy leaves and stalks. Before transit to Bombay, each chest of opium exported from Malwa required a pass is-sued by the British opium agent at Indore, the major commercial cen-ter on the Malwa plateau. In exchange for this pass, a bill for payment of duty was drawn upon the parties to whom the chest was consigned. In 1845 the duty was two hundred rupees per chest. These bills were forwarded to the British opium agent in Bombay and presented to the consignees, who paid the duty to the treasury. When the consignee presented a receipt for this payment, the agent cleared the opium for export.[19]

Export of the opium crop grown during the winter of 1843–44 and processed during the subsequent spring and summer began the following October, when the first chests reached Bombay. Just as production of the crop and its transport from Malwa were dependent on the weather, so was its export to China. The southwest monsoon, bringing summer rain to western India, lasted from June to September. Opium clippers did not visit Bombay during this period, as they would have been trapped in port by four months of impenetrable headwinds. But between October and May, a streamlined opium clipper with a driving captain could carry up to three cargoes of Malwa to China before Bombay Harbor was again blocked by bad weather.

When the *Frolic* finally arrived at Bombay on March 28, 1845, it was already late in the season, and the Kessressung Khooshalchund firm, after waiting in vain for her, had apparently exported its opium to China aboard other vessels. As Martin Murray & Co. began to seek another outgoing cargo for the *Frolic*, the major stock of Malwa remaining in Bombay was the four thousand chests held by Sir Jamsetjee Jejeebhoy. As the preeminent opium speculator in Bombay, Sir Jamsetjee's operations were so large that he could corner a significant portion of the available supply, and in April 1844 he brought the market to a standstill by refusing to allow buyers to inspect his drug prior to purchase.[20] Kessressung Khooshalchund and other speculators who had contracted in advance to receive consignments from Sir Jamsetjee's stock refused to accept significant amounts of uninspected Malwa, since much of the drug would likely prove too adulterated to bring full market price in China. During the protracted negotiations, which lasted until the third week of April, Kessressung Khooshalchund, Martin Murray, and the *Frolic* were all held hostage to Sir Jamsetjee.

As Martin Murray & Co. began to seek a cargo for the *Frolic* on the open market, they found—as they wrote the Heards—"a prejudice against American vessels on the part of some influential parties in the trade who own English clippers."[21] This bias effectively prevented the Martin Murray firm from assembling the *Frolic*'s first outgoing cargo until the opium dispute was finally resolved and the Kessressung Khooshalchund firm took delivery of its consignments from Sir Jamsetjee. On April 24 they reported to the Heards, "After considerable difficulty and negotiation we succeeded in getting Kessressung Khooshalchund (through your friend Jehangeer Cursetjee) to agree to give us 400 chests."[22]

Captain Faucon had determined that the *Frolic* could carry at least eight hundred chests, and now there was a clear risk the vessel would sail only half full. Martin Murray placed a classified advertisement in the *Bombay Times* soliciting additional cargo of opium, but this brought only 36 chests. Meanwhile, Jehangeer Cursetjee pressured Kessressung Khooshalchund to increase its shipment. On May 8, when the *Frolic*'s list of freight was certified, the cargo totaled 647½ chests of Malwa opium.[23] Of these, Kessressung Khooshalchund shipped 542½, consigning 437½ to the Heards and 105 to Russell & Co. The chests shipped by Kessressung Khooshalchund were the separate property of nine different speculators, each of whom could consign his portion to be sold by his favorite firm in Canton, and, of these, five had chosen to consign with Russell & Co. The Heards would have received only minimal earnings if Kessressung Khooshalchund had not purchased 191 chests on their own account and consigned them to the firm.

The Kessressung Khooshalchund firm had initially agreed to a freight of $5.50 per chest from Bombay to China, but at Jehangeer's insistence they made out bills of lading at $6.00, in order to—as they put it— "give every advantage to your clipper on its first voyage."[24] But the Hindus were sharp businessmen, and even as they agreed to pay an extra 50 cents they levied a one-rupee, or 46-cent, "Bazar brokerage" charge on each of 611 chests.[25] This granted no immediate advantage to either party. It allowed the *Frolic* to show a higher income on the company books, but the long-term advantage fell to the Kessressung Khooshalchund firm. To the Heards' consternation, they continued charging the same gratuitous brokerage fee on subsequent voyages while paying only current market rates for freight.

As the *Frolic* prepared for her May 8 departure, Kessressung Khooshalchund drafted two letters of instructions for the Heards. The opium, they noted, was of "picked" quality, three-quarters of it having been examined by Jehangeer Cursetjee. For this reason it had been expensive, costing about $750 per chest.[26] At that rate, Kessressung Khooshalchund's shipment of 542½ chests represented an investment

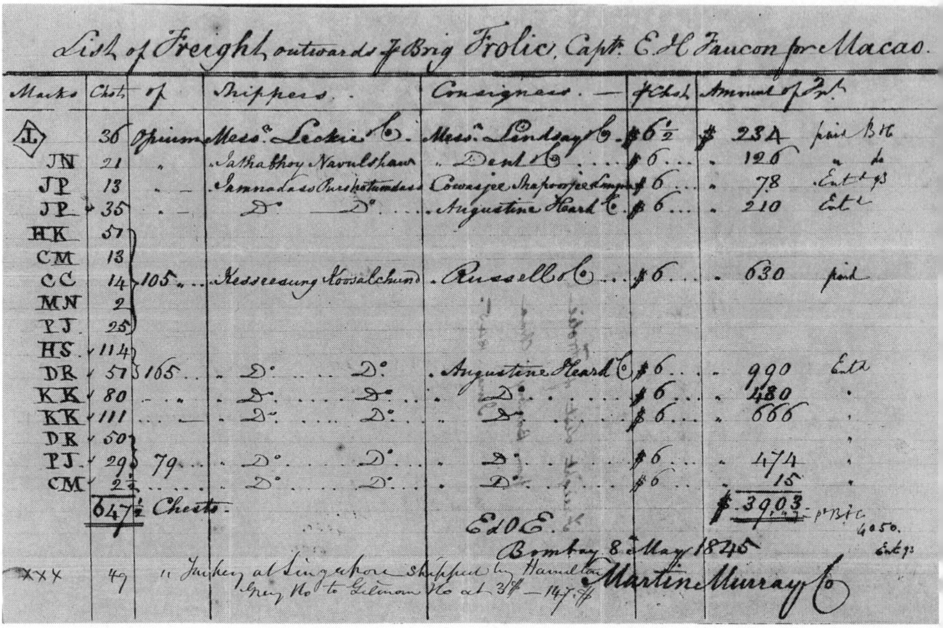

List of Freight, outwards ℘ Brig Frolic, Capt. E. H. Faucon for Macao.

Marks	Chests	of	Shippers	Consignees	℘ Chest	Amount of Frt.
(L)	36	Opium	Messrs. Leckie & Co.	Messrs. Lindsay & Co.	$6½	$ 234
JN	21	"	Jathabhoy Navulshaw	Dent & Co.	$6	126
JP	13	"	Jamnadass Purshotumdass	Cowasjee Shapoorjee Lungrana	$6	78
JP	35	"	Do.	Augustine Heard & Co.	$6	210
HK	57					
CM	13					
CC	14	105	Kessressung Khooshalchund	Russell & Co.	$6	630
MN	2					
PJ	25					
HS	114					
DR	51	165	Do.	Augustine Heard & Co.	$6	990
KK	80		Do.	Do.	$6	480
KK	111		Do.	Do.	$6	666
DR	50					
PJ	29	79	Do.	Do.	$6	474
CM	2½		Do.	Do.	$6	15
	647½ Chests					$ 3903

E. d. O. E.

Bombay 8th May 1845

Martin Murray & Co.

Figure 21. Freight list for the *Frolic*'s first outgoing cargo from Bombay, 647½ chests of Malwa opium, May 8, 1845. Courtesy Baker Library, Harvard Business School.

of over $400,000, leading to an understandable concern for its safety. Khooshalchund purchased insurance in Bombay with the risk coverage to continue 30 days after the *Frolic*'s arrival in China, and they instructed the Heards to keep their opium insured whenever it was subsequently on water.

Kessressung Khooshalchund asked the Heards to act for them during the sale of the opium in the same manner that the Heards would act for themselves. In payment, the Bombay firm asked for "Good Bills on London at a fair rate or Sycee silver in large ingots at moderate premium." There was some concern, as Sycee silver had lately "turned out very inferior, and mixed with other base metal." They urged the Heards to be careful in purchasing it and, of course, to insure it during shipment. Finally, as the southwest monsoon and attendant summer rains were about to start, Kessressung Khooshalchund asked that the *Frolic*

Figure 22. Loading trunks of Malwa opium aboard the *Frolic*, Bombay,
May 1845. Original illustration by S. F. Manning.

not be returned to Bombay until November or December. Until the new crop arrived in the fall, only inferior drug would be available. Meanwhile, it would be best to run the vessel between Calcutta and China.[27]

The Hindus had not yet received the bad returns on their fall 1844 shipments, but as they continued negotiations to purchase shares in the Heards' clippers, they could see the *Frolic*'s first cargo was almost entirely their own. Pressing this advantage, they pointed out that Martin Murray & Co., acting as the Heards' Bombay agent, had been able to procure only 36 chests of opium for the *Frolic*. The Kessressung Khooshalchund firm did not want to be responsible for providing the *Frolic*'s entire cargo every time she visited Bombay. They pointed out that sometimes "the owner must give a lift to the vessel . . . to induce other shippers to come forward" to help fill her, or else she "might be detained for a length of time and run up a great deal of expenses." The Indians thus informed the Heards that they would sometimes be "obliged to buy a couple of hundred chests" on the Heards' account "to help the Frolic," and for the money thus advanced the Heards would be charged six percent interest.[28]

On May 8, 1845, when Captain Edward Faucon dismissed the Bombay harbor pilot and took command of the *Frolic*, both his reputation and that of his vessel were on the line. Everyone knew the *Frolic* had been built for speed, and competing firms and prospective shippers would be noting her performance. A good passage would bring increased consignments, while a bad one could spell disaster. A clipper's reputation in the opium trade often rested on the elapsed time between India and China, but that could depend on weather. A slow vessel enjoying ideal conditions might have a much quicker passage than a fast vessel handicapped by calms. Thus the best way for a clipper to build a reputation was to race directly against a highly touted fast vessel owned by a competing firm. For the *Frolic*, this opportunity came on her first passage to China.

The *Frolic* was scheduled to sail three days before the 257-ton brig *Anonyma*. This sleek vessel, formerly belonging to the Royal Yacht Squadron, was now owned by Sir Jamsetjee Jejeebhoy and carried the house flag of Jardine, Matheson & Co.[29] In her three years in the opium trade the *Anonyma* had compiled an outstanding record for fast passages. When news of the match reached Canton, John Heard felt both excitement and dread: "I would give a great deal to have the 'Frolic' beat the 'Anonyma' on this passage," he wrote to his uncle. "It would be worth $5000 to her and more. But I fear there is little prospect of this, as the 'A' is a much more powerful vessel." As if to prepare himself and old Mr. Heard for the *Frolic*'s defeat, he pointed out, "Besides, Faucon cannot be so well acquainted with the navigation of the Straits as the captain of the 'A' who is an old hand in these waters."[30]

Confidence in the captain of an opium clipper was at best evanescent. Indeed, Captain Kennedy of the *Dart* had lost his reputation in only 40 days. On April 20, John Heard had described him as "an intelligent, well behaved, and well educated man, very temperate and decent, and anxious to prove by future efforts that his long passage out [from Baltimore] was not his fault." Captain Kennedy had informed the Heards that the *Dart* would "sail eight knots in a sea-way within five points, and tack," so clearly it was not the vessel that was slow, and Heard already wondered if Kennedy would ever "develop that decided go-ahead principle" so necessary to the opium trade.[31] By May 30, George Dixwell had seen enough to conclude Kennedy was incompetent. "I wish I could get rid of Kennedy," he wrote to Mr. Heard in Boston. "Entre nous, I damn Bowditch once a week for recommending him." Dixwell, in his anger, went on to impugn Kennedy's ancestry: "It is against all precedent for a rotten tree to bring forth good fruit; and K's father, to my certain knowledge, is rotten through & through."[32]

George Dixwell had more confidence in Faucon and the *Frolic*. "A good deal of our success depends upon her performance," he wrote to Mr. Heard, predicting that Faucon "would drive her well. . . . If he should bump her on a rock, that will be a small matter compared to making bad passages." The *Frolic* arrived at Macao on June 13, 1845, completing the 4,470-mile passage via Singapore in an impressive 34 days. Six days later, the *Anonyma* had still not arrived, and John Heard exulted: "The Frolic has beaten her!"[33]

George Dixwell was working feverishly to secure a greater role in the opium trade for the Heard firm. In late April, he had moved from the firm's headquarters in Canton to a rented house in Macao, for health and business reasons. During previous summers in hot, humid, riverine Canton, Dixwell had been devastated by chronic dysentery and diarrhea. He wrote to Mr. Heard that "sea air and bathing" at coastal Macao would enable him to "confirm" his health and "get into fine condition." Furthermore, from Macao he would be able "to watch the coast trade in drug" better than he could from Canton, and he could also more easily "consult occasionally" with Mr. Heard's old friend, James Perkins Sturgis, whom he found "very shrewd in the illicit traffic."[34]

George Dixwell's move to Macao proved timely. That same month, after Chinese authorities complained about blatant smuggling, the British consul dismantled the opium receiving station at Whampoa, twelve miles below Canton, and ordered British-owned vessels out of the Pearl River.[35] The opium receiving vessels responded by moving to outer anchorages 20 to 30 miles south of the Pearl River delta. In anticipation of this dislocation, the *Frolic*'s first shipment of opium was directed to Dixwell in Macao. When the *Frolic* arrived, Dixwell had just returned from a trip to Shanghai aboard the *Dart*. There he had personally "worked off" the old stock of Malwa opium Harding had stubbornly hoarded almost to the point of disaster. Of the 472 chests on the *Frolic* consigned to the Heards, Dixwell shipped 250 to Shanghai on the *Dart* and sold the remainder in Canton.[36]

By purchasing the *Frolic*, the *Dart*, and the *Don Juan*, George Dixwell had positioned the Heard firm to earn most of its profits from freight and commissions from opium. To ensure that his new fleet would pay for itself, he would have to consistently bring large consignments from Bombay. But there was an obstacle. Kessressung Khooshalchund had given specific instructions that the *Frolic* not be returned to Bombay until November or December, suggesting she be run to Calcutta in the meantime. But such a voyage could not be profitable because the Heards had nothing to ship to Calcutta and no agent to secure an outgoing cargo there. Moreover, the Patna opium market in Calcutta was already dominated by Parsees willing to sell to the Chinese on credit.

Dixwell decided to take a calculated risk. He would ignore Kessressung Khooshalchund's orders and return the *Frolic* to Bombay, where he hoped the Hindus would feel obliged to find her another cargo. Twelve days after her arrival in Macao, Dixwell dispatched the *Frolic* for Bombay with a cargo of treasure.[37] The 8½ tons of Sycee silver ingots and miscellaneous coinage were valued at over $270,000 and would earn the firm $3,200 in freight charges. Faucon, eager to build a reputation for his vessel and to please his employer, drove the *Frolic*

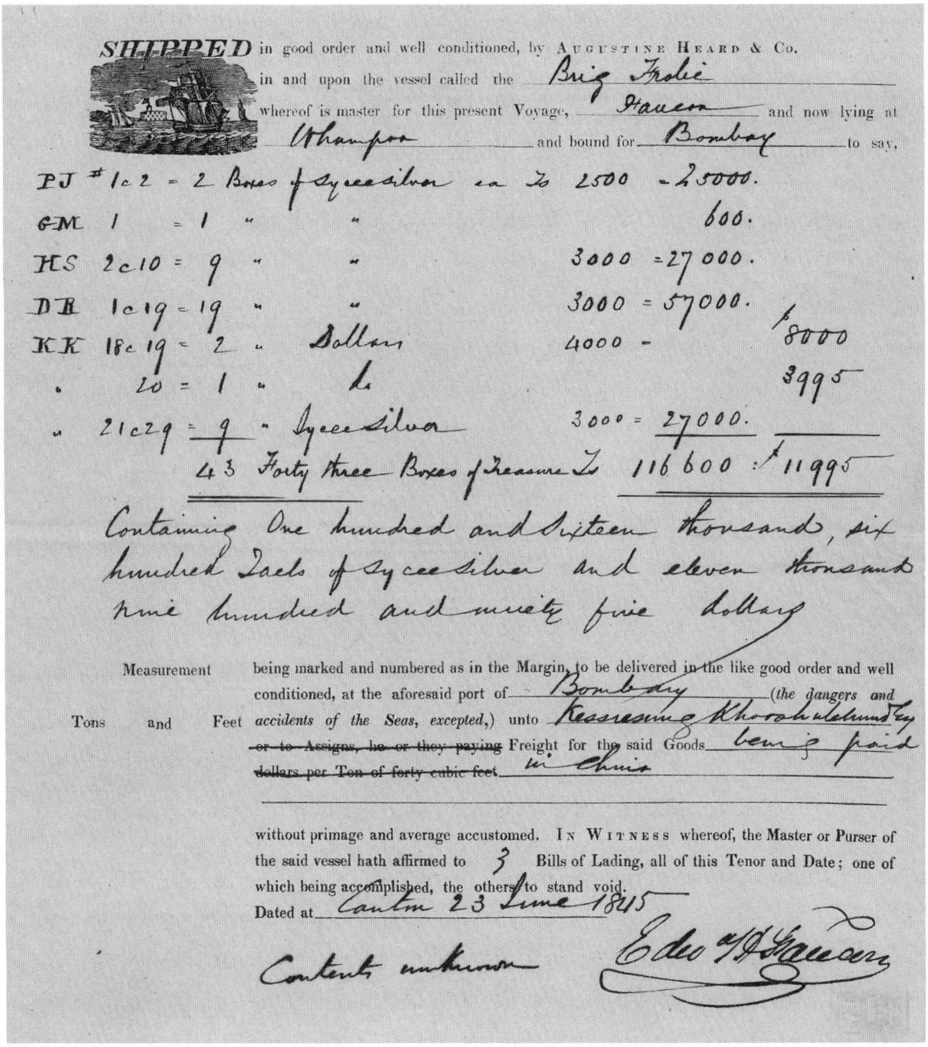

SHIPPED in good order and well conditioned, by AUGUSTINE HEARD & Co. in and upon the vessel called the _Brig Frolic_ whereof is master for this present Voyage, _Hauen_ and now lying at _Whampoa_ and bound for _Bombay_ to say,

PJ #1 c 2 = 2 Boxes of Sycee silver ea 2500 ~25000.
GM 1 = 1 " " 600.
HS 2 c 10 = 9 " " 3000 =27000.
DB 1 c 19 = 19 " " 3000 = 57000. /8000
KK 18 c 19 = 2 " Dollars 4000 -
" 20 = 1 " d. 3995
" 21 c 29 = 9 " Sycee silver 3000 = 27000.
43 Forty three Boxes of Treasure Ts 116 600 / 11995

Containing One hundred and Sixteen thousand, six hundred Taels of Sycee Silver and eleven thousand nine hundred and ninety five dollars

being marked and numbered as in the Margin, to be delivered in the like good order and well conditioned, at the aforesaid port of _Bombay_ (the dangers and accidents of the Seas, excepted,) unto _Ressressung Khooshalchund Ey_ ~~or to Assigns, he or they paying~~ Freight for the said Goods _being paid in China_ ~~dollars per Ton of forty cubic feet~~

without primage and average accustomed. IN WITNESS whereof, the Master or Purser of the said vessel hath affirmed to _3_ Bills of Lading, all of this Tenor and Date; one of which being accomplished, the others to stand void. Dated at _Canton 23 June 1845_

Contents unknown

Measurement
Tons and Feet

Figure 23. One of three bills of lading for the _Frolic_'s first return cargo to Bombay: 116,600 taels of Sycee silver and $11,995 in coinage, weighing over 5.1 tons. The total cargo from all three bills of lading was over 8½ tons of silver. Courtesy Baker Library, Harvard Business School.

mercilessly down the China Sea, tacking southeast against the southwest monsoon.[38] On August 17, after a 51-day passage, Faucon brought the *Frolic* into Bombay Harbor. Immensely proud of this passage, Faucon later informed Dixwell that the ship *Sultana*, which left China a few days before the *Frolic*, required 108 days to reach Bombay.[39]

Hoping this good news would soften Mr. Heard, John wrote: "You will think us mad when I tell you that we have bought another vessel." He had just contracted to buy the *Snipe*, a 169-ton, British registered, teak-built brig.[40] The cautious Mr. Heard had not been pleased with the firm's purchase of the *Frolic* and the *Dart*, so George Dixwell wrote to him attempting to justify the purchase of a fourth vessel in less than a year. Negotiations had not yet been concluded, but Dixwell was optimistic and confidently explained, "Kessressung Khooshalchund has taken half of the Don Juan, Dart and Frolic off our hands so that we have not now much in vessels." Noting the increasing consignments from Bombay, Dixwell pointed out that the firm now had "enough drug to make a receiving vessel pay, and being very much embarrassed for the want of a person who could report on the quality of the drug . . . take care of it and sell inferior," the firm had purchased the *Snipe*. Costing less than $5,500 after repairs, the *Snipe* should be "considered the greatest bargain which has been made in China for years."[41]

By midsummer 1845, George Dixwell's opium fleet was fully in place. The *Frolic* would carry Kessressung Khooshalchund's consignments from Bombay to Cumsingmoon, an outer anchorage fifteen miles north of Macao. There her cargo would be placed aboard the receiving vessel, *Snipe*, to be graded under the supervision of the *Snipe*'s new supercargo, William Endicott. Inferior opium would be sold locally and the better drug transported north on the *Dart* to coastal selling points. The *Don Juan* would be kept supplied by the *Dart* to serve Shanghai as a station vessel in Woosung Harbor.

When the *Frolic* arrived in Bombay, the Kessressung Khooshalchund firm was in mourning. Only a few weeks earlier Huttasung Kessressung, the firm's senior partner, had died in Ahmedabad. Then word had come from Poona that on August 24 Jehangeer Cursetjee had died of cholera.[42] On September 5, Tamooljee Rustomjee, the Parsee who handled Kessressung Khooshalchund's English correspondence, wrote to the Heards that the deaths "had thrown a gloom over all who were acquainted with these worthy men," but the "old firm" would continue, as before, in conjunction with "members of Huttasung relations." The firm's principals had, however, not been pleased with the "unexpected early return of the 'Frolic.'" It had caused "a good deal of uneasiness to get freight for her" at a time of the year when, as Tamooljee expressed it, "good opium is scarce, and inferior drug unsaleable."[43]

George Dixwell's gamble paid off nonetheless, for the Hindus succeeded in assembling a cargo of 541 chests at $6.00 each, for a freight of $3,246.[44] Only 75 of these, however, were consigned to the Heards. For the balance, wrote Faucon, "there is nearly a consignor for each chest . . . most all by natives & consigned to natives." Kessressung Khooshalchund had been right: September was indeed a bad time to secure a cargo of high-quality drug. Faucon judged almost all he had taken aboard the *Frolic* was of second quality, noting "I don't believe there are 5 of No 1 in the whole cargo."[45]

Despite the deaths of the old partners and the disagreement about the earlier-than-expected return of the *Frolic* to Bombay, the new management of Kessressung Khooshalchund wanted to reassure the Heards that their business relationship remained secure. Tamooljee therefore appointed the Heards as Kessressung Khooshalchund's sole agent in China and confirmed that his firm would pay $18,562.05 for shares in the Heards' clippers, taking two-fifths of the *Frolic* for $8,283.90, half of the *Dart* for $6,715.65, and three-eighths of the *Don Juan* for $3,562.50. On the Heards' advice, Kessressung Khooshalchund agreed not to require a bill of sale, because as they were British subjects the transaction would "destroy the national character" of the American vessels. They did, however, approve the Heards' idea of a "proforma sale" of the *Frolic* to the Khooshalchund firm, making her a "British bottom." This ruse was devised by the Heards to circumvent a new British tariff.[46]

When the Heards dispatched the *Frolic* to Bombay, her hold had been virtually empty. The treasure she carried was of great value, but it occupied little space. Unused cargo capacity represented not only unrealized income but additional expense, because of the need to purchase ballast. If the *Frolic* carried opium regularly from Bombay to China, she would profit doubly if she also carried freight on her return voyages. The British, however, were preparing to levy a new tariff in India, doubling the duty on foreign goods imported in foreign vessels. The Heards hoped that disguising the *Frolic* as a British vessel by a pro forma sale to Kessressung Khooshalchund would deceive the Bombay customs authorities and thus avoid the duty.[47] But after making inquiries, the Hindus vetoed the duty-evading scheme, for, as they explained, "the System of carrying on business in our customhouse, is now so very strict, and the reverence officers, many of them old season, who are not easily to be deceived, it would be a dangerous business to change the colors of the Frolic."[48]

Faucon and the *Frolic* had established a reputation for fast passages by outrunning the *Anonyma* in June 1845. By the fall of the same year, the rhythm of her subsequent life had begun to emerge. Between October and May, she would make three voyages carrying chests of Malwa opium from India to China and tons of silver bullion on each return. These ventures were important to the Heards in their own right, but they constituted only a small part of a much larger network of international trade.

CHAPTER 5

Canton

AUGUSTINE HEARD, back home in Boston on January 1, 1840, would have been surprised to know that six years later his newly established firm would own four opium clippers. At that time the Opium War was still in progress, and Mr. Heard considered sale of the drug in China to be a subsidiary activity at most. In his view, the primary purpose of his agency house was to purchase Chinese goods for American clients and arrange for their shipment to the United States. The opium trade, he felt, served chiefly to complement the firm's other business operations.

The Heards were commission merchants providing a number of essential services to American clients within an international system of credit and exchange. Their letters and circulars furnished market news and advice, particularly concerning teas and silks. For teas, this information included regular estimates of the size of the crop, tonnage being exported, current prices, and anticipated price changes. The Heards' American clients placed orders based on these reports and on their own assessment of market conditions in the United States.

Once the Heards received an order they went shopping.[1] For teas this required "bargaining, tasting, inspecting, weighing, transporting," and also, probably, a good deal of bribery. The Heards then arranged for storage of the tea until space could be found aboard an outgoing vessel, whereupon they insured the cargo and supervised its loading for shipment. The Heards charged commissions on the total value of the products they bought, sold, or otherwise managed. Separate commissions were taken for purchasing, selling, exchanging currencies, handling, insuring, and arranging shipping. Altogether, these commissions might total 8 percent of the value of the products bought or sold.

During the early 1840s, the Heards earned most of their profits from commissions and fees. The partners' own capital was at little risk, as they generally did not share in the ultimate profit or loss on the teas or other commodities.[2] Indeed, the partnership agreement specifically placed restrictions on speculative operations in which house capital might have been ventured.

When the Heards made purchases for their American clients, however, they needed to arrange for payment. This was effected through a worldwide exchange system mediated by Anglo-American banks based in London. The English bought cotton from the United States and tea and silk from China. They paid for some of this with manufactured goods and for the balance with silver earned from the sale of Indian opium in China. The United States bought tea and silk from China, paying for a small portion of these with exports but the larger share with hard currency earned from selling cotton to the British. By the early 1840s exchange between England and the United States, and between these two countries and China, was being balanced by sales of immense quantities of British-controlled Indian opium, paid for in silver by the Chinese.[3]

The largest Anglo-American banking house of the time was Baring Bros. & Co., based in London. In 1843 the Heards asked for, and received, £20,000 of "uncovered" (unsecured) credits from Barings. They hoped to use these credits to increase the volume of their business in China. As George Dixwell observed, "It is very convenient to hold such a means of replacing funds here without the delay of a year and a half, which is necessary in getting back remittances from America."[4]

The unsecured credits issued by Barings were extremely important to the growth of the Heard firm, since they allowed the Heards to make advances to their American clients in amounts exceeding their own limited capital. As commission merchants, the Heards' earnings depended directly on the volume of business transacted, and the credits from Barings enabled them to increase purchases by their American clients. The major risk to the Heards in making these advances was bankruptcy of a client, so it was essential to find clients with enough capital to cover any possible loss.

Both Augustine Heard and George Dixwell's brother John used their connections in the American business community to find reliable clients. When John Dixwell traveled to Baltimore in September 1844 to inspect the *Dart* and the *Frolic*, he took the opportunity to establish a formal business relationship with Henry Oelrichs and Gustavus Lurman. This association was typical of the Heard firm's relationships with client firms in America.

Oelrichs & Lurman had a substantial trade, exporting tobacco and grain to England and importing teas and silks from China. Since the early 1830s, the firm had also engaged in joint speculations with Barings.[5] Barings maintained what was probably the first extensive credit rating system for American businesses, and they probably provided John Dixwell with a confirmation of Oelrichs & Lurman's soundness. While we do not have Barings's rating of Oelrichs & Lurman, we do have R. G. Dun & Co.'s 1847 rating commentary on the firm.[6]

The commentary noted that Oelrichs and Lurman were 40 and 45 years of age, had been in business for fifteen years, and had an operating capital of $100,000. But reliability was judged on more than figures, and the Dun & Co. reviewer, in telegraphic style, provided the following penetrating profile: "Do a lar & somewhat hazardous bus.— Char & Cus Capac. good—'L's' wife has say $75m settled on her—'L' dir in one of the banks—'O' of extrav. habits—both are inclined to spree & some cautn. sh'd be observed."

John Dixwell negotiated the agreement with Oelrichs & Lurman in Baltimore on September 9, 1844, and announced it to the Heard firm in Canton by a letter carried aboard the *Dart* on her maiden voyage.[7] He considered the agreement important enough that he sent a duplicate letter via Bombay and a triplicate via Calcutta. Dixwell's evaluation of Oelrichs & Lurman was somewhat more generous than that of Dun & Co. "You will find them liberal and agreeable persons to do business with," he wrote. "The house has command of large means & has a high reputation here for enterprise, activity, shrewdness & intelligence." Dixwell also noted that Oelrichs & Lurman owned a fleet of vessels and had already sent several of them on voyages to Canton.

The agreement stipulated that Oelrichs & Lurman would consign their ship *Stephen Lurman* to the Heards in return for the Heards' guarantee to supply 450 tons of paying freight to fill the vessel to half its capacity at a minimum rate of $20 per ton. Oelrichs & Lurman also agreed to make purchases through the Heards to fill the other half of the vessel. Oelrichs & Lurman were thus guaranteed a full ship, while the Heards would earn large commissions on the purchase and handling of 900 tons of cargo.

The Heards made similar agreements with other American firms, obligating them to supply specific tonnages of paying freight. Even before word of the Oelrichs & Lurman agreement reached China, the Heards had a contract "to advance two thirds of the cost on 500 tons of teas" to help fill the *John Q. Adams*, another vessel consigned to them. "I think the Ninyongs [teas] may hardly . . . go to pay the advance," George Dixwell later explained. "But we had to fill up the room; and if the teas do sell for more than enough to cover the advance, we make a comm. both ends."[8] Dixwell had obtained the funds to fill the *John Q. Adams* by drawing on the firm's £20,000 credit with Baring Bros. He minimized the risk, however, noting, "If the teas shipped . . . do not cover the advances we may get something back from the shipper here. The only doubt is whether the shipper may not break first."

John Dixwell's investigation of Oelrichs & Lurman's solvency was essential, as the Heards' credit business depended on the solvency of their clients. In January 1845, when George Dixwell learned that the *Stephen Lurman* was already on its way, he had no time to further examine Oelrichs & Lurman's soundness before the hurried purchase of "2500 half chests of good Hysons" on short credit, because he feared "good teas might not be obtainable" by the time of the vessel's arrival.[9] The transaction was risky since tea prices were subject to marked fluctuation, but as the Heards' business depended upon filling the vessels consigned to them, Dixwell had no choice. The Heards were taking a chance by advancing the firm's working capital to cover client purchases, but the market in China was changing. By mid-1845, it was increasingly difficult to sell—or even barter—cargoes of American goods, particularly the cotton textiles that the Heards' clients insisted on sending over.

George Dixwell first recognized the magnitude of the change in the market when he traveled to Shanghai in June 1845 to help Captain Harding sell the firm's old stock of Malwa opium. Part of Harding's problem, George soon discovered, was that both Dent & Co. and Jardine, Matheson "had been exchanging their Malwa for silk," making "cash sales . . . rare and difficult to effect."[10] "In fact," he informed Mr. Heard, "opium is cash in such transactions and people who have no opium trade will find it extremely difficult to do anything here. Even barter trade does not go well, if you cannot give the Chinaman enough opium, with goods, to enable him to pay his duties!"

George Dixwell had argued for years with old Mr. Heard's objections to acquiring an opium fleet, and at last he felt vindicated. As the recipients of large consignments of Indian opium carried aboard their own vessels, the Heards were serendipitously positioned to trade for their American clients, having Malwa opium to barter in place of hard currency. "The American houses, except R[ussell] & Co. cannot do anything here without great difficulty," he bragged, "for not being engaged in the opium business it would cost them much more to get funds here."

When Dixwell returned from Shanghai to Macao, a letter awaited him from Mr. Heard, who, not knowing how the market had changed, urged once again that he consider selling the *Frolic* and the *Dart*. Dixwell responded with all the respect due to a senior partner, while noting, with diplomatic resolve, "As far as I am concerned, I would be quite willing to sell them providing you wished it; but I am sure you would not wish it if you were here and conversant with all the circumstances."[11]

As John Heard waited with George Dixwell for the *Frolic*'s first cargo of Indian opium, he wrote to his uncle to allay old Mr. Heard's doubts about the firm's heavy investment in opium clippers: "The opium business is the best business we have, not only from the direct, but for the collateral profit it induces. It also affords an excellent vent for exchange from America, rendering us independent of the demand for bills. We shall do all in our power to transact it well, and as we have much time to devote to it, and our arrangements on the coast enable us to command all markets, I think we shall succeed."[12]

The Heards were already successfully integrating their drug business with the more traditional services they provided. In the summer of 1845 they were using Kessressung Khooshalchund's Indian opium as advance payment to Chinese brokers in Shanghai for their American clients' purchases of teas and silks. During the following summer George Dixwell went one step further. He convinced Kessressung Khooshalchund to allow up to $60,000 of their opium proceeds to be bartered for teas to be sold in England. The Hindus, as British subjects, felt secure in speculating on teas for sale in England. But Dixwell, "taking the responsibility of a slight deviation from old K.K.'s instructions," shipped the tea to the United States instead. To mute criticism for having taken this unauthorized liberty, and to give the Indians "confidence," the Heards took a one-third interest in the operation themselves.[13]

During 1845 and 1846, George Dixwell gradually convinced Kessressung Khooshalchund to allow its capital to be used to support more and more of the Heards' overall operations. In the fall of 1846, the Heards asked Kessressung Khooshalchund to authorize purchase of an additional $80,000 in teas to be sold in the United States. Eventually, the Heards asked for an unfettered "general authority" to barter the Indians' opium for Chinese products to be sold in England and America.

In November 1846, John Heard described in a letter to Augustine Heard the firm's increasingly complex relationship with Kessressung Khooshalchund. He wrote that the Heard firm, in order to demonstrate good faith, would continue to take a one-third interest in the Indians' shipments of tea to the United States.[14] "The idea," John noted, had "emanated entirely from Dixwell at Shanghai." George Dixwell had, of course, carefully calculated the risk to which he was exposing his partners' capital. As paraphrased by John Heard, Dixwell had concluded: "We must take some interests of this kind in order to help the opium business, and if we do not go beyond $100,000 . . . during one year on our own a/c [account], there cannot be much harm done if the teas are well bought. Besides," he explained, "we should get 3% [in commissions] on $300,000, say $9,000, and so could afford to loose 9% and yet be square."

In late October 1845, when the *Frolic* arrived in China with her second cargo of opium from Kessressung Khooshalchund, George Dixwell's carefully planned opium strategy was already in place. Kessressung Khooshalchund had paid for its shares in the *Frolic*, the *Dart*, and the *Don Juan*, and the Heards felt assured of a steady flow of opium consignments. John Heard estimated that Kessressung Khooshalchund shipped two thousand chests of Malwa opium to China each year.[15] "I do not expect that, altho' his sole agents, we shall get all his consignments," Heard wrote to his uncle, "but we will get the greater part of them." John concluded that, "Parsee fashion," Kessressung Khooshalchund would probably ship the remainder of its consignments to other firms as an ongoing test of the Heards' ability to obtain competitive prices.

Success in the opium trade required more of the Heards than passive receipt of regular consignments. In order to compete, the Heards also had to deliver a product of acceptable quality to knowledgeable Chinese opium brokers. These deliveries were made at a multitude of secret offshore locations spread out along the dangerous coast stretching 980 statute miles between Canton and Shanghai.

As the *Frolic* arrived at Cumsingmoon with a fresh cargo of Indian opium, she first drew alongside the Heards' receiving vessel *Snipe*. The *Frolic*'s hatch was unsealed, and Captains Faucon and Endicott supervised transfer of between 500 and 850 wooden chests. Each chest carried the mark of its consigner and a registration number. As the chests were off-loaded, clerks checked these numbers against the *Frolic*'s cargo manifest so that Captain Endicott could certify the cargo had arrived intact. The American, British, and Parsee merchants to whom the opium was consigned generally negotiated sales to Chinese brokers in Canton. Payment was made either there or aboard the receiving vessel. Once the deal was struck, the merchant firm provided the buyer with a written order to be presented to the captain of the receiving vessel. There, after weighing and inspection, he would take delivery.[16]

Before accepting a chest of Malwa, the Chinese broker carefully tested the opium to evaluate its relative purity. Raw opium was valued in direct proportion to the amount of hot-drawn watery extract that could be obtained from it. The testing process was highly standardized. A gunny-covered wooden chest was opened, the dried poppy leaves cleared away, and three cakes selected. Ideally, a cake would have a hard, thin skin and a firm interior the texture of cream cheese. A small measured weight was taken from each test cake and placed, together with fresh water, into one of three small brass pots where it was prepared for smoking.

This process, carried out on the deck of the receiving vessel, took about half an hour. Each pot was brought to a boil. After simmering, the liquid was filtered and then washed through bamboo paper. The weight of particulate matter collected on the filter was a measure of adulteration. Meanwhile, the filtrate was examined for proper color,

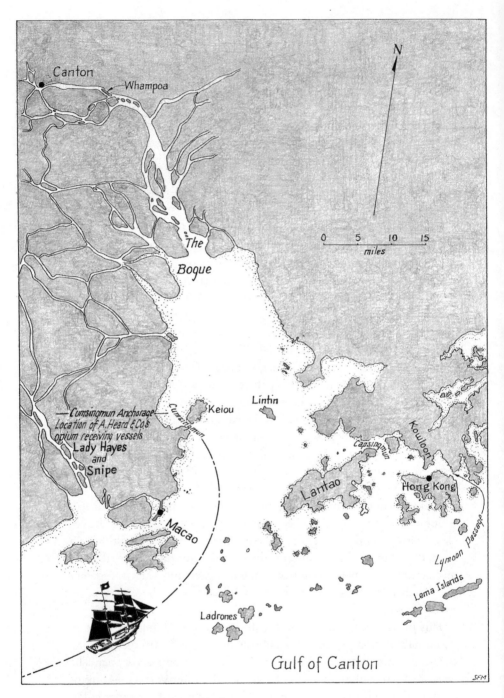

Figure 24. Map of the Gulf of Canton.

preferably black. It was then kept boiling until it was reduced to a trea-
cle-like extract. A small sample of this was smoked in a pipe to evaluate its flavor and potency. These tests were necessary for all Malwa
opium since there were no controls over its quality during production.
Patna opium, on the other hand, was rarely, if ever, tested. Every hide-
covered chest of Patna, in addition to the 40 balls of equal weight, each
packed within a protective partition, carried a certificate from the
British East India Company that guaranteed quality.[17]

Most of the opium consigned to the Heards was Malwa, and thus of
questionable quality. Because no test by a previous holder of the drug
was accepted by a subsequent purchaser, testing was repeated at every
transaction point during the long journey of the product from producer
to consumer. The Heards' Malwa drug was first tested at the time of
its purchase by Kessressung Khooshalchund, but before the Heards accepted any of it on consignment, they tested it themselves. The quality
of the product had to be independently verified because if the Hindus
had paid for first quality drug in Bombay, they would expect first quality prices in China. If the buyer in China found the drug inferior, and
thus paid a low price, the Heards would be blamed.

The Heards' best defense against such recriminations was Samsing
"Chinaman," their opium examiner in Bombay. Like other Chinese
opium inspectors, he was to be provided with board and lodging in addition to fees for the opium he inspected, and after twelve months, an
allowance of $100. Samsing arrived in Bombay in August 1845 to in-
spect the *Frolic*'s second outgoing cargo. The Heards had instructed
him to be conservative, but he did his job so well that Kessressung
Khooshalchund was obliged to send by other shippers 140 chests that
Samsing rejected. Kessressung Khooshalchund complained to the
Heards that Samsing and his assistants were damaging the business by
"being too particular."[18] The firm on its own account had purchased
an additional two hundred chests to be consigned to the Heards, but
of these, the Chinese inspector had found none of first quality, only 60
of second quality, and all of the remainder inferior. In fact, what the inspector for Dent & Co. called first quality, Samsing called second. Tamooljee, the Hindus' Parsee correspondent, judged that as a consequence it would be difficult to find anyone willing to ship aboard the
Frolic. He recommended, "It would therefor be well if you could get a
letter written in the Chinese language to Samsing, to do what is right,

because by being too particular a deal of time will be lost."[19] The truth of this complaint was confirmed in November when the *Frolic*'s cargo was off-loaded into the *Snipe* at Cumsingmoon. There, William Endicott reexamined the drug and reported to the Heards: "Altho Capt Faucon informs that the whole of it was passed in Bombay as 2nd quality opium, I have examined it pretty closely today & must say that I can see nothing inferior in it otherwise than its being rather thick skin & boils somewhat thicker than usual, which sometimes occasions a reduction of $20 to $50."[20]

On his return to Bombay, Faucon discussed the matter with Samsing. "I have told Samshing," he wrote, "that while he was to be careful in selecting the drug, it was not desirable that he should be too rigid."[21] Samsing was in the unenviable, no-win position of a subordinate expected to meet conflicting sets of expectations. Faucon attempted to help the perplexed inspector resolve the contradiction. "The distinction between 1st & 2nd quality is of course proper to make," Faucon wrote to the Heards, "but where the quality was a little inferior to No. 1 & not decidedly No. 2, I have expressed to him my opinion that he had better pass it as No. 1."

Quality control was the most important duty of the captain of the receiving vessel. The staff aboard the *Snipe* opened, inspected, weighed, and repacked every chest of Malwa consigned to the Heards. Inferior opium was identified for quick discount sale on the otherwise impacted local market, and high-quality drug was dispatched aboard the *Dart* up the coast where it would obtain the highest prices. For each chest, in ledger-like format, the receiving vessel's staff listed the consigner's mark, the chest number, gross weight, net weight, results of test-boiling, quality of cakes, and, in the largest space, pertinent remarks. These comments enable us to see Malwa opium through the critical eyes of the Heards' examiners. "This batch boils well, some of it thick and black." "This lot of drug . . . has the appearance of gum in the cake which prevents it passing the paper." "All this opium is more or less red & thick skin, some quite soft and mouldy. . . . It cannot be called first rate." "Some of this opium has a muddy appearance on being boiled." "This lot . . . has a strong smell of fish oil."[22]

The Heards' examiners aboard the *Snipe* were also expected to recognize shipping damage so consigners could be indemnified by their insurance carriers. Water damage occurred aboard the *Frolic* during a passage from Bombay to Singapore in the spring of 1846. As Faucon explained to the Heards, when the *Frolic* was loaded at Bombay "I was advised that I should be deep with 800 chests & was recommended to take out all my ballast." Faucon considered the advice "imprudent & kept in 20 tons." Unfortunately, this was still not enough ballast to stabilize the vessel, for, as he later recounted, during her 37-day passage to Singapore the vessel "had the NE monsoon pretty fresh," and "she laid over so much that the water could not get to the pumps." Faucon confessed that his "apprehensions" were later aroused "by the water pumped out smelling very strong of opium."[23] In defense of his vessel, Faucon noted that the *Frolic* had "leaked but little," yet he judged it probable that chests carried in the "front tier or in the wings" had probably been damaged.

Captain Faucon phrased his report carefully to protect his firm from liability and ensure that the Heards' damage claim would not be contested by the insurance company. There could be no charge of negligence against him since he had exercised good judgment by placing twenty tons of ballast aboard the vessel in spite of the bad advice of Bombay port officials. There could be no complaint against the *Frolic* since she had "leaked but little" and her pumps had fully operated. As Faucon crafted his report, the ultimate culprit was the northeast monsoon—an act of God—precisely the cause least likely to be contested in court.

It was soon apparent that the 169-ton *Snipe* was too small to be very profitable. In 1846, in response to the expansion of their opium business, the Heards bought a three-fourths interest in the 314-ton *Lady Hayes* for $9,000. "She is a teak ship, can stow 2000 to 2500 chests as a receiving vessel and," as John Heard hastened to reassure his uncle, "we got her cheap."[24] Captain Langley, who would command her, held the remaining quarter of the vessel. "He is one of the best captains in China," John wrote, "a man of intelligence, and long in J[ardine] M[atheson] & Co's employ, who give him high character." The *Lady Hayes* was too large to be kept supplied by the *Frolic* alone. In order for her to become profitable, she would have to attract business from other shippers, and the Heards hoped that her well-liked and well-connected captain would bring that business with him. "We think she will

Figure 25. The *Frolic* delivers a cargo of opium to the Heards' receiving vessel *Lady Hayes*, moored at Cumsingmoon in 1846. A 30-oared fast crab will speed purchases to Chinese brokers near Canton. Original illustration by S. F. Manning.

make money at Cumsingmoon," wrote John Heard. "Langley is well known among the English houses and will get drug from them and from the Parsees."

Upon installing the *Lady Hayes* at Cumsingmoon in 1846, the Heards dispatched Captain Endicott and the *Snipe* to Woosung anchorage, just a few miles from Shanghai. This freed the *Don Juan* to travel more regularly to far-flung coastal locations where smaller lots of drug could be sold for hard currency. The *Don Juan*, under Captain Harding, had regularly visited these remote outposts since the summer of 1844.

The coastline was so vast it is hard to envision. Chusan was over 400 miles north of Chin-Chew, and Shanghai over 100 miles beyond Chusan. One of Harding's few surviving letters, dated February 2, 1845, written to the Heards from Chusan Island, preserves the flavor of this small-scale coastal trade. "I arrived in this post," wrote Harding, "in ten days from Chin-Chew. . . . There are a few purchasers from 'Chappu' (a place some eighty miles from this) & as this will be the last purchase before China new year they are in no hurry to conclude the bargain . . . they offering $400 & I asking $450. Most likely they will buy tomorrow somewhere & I am off at once for Shanghae."[25]

The Heards made a change in their coastal operations in the summer of 1846. As he had the previous year, Harding had again held old opium too long in hopes of higher prices, and now he was having difficulty disposing of it. In August George Dixwell replaced him with Charles A. Fearon as the firm's Shanghai agent and for $5,000 purchased a building from which Fearon could conduct company business. Reflecting on Dixwell's decisive action, John Heard reported, "I have no doubt that had Mr. Fearon been in Shanghae six months earlier he would have saved us at least $10,000." Fearon, an experienced businessman, took firm control over the Shanghai office. In less than two months he sent the Heards over $200,000 in cash sales. "Harding," John Heard complained to his uncle, "would not have sold a chest: indeed he is lazy, pig headed and obstinate, besides being quarrelsome."[26]

Shortly after the *Snipe* was established as a receiving vessel at Woosung, she began to attract consignments from independent shippers whose opium had not been inspected. Before this, most poor-quality drug consigned to the Heards had been identified and disposed of at Cumsingmoon. Now it would be necessary to institute the same thorough testing at Woosung. Late in the summer of 1846, shortly after the *Snipe* began her new assignment, two instances of outright fraud were discovered.

The first instance came to light when the *Snipe*'s supercargo opened a suspicious chest marked "GSC No. 605" and discovered that it did not contain opium. As in all such cases, an outside examiner was called aboard the vessel immediately to determine who would bear the financial liability. The contents of chest 605 were quickly revealed to be balls of "Moonghy rice and opium dust." The examiner concluded "from the fact of the gunny being sewn with Bombay twine" that the chest was "an original package," and thus the tampering must have occurred in Bombay.[27] In this case the detective work was straightforward and responsibility assigned to the Bombay consigner and his insurer. Only a month later, however, a far more complex fraud was discovered, and Fearon had to act quickly to absolve the *Frolic* and her owners from liability.

The *Dart* was laid up for repairs during the summer of 1846. It was the off-season at Bombay, so the *Frolic* was dispatched in her place to deliver a cargo of drug to the *Snipe* at Woosung. Part of this cargo was Patna opium belonging to Bush & Co., an American firm headquartered in Hong Kong. As these were sealed chests of Patna drug, carrying the British East India Company's guarantee of quality, they required no testing.

But on September 11, Charles Fearon in Shanghai wrote to Bush & Co.: "I regret to inform you that one chest of Patna shipped by you p[er] 'Frolic' has turned out to be clay. The balls are well made and covered with China paper which so closely resembles the appearance of Patna's skin, that the fraud would not have been discovered, had not the attention of Capt Endicott been arrested by the extraordinary weight of the Balls." Fearon noted that other Shanghai firms receiving drug from the Bush warehouse in Hong Kong had found "mud and rice instead of opium." Chinese laborers working for Lindsay & Co. in Hong Kong had recently been discovered substituting similar balls for real Patna. This led Fearon to suspect that the fraud had occurred in Hong Kong, "either on shore or in the cargo boats."[28]

Fearon informed Bush & Co. that he would return the bad Patna to them aboard the *Don Juan*. The evidence against the Bush firm's Chinese laborers was, of course, only circumstantial. There remained a lingering possibility that the substitution had occurred in India—and, if so, the exporter, and not Bush & Co., would be responsible for the $1,000 loss. Having first attempted to clear the *Frolic* from liability, Fearon graciously guided his friends at Bush & Co. out of an expensive embarrassment, pointing out that "if there is any person in China capable of analysing the clay, it will be easily decided whether it comes from China or Calcutta."

The Heards maintained quality control over the opium they sold by constant testing. But it was also necessary to verify the purity of the silver bullion they received in payment. On November 2, 1846, when the

Heards dispatched the *Frolic* to Bombay, she carried over ten tons of silver bullion valued at $350,000, almost all of which was proceeds from the firm's drug sales on the coast.[29] Since the Chinese had no standard silver coinage of their own, payments in silver were made in a bewildering mix of locally cast "Sycee" silver ingots and silver coinage from a multitude of nations. Sycee ingots were not standardized, and their real value could be determined only by assaying their weight and silver content. Coinage also varied in silver content as well as denomination, and to make matters even more complicated, the Chinese did not consider all silver coins to be equally desirable. During the mid-1840s the preferred coin was the Carolus dollar, minted in Spain and Mexico between 1759 and 1808. Because of its popularity, the Carolus dollar often sold at a premium of up to 15 percent above its silver content.[30]

To calculate the value of the varied forms of silver paid for their opium, the Heards hired "shroffs," professional Chinese money changers. Shroffs were trained to identify the authentic marks that reputable money houses stamped on silver ingots, and they were able to distinguish counterfeit from legitimate coinage. When necessary, they arranged for assays. They also factored in the current premiums and discounts on the varied forms of silver in order to calculate the true value of a payment. They were paid a commission based on the total value of the bullion they inspected. In exchange, they were held financially accountable for the silver content of any coin into which they had hammered their chisel-mounted seal or "chop." While transactions were negotiated, the vessels' decks would be crowded with company clerks, shroffs, interpreters, porters, and heavily armed sailors, as well as opium buyers, their accountants, and drug testers.

Bad silver did get through, despite the shroffs. Sometimes a Sycee ingot, on being broken, was found to contain lead or even small stones.[31] In January 1846 the Kessressung Khooshalchund firm objected to the debased quality of the first eight-ton cargo of silver bullion they received from the Heards. "The Sycee silver pr Frolic," the Hindus' correspondent Tamooljee complained, "is very much mixed with inferior metal and I was forced to send the whole to the Mint, there being no purchaser in the market." To document his case, Tamooljee sent "an attested copy" of the unfavorable assay, signed by the Bombay mint master.[32]

Much of the Heard firm's considerable success in the illicit opium trade depended on the individual reputations of its captains. For these men, virtually every passage was a race, either against the calendar or against clippers owned by competing firms, with outcomes noted and discussed by prospective shippers. Speed meant money, for as the Heards well knew, a vessel whose captain established a record for swift passages almost always attracted more cargo at higher rates than did a vessel with a plodder for a captain. Indeed, when the *Frolic* had beaten Jardine, Matheson's *Anonyma* to China in June 1845, John Heard confidently predicted the victory would be worth $5,000 to the *Frolic* in new business.[33]

The Heards rewarded their captains with high salaries, generous perquisites, and opportunities to speculate on their own accounts, but they were quick to dismiss those who did not measure up. Captain Kennedy of the *Dart* had been discharged early in 1846 and Captain Harding of the *Don Juan* later that fall. A contract signed by Captain Porter on June 26, 1846, when he took over the *Dart*, defined the Heards' expectations.[34] Captain Faucon's contract as master of the *Frolic*, though not extant, was probably similar.

Captain Porter's salary was to be $150 per month, with an allowance of $50 more for mess. When passengers were aboard, the captain was to keep half of the passage money and credit the firm with the balance. "In this case," cautioned the Heards, "you must provide good mess, and enough Beer and Wines, charging the whole expense to the vessel." Accommodations, however, were to be held first for staff and for friends of the company. "You are at liberty to trade to such an extent and in such articles, as not to interfere in any way with the business of the Schooner: but we shall immediately make new arrangements if you should suffer your business to interfere with ours, or to cause a moment's delay."

The captain's first order in sailing the vessel was "to carry cargo safely and without damage. . . . Everything must yield to this." The second object, "and a most important one," the Heards added, "is dispatch. We expect you to spare no exertions which will tend to shorten a passage or hasten business in port." The vessel was to be "kept in complete order and fit in every respect," and all necessary expenses were to be "incurred without hesitation." At the same time, the captain was to "avoid all extravagance" and make no alteration to the vessel without first obtaining company consent. "We look for the strictest economy which can be practiced without suffering the Schooner to get into bad order," the Heards concluded.

Since Captain Porter did not own a share of the *Dart*, he could carry only two chests of opium per trip on his own account. Faucon, however, as one-fifth owner of the *Frolic*, had greater privileges. In January 1846, for example, the Heards advanced Faucon $14,466.72 to purchase 22 chests of first-quality Malwa from Kessressung Khooshalchund on his own account.[35] For Faucon this represented an immense risk, more than eight times his annual salary, and he felt uneasy about it. Six months later, increasingly tense as he awaited news from the coast, Faucon wrote to the Heards, "Please inform me if any of my drug has been disposed of. I am shaking in my shoes abt it."[36]

Faucon made every effort to please his employers. He drove the *Frolic* hard to achieve fast passages and avoided "all extravagance" to keep down operating costs. In this latter effort he succeeded almost to a fault. "Faucon seems to get her along as fast as any one, but he does not seem to keep her in very nice order," John Heard complained to his uncle. "She looked like the *deuce* when she was last in China." The company gave Faucon "a hint that he need not economize quite so much in paint &c."[37] Faucon, who took great pride in the *Frolic*, acted quickly. He cleaned up the vessel so well that he asked to have a portrait of her done when he returned to China. "Don't forget to send a painter to take the Brig at Whampoa," he reminded the Heards, "someone who will make a decent picture."[38]

By the fall of 1846, Faucon and the *Frolic* had achieved an outstanding record for speed. They had attracted enough business from other shippers that Kessressung Khooshalchund was now willing to cancel their emergency authority to buy opium on the Heards' account to fill the vessel. "I give up with much pleasure," wrote the Hindus' correspondent. "I see no cause for putting you to any risk, as there will be plenty of shippers that will avail themselves of her well known sailing qualities."[39]

Kessressung Khooshalchund was emphatically optimistic about the *Frolic*'s continued earning power. While the Hindus had been mildly concerned that it had taken more time than usual to get the *Frolic* off, this was only because Samsing "Chinaman" had been "so very particular" about the shape of Malwa cakes. He had rejected many that he

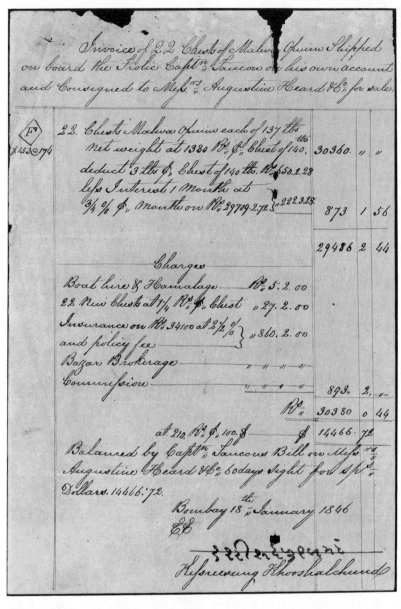

Figure 26. The Heard firm advanced $14,466.72 to Captain Faucon on January 18, 1846, enabling him to purchase 22 chests of Malwa opium on credit in Bombay. Courtesy Baker Library, Harvard Business School.

had otherwise found to be of good quality simply because they were not shaped "according to his idea of his countrymen." "But on the whole," the Hindus' correspondent confidently assured the Heards, "I believe [from] the influence I have among Native friends, . . . the 'Frolic' will earn a fair freight and put a very fair commission in your pockets."[40]

In early January 1847, as he prepared to return to Boston after five years in China, George Dixwell was confident that Augustine Heard & Co.'s opium business was secure. John Heard, now almost 24, had gained sufficient experience to become the managing resident partner, and it appeared the transition would be smooth. At 33, George Dixwell had made so much money in China that his older brother, Epes, could take playful pleasure in teasing him about it. "I have looked over all my paper," wrote Epes, "and selected a sheet of the nicest to write to the rich old cock who has made his fortune and is now on his way home. I hope that this sheet will not offend your money-bags . . . and pray be satisfied to know that I write with a gold pen."[41]

Yet even as Captain Faucon and the *Frolic* were achieving widespread recognition for fast passages to China and George Dixwell was returning to Boston a rich man, the shipping business was changing. In less than three years, these new developments would end the *Frolic*'s useful life as an opium clipper. On January 26, 1847, an unsuspecting Faucon wrote to the Heards that the steamer *Sir Charles Forbes* was about to sail from Bombay with four hundred chests of Malwa opium. "She is a new boat," wrote Faucon, "and her owners are desirous of selling her in China."[42]

Five months later, in early June, the Heards received letters from two of their largest Bombay consignors that made them abruptly aware of the consequences of the entrance of steamers into the opium trade. In the first letter, the Parsee firm of B. & A. Hormujee noted that steamers would soon be traveling regularly from Bombay to China and inquired whether there might exist "any prejudice in China amongst the Chinese for opium transmitted by a steamer instead of a sailing vessel." They wondered whether good opium might deteriorate if carried on a steamer.[43] Kessressung Khooshalchund's letter, arriving a week later, was more direct. "As we shall have very soon a number of extra steamers running to China," wrote the Hindus' correspondent, "I fear the

'Frolic' will, in the course of some time, have very little chance of getting a full cargo and if she cannot sufficiently & profitably be employed in the Coast of China, it will be better to sell her when a fair opportunity offers."[44]

By October it had become apparent that the *Frolic*'s future earning power was already undermined. "Steamers have now begun running from here to your place with opium freight at Rs 26 per chest, and I do not know what will become of so many Clippers employed in the China Trade," wrote Kessressung Khooshalchund's correspondent. Insurance rates for steamers were much lower than for sailing vessels, as the Indian firm ominously noted: "The underwriters will take risk in these steamers at 1% per chest which is . . . a very light rate and thus the utility of shipping opium per Clippers has been totally effaced."[45]

Using Kessressung Khooshalchund's figures, we can calculate the overall cost differential of shipping a $500 chest of Malwa opium aboard a steamer rather than a sail-driven clipper. On a steamer, at 26 rupees ($12.22) for freight and 1 percent ($5.00) for insurance, the total shipping cost was $17.22 per chest. Aboard the clipper *Frolic*, at $6.00 for freight and 2.5 percent ($12.50) for insurance, the cost was $18.50. Clearly, there was already a $1.28 advantage in shipping aboard a steamer. As insurance was a fixed cost, steamers only needed to lower their freight rates by small amounts to substantially increase their advantage.

The new competition from steamers was only one of several problems confronting John Heard during the summer of 1847. John was also concerned about persistent rumors that the British East India Company was pursuing a new policy to discourage growth of the Malwa drug trade. The Company had already announced its intent to sell 31,000 chests of Patna opium during the 1847–48 season, 9,000 chests more than the preceding season. This glut of opium would depress prices, but an even greater worry was the rumor that the Company planned to again raise the export duty on Malwa opium. "A couple of years since," John informed his uncle, "they raised it from 300 to 400 Rs, and the infliction of a heavier tax would kill the trade almost entirely."[46]

Sales of Malwa drug had thus far remained strong despite pervasive adulteration, mainly because it was always possible to undersell the Company-produced Patna product. But the combined effect of lower prices for Patna and higher fixed costs for exporting Malwa would erase this price advantage and favor the sale of Patna drug. "The adulteration of Malwa," John wrote, "has induced already a change of taste among the Chinese, making them prefer the guaranteed article of the Company."

"It has occurred to me," John explained to old Mr. Heard, "that an important branch of our business is menaced by this change, and that we ought to knit ourselves as closely as possible to K. K. in order that the capital that he wields, when thrown out of Malwa, may be employed in some other manner that may bring fish to our net." John decided to visit Bombay to become personally acquainted with the head administrator at Kessressung Khooshalchund, with the hope of "prevailing on him, not only to continue using his money, through Calcutta, in Bengal [Patna] opium, but to permit [the Heards] to extend his shipments of China Produce to England and the United States."

Late in the summer of 1847, the *Don Juan* was lost on the China coast without a trace. Suddenly, John needed to develop his own strategy to keep the firm active in that lucrative traffic. At the same time he had to be in a position to enter the Bengal trade if necessary, carrying British East India Company–produced Patna drug from Calcutta. Following Kessressung Khooshalchund's orders, John Heard dispatched the *Frolic* to Calcutta in October 1847, though he had misgivings. "She will not make so good a voyage as though she loaded at Bombay with a full freight," John informed his uncle. "She carries too little for a Bengal clipper, but we had no alternative after the orders were received." John tried to put the venture in a more positive light: "It may in the end be advantageous, by introducing her and us to a, comparatively, new line of business."[47]

By the spring of 1848, John Heard had developed his new plan for the fleet. He calculated that the steamers, even if full on every trip, would be able to carry only 17,000 of the 45,000 chests of opium imported annually into China, leaving a balance of almost 30,000 to be transported aboard sailing vessels. Accordingly, he proposed to Kessressung Khooshalchund that the Hindus take a half or a third interest in a new clipper of 400 to 450 tons. John Heard believed a new and larger clipper, built to company specifications, would be more versatile than the *Frolic*, which was too small to earn a profit carrying anything but opium.

John, of course, had to convince old Mr. Heard of his plan as well. "She could be used on the Coast, where the business, at present, is good," John wrote. Moreover, "she could go to Bombay or Calcutta, take as much opium as could be had, & fill up with cotton." And, as if that were not enough, "She could go to Penang, Arracan & Singapore and obtain freight to Canton and Amoy and . . . [still] be on hand to avail of a good chance and high freights to the United States."[48]

Russell & Co.'s new vessel, the 600-ton *Houqua*, had been built and outfitted for $36,000. John concluded that a 450-ton vessel, costing much less, would be a very safe speculation. "But to insure this," John wrote, "there must be *no mistake* about her. She must *be an out and out clipper*." John Heard was intensely competitive, and the opium clipper he most wanted to beat was Russell & Co.'s 450-ton, Boston-built *Coquette*: "The 'Coquette' is the best vessel in China and one that is faster, prettier, and can carry nearly as much, might be built." Faucon, he added, "should have the command, as he deserves it from his services. Besides, his address and knowledge of the business would make him particularly desirable in a vessel of which the Captain might sometimes be the Agent."

John Heard also wrote enthusiastically to Kessressung Khooshalchund, urging the Indians to take an interest in the proposed new clipper. However, there were increasing problems with the Heards' opium business, and John's letters to his uncle were somewhat less buoyant. His final accounting for the 1847–48 fiscal year reported: "You will perceive by the Profit & Loss a/c [account] that the balance of division is much less than ever before." The Shanghai expenses had contributed a great deal to the unfavorable outcome, he explained, with the balance against them totalling $9,698.35.[49]

When George Dixwell had first proposed a Shanghai branch, the Heards had expected its expenses to be offset by increased drug consignments and storage fees from Parsee firms in Canton. But the Parsees had sent their own agents to Shanghai and developed their own storage facilities. As a consequence, both the Shanghai office and the receiving vessel *Snipe* showed losses for the year. The *Frolic* had not done well either. "The Frolic has had heavy repairs," John wrote, "and her business has been a losing one, from the fact that no treasure freights have been obtainable." The *Frolic* had made only two voyages during the year, and one of these "was to Calcutta which did not yield nearly so much as if she had gone to Bombay." She had completed only two voyages for the fiscal year because she had not yet returned from the third, and John pointed out that had those "proceeds been included in the . . . statement she would have lost little or nothing."

Regardless of John Heard's explanations, the *Frolic* had run at a loss. When the year's accounting for the vessel finally reached Kessressung Khooshalchund, the only entry the Indians' administrator noted was the bottom line. "On a glance to the statement rendered by you . . . it appears that the profits have now given way," he responded, "and it is very much to be feared that the present unhealthy circumstances of our freight market would be an additional discrepancy to benefit the interests of the owners." The Indians saw plainly that sailing vessels had no real future, and in an attached note Kessressung Khooshalchund's spokesman attempted to quash any further discussion of a new clipper. "In reply to your enquiry," he wrote, "I beg to state that intimation from Ahmedabad [the residence of the firm's owners] does not warrant to have any share in the new clipper adverted by you. At present, there appears no prospect in having any interest in the clippers which have lost entirely the advantage of securing better freight in the present precarious times owing to the innumerable steamers now running from Bombay."[50]

John tried once more to convince Kessressung Khooshalchund to invest in the new clipper. For his efforts he received a carefully worded rejection which barely masked the always polite Hindus' growing exasperation with him. "You will observe the advantage of the China Clippers has entirely been reaped by the frequent running of steamers to your port with opium and other cargo which, I fear, may probably tend to render the voyage of the 'Frolic' to China most miserable. . . . It is no use now adays to have any interest in the Ships and with this view I have declined a share in the new American Clipper to which you crave my attention, and from a separate letter by the last conveyance you must have read the unwillingness in joining you in the said clipper."[51]

As one-fifth owner of the *Frolic*, Captain Faucon was likewise concerned that profits had given way. Although he had now paid off his share in the vessel, unlike George Dixwell he had not yet made his fortune, and he could see that his prospects for doing so were rapidly diminishing with the growing obsolescence of his vessel. Faucon had al-

ways manned the *Frolic* with highly paid English and American seamen, but in the summer of 1848 the new and unfavorable economic
reality forced him to cut operating costs by hiring, for the first time, an
all "native" crew.[52] From now on, the *Frolic* would sail with two English or American officers, a carpenter and a cook (who might be Anglo or Chinese), a Chinese "boy" to look after the needs of the officers,
and fourteen to sixteen native seamen. Those from the west coast of
India were called "Lascars"; those from Singapore (modern Malaysia)
"Malaymen." All spoke Portuguese, the old trade language of western
India, Malaysia, and Macao.

Faucon had been too cautious an investor to make money in his own
opium speculations. Now he had become the master of an obsolete vessel and a native crew. His hopes of wealth dimming, he was disaffected
and depressed. Unfortunately, news of his complaints leaked back to
Canton. John Heard responded angrily. "We are well off in our captains, except Faucon," John wrote to his uncle. "I always had a high
opinion of him until lately, altho' I hated the sight of him, for his appearance was only the signal for a growl about his hardships and mis-
fortunes." Faucon's remarks, John went on, "were not of much consequence, except as evincing a very ugly state of feeling. The fact is, he is
an unfortunate man and visits his spleen which ought to be directed on
himself, on others. He has had every opportunity which a man could
have in our employ, the highest pay, credits always, and 'tis not our
fault that he has not made money."

Faucon was finding it difficult not to allow his disappointments to
show themselves, and John Heard feared his sour mood was compro-
mising his effectiveness as a captain. Commercial success was closely
tied to personal relationships and the facility for "getting along." Thus
John observed in his letter to Mr. Heard: "His temper is so disagree-
able that he is disliked by all his brother shipmasters & he is only valuable on account of his education & intelligence making him competent
to act as an Agent." But, John went on, "this is not likely to happen,
and there is such a thing as paying too dear for the whistle." In an effort to support his case with a few facts, John proceeded to compare
Faucon with Captain Porter of the *Dart*. When Faucon had come down
from the Coast, John revealed, he had carried $370,000 in treasure,
and the rival *Torrington*, sailing the same day, had carried $160,000.
John blamed Faucon for failing to obtain the entire shipment for the

Frolic. "Had it been the Dart instead of the Frolic," wrote John, "every dollar would have come by her, as Porter is as popular as the other is the reverse." The *Torrington*'s treasure, John argued, had been lost "by [Faucon's] sheer incivility," and, as the Heard firm charged .5 percent to transport treasure from Shanghai to Canton, John calculated that "in the above case Porter would have been just $800. better to us than Faucon."[53]

In retrospect, this incident reveals an immature, defensive John Heard overreacting to gossip. He himself had conceded that Faucon's complaints "were of not much consequence." The two men apparently soon worked out their differences amicably, and Heard's subsequent correspondence about Faucon expressed no further rancor. Yet in the fall of 1848, even as the *Frolic*'s future was clouded in uncertainty, events were occurring in California that would determine the last chapter of her life.

ꝶhe Final Cargo

ON JANUARY 24, 1848, gold was discovered at Sutter's Mill in California's Sacramento Valley. By summer word of the discovery was out, and on December 5 John Dixwell wrote from Boston to the Augustine Heard firm in Canton that the Gold Rush was already well under way. "We have extravagant accounts of the quantity of gold lately found in the whole valley of the Sacramento in California," wrote Dixwell. "The handful of inhabitants now there is said to collect at the rate of $60,000 a day. . . . Shiploads of emigrants are already started from the Atlantic ports to share in the pickings."[1]

John Dixwell was primarily interested in the benefits the massive migration to California might provide to the firm's shipping business. In January 1849 he sent additional information to John Heard in Canton, including a market analysis. Dixwell reported vessels "loading from Bangor to Baltimore," with at least a hundred already on their way around Cape Horn, as well as "other expeditions . . . going from the Western Country overland." All of this, he wrote, "must have a serious effect on the China & India trades." Dixwell predicted that although some of these outbound vessels would remain on the California coast, at least 50, some carrying enough gold to purchase complete cargoes, would cross the Pacific seeking freights in China, Manila, and India. This would result in a drop in freight rates, while the price of China goods would rise. Augustine Heard & Co. could seize this opportunity for "valuable business" if they entered aggressively into the trade between California and China.[2]

California merchants did not ignore the prospects of profits from importing China goods. Even as John Dixwell was urging the Heards in China to investigate the burgeoning California market, merchants in California had dispatched the brig *Eveline* for a China cargo. In addition to the gold she carried, the *Eveline* would also bring Jacob Leese— a friend of Faucon's old friend John Everett—to China.

John Everett and Edward Faucon were connected through social ties that had been established years before in the California hide and tallow trade. It had, in fact, been Captain Faucon's friendship that first brought John Everett to China. Everett had come to California as clerk aboard the Bryant and Sturgis brig *Chalcedony* in 1831. On the two-year voyage, the 21-year-old Everett had become acquainted with Faucon, the *Chalcedony*'s 25-year-old first mate. In 1834 Faucon, now captain of the *Alert*, returned to California with John Everett as clerk. Faucon and Everett made three hide-collecting trips along the California coast from San Diego to San Francisco, and the two men formed a lasting bond of friendship.

By 1837 the hide market was weakening, and Faucon, seeing no prospects for making his fortune in California, left to enter the China trade. Everett remained in the hide and tallow trade for seven years more. His final trip to California was as supercargo of the bark *Tasso* during her 1841–44 voyage. Over the years, Everett had made repeated visits to pueblos and ranchos along the old mission strip from San Diego to San Francisco in the course of bartering New England manufactures for cowhides, and he had developed lasting friendships with some of California's leading citizens, including Abel Stearns in Los Angeles and Thomas Larkin in Monterey. Joint commercial ventures in the nineteenth century were based on long acquaintance and shared history. The friendship and business relationship linking John Everett and Thomas Larkin exemplifies this dynamic.

Everett's friend Thomas O. Larkin, originally from Charlestown, Massachusetts, established a store in Monterey in 1832 and became wealthy selling manufactured goods smuggled ashore from visiting vessels.[3] Everett often stayed with the Larkins when traveling in California, and when he returned to Boston after the *Tasso*'s voyage, he attempted to repay some of the many courtesies he had received over the years. Everett's letters to Larkin are full of news and gossip, written with the warmth of a well-seasoned friendship. "All your friends appeared to think I must be an everlasting clever fellow to take the trouble to hunt them up on your a/c," he wrote, " . . . but I told them I had been paid beforehand in sundry dinners, suppers, lodgings, &c." Of Larkin's relatives Everett wrote, "they all with true New England curiosity wanted to know how much money you had made during your long absence." Everett guessed "thirty or forty thousand dollars," adding, "if I have erred it is not from intention I can assure you."[4]

John Everett was at loose ends when he returned to Boston in 1844. Hide prices had sunk to 9¾ cents per pound, and thus, as he informed Larkin, "the voyage of the Tasso did not pay simple interest, to say nothing of insurance."[5] The energetic and ambitious Everett did not hesitate to look for new employment. In about July 1845, he wrote to his old friend Edward Faucon in China to announce his availability, and a few months later he wrote to Larkin in California. Everett's letter to Faucon has not survived, but in his letter to Larkin he confessed: "I am doing nothing more than going from one place to another amusing myself, but shall embrace the first good offer to become again a commerciante." Always jovial, Everett added, "I am still open to offers & the first pretty girl, who has a cool hundred thousand as her portion, can have me by asking. Do you know one out in your direction?"[6]

Meanwhile, Thomas Larkin was becoming embroiled in international politics in California. On April 22, 1844, he had received a commission from President John Tyler to serve as United States consul.[7] Relations between the United States and Mexico were tense. Only a week earlier the United States had signed a treaty with the Republic of Texas, proclaiming that portion of Mexico to be a possession of the United States. War was expected, and Larkin's consular duties soon included those of spy and secret revolutionary. In October 1845 President James K. Polk let Larkin know that he would support a movement by Americans in California to form a state, if it could be done surreptitiously, "without causing Mexico just cause for complaint."[8]

Everett had a healthy cynicism regarding the annexation of California by the United States. "*We* only want a slight pretext to drop in on you," he wrote, "& even a minority expression of willingness on your part will be considered powerful enough to call US to your aid & once the job is done, you of course are *the* big man & get office & pay & a large share of the government plunder."[9]

While Everett took the prospect of war lightly, John Dixwell was extremely concerned with the possible effects of international conflict on the interests of Augustine Heard & Co. In 1845, only five months after the *Frolic*'s maiden voyage from Baltimore to Bombay, Dixwell had warned the Heards in Canton of an "approaching war with England on the one side, and Mexico on the other," with "Texas and Oregon being the subjects of dispute." With war imminent, John Dixwell feared for the *Frolic*'s safety. In May, acting on information received in a "confidential" private letter from Washington, D.C., Dixwell had abruptly sold all his holdings of marine insurance company stocks and wrote his colleagues in Canton. "If Mexico issues letters of Marques, it will be authorizing & legalizing the most extensive system of Piracy. She has no navies of her own . . . and all the disconnected & unprincipalled in the world will enlist under her flag to rob and destroy."[10] John Dixwell believed the Heard vessels on the coast of China would be seized at the outset of the war. "If this proves true our insurance companies are good for nothing," he added, concluding, "P.S. I should advise you certainly to sell the Frolic."[11] In Canton, however, George Dixwell, enmeshed in the firm's opium business, ignored the entreaties of both his older brother and old Mr. Heard, and did not sell the *Frolic*.

When Thomas Larkin received John Everett's letter seeking employment, he had a position to offer him. Larkin was purchasing a cargo of "New England domestic goods" to sell in California and offered Everett the job of supercargo. Only three days earlier, in Sonoma, the Bear Flag Revolt had declared California independent from Mexican rule. Uncertain of the political future, Larkin advised his old friend, "Times are fast changing here. Whether the Vessels in 1847 may pay duties or not I cannot fortell."[12] Larkin also wrote to Rev. William M. Rogers, his cousin in Boston, with secret instructions to be shown to Everett only if he joined the venture.[13] These secret instructions were typical of the subterfuge which was an integral part of commercial life in Mexican California. Larkin had, after all, made his first fortune selling smuggled goods in Monterey.

"The Vessel," Larkin instructed Rev. Rogers, "should have a list of stores, rigging &c for 3 years, but laid out, double or more what might be supposed to be used, as this list pays no duties, and the surplus can be sold as cargo." Larkin recommended two invoices for the vessel's cargo, one in Spanish and one in English: "The one in English should be headed as going to the Columbia River and a market not naming California." This deception would enable the supercargo to secure the lowest possible duties, "by the authorities supposing its a chance vessel and not bound direct to California."

Larkin elaborated: "The Supercargo should convene with some shore Merchants before anchoring." When approached by port officials he should tell "the Boarding Officer, he put in for news, for wood & water, in distress, or to land dispatches for the U.S. Consul. . . . Private letters may do, public are better." Larkin advised Rev. Rogers that if he informed the secretary of state of the vessel's departure, government letters might be obtained. Larkin ended his letter by noting, "Mr. Everett can explain all this."

But Everett, in the end, did not wind up as agent for Thomas Larkin. He had responded to an offer from an old shipmate and had already sailed for China. As he had written to Larkin three months earlier: "At the moment this comes in to your hand I shall probably be on my way to the Eastern Indies, having recently determined to let that portion of this globe rejoice in the light of my countenance. I am off for Canton in the first boat to be absent Heaven knows how long." Everett explained, "I have recently heard from Faucon who is doing very well out there & wishes me to join him."[14]

Everett's departure for Canton was delayed for six weeks while he waited for remittances from California for his sales of merchandise aboard the *Tasso*. On April 26, just prior to embarking, he wrote again to Larkin, addressing him as "Amigo mio." "I shall be on my way to [the] land of the 'celestials' where the women have small feet & the men wear long quees." Everett had heard again from Faucon, who "was well & doing well" and didn't "expect to return to the United States for some years . . . not 'till he has made a fortune."[15]

John Everett arrived unannounced in Canton in September 1846. A month later John Heard wrote to old Mr. Heard. "There is a Mr. Everett here who came out in the 'J. Q. Adams' whom we may take as a bookkeeper if Roberts does not remain. He is a Bostonian—a man of about 40, and highly recommended by Faucon as an accountant."[16] Everett was hired by the Heards on January 1, 1847, and only two months later John Heard informed his uncle, "I think we have a prize in old Everett."[17]

But John Everett had not come to China for a bookkeeper's salary. Everett properly viewed his position with the Heards as a sinecure, from which he could speculate on his own account and receive a share in the commissions for any business he might bring to the firm. To this end, Everett quickly reestablished contact with his merchant friends in California. Contemplating a joint venture with Thomas Larkin, Everett wrote to him in September 1847. "What is the prospect for direct trade between China & your place," he inquired. "Could a cargo of China goods, silks, trunks etc. be sold & the payment realized in specie—or has the taste changed with the new arrangement of Govt. & coarser articles to be used in their places."[18]

John Everett wanted to establish commerce with California, but he certainly did not want to receive payments in cowhides. There was no market for cowhides in Canton, and because California produced no other commodity for export in the fall of 1847, this was a major obstacle to direct trade. By the spring of 1848, the discovery of gold at Sutter's Mill would fundamentally change this situation. With payments in gold, extensive direct trade with China was possible, and throughout the summer and fall of 1848 Thomas Larkin considered John Everett's proposal.

Thomas Larkin was in a good position to profit from the rapidly increasing pace of business in California. He had large stocks of cheaply purchased merchandise to sell at inflated prices and additional cargoes on their way. He also owned valuable real estate in San Francisco. More important, by the end of 1848 he held enough gold to purchase a cargo of luxury goods from China. Larkin preferred to share the risks in speculative ventures, so he entered into a partnership with his friend Jacob Leese to finance the voyage of the brig *Eveline* to Canton.

Jacob P. Leese had been in California since 1833. After settling in Sonoma he had married the sister of Mariano Vallejo.[19] The Vallejo family owned enormous tracts of land north of the San Francisco Bay, and with his marriage Leese became a man of property. By the fall of 1848 Leese also held large amounts of gold he had earned from sales of land and supplies. Like Larkin, he was seeking a speculative venture.

On January 16, 1849, Larkin and Leese purchased the 196-ton brig

Figure 27. Jacob Leese (seated at left) and Thomas Larkin (seated at center) pose for a portrait with business associates circa 1850. Courtesy Bancroft Library, University of California, Berkeley.

Eveline for $15,000 in placer gold dust.[20] Each agreed to advance an additional 1,500 ounces of gold—with a value of $24,000—to purchase a cargo for the vessel in China. Without knowing the market in China, however, they did not know whether they were sending enough gold for a complete cargo; thus they authorized purchase of up to $30,000 of additional goods on credit.[21] Leese would sail with the vessel as supercargo, and Larkin's half brother, Captain John B. R. Cooper, would be her master.

Neither Larkin nor Leese had connections in China, but they knew that John Everett, their old and trusted friend, now worked as bookkeeper for Augustine Heard & Co. Two days after he signed his agreement with Leese, Thomas Larkin addressed a long letter to John Everett in Canton. "Our old friend Jacob P. Leese, joint owner in the Eveline, leaves this [place] for your port to purchase 50 to 70,000 dollars cargo for himself and me," wrote Larkin. He explained how he had accumulated such a large amount of working capital: "Land in San Francisco is going up in price beyond all precedent." Larkin added that he was still unwilling to sell his old adobe there, even for $40,000. "The men and times are rich, golden rich," wrote Larkin, also noting that he and a partner had just cleared 120 percent on one Mexican cargo and were soon expecting another.

Larkin invited Everett to join in the *Eveline* venture. "Should you see fit to put into Mr. Leese's hand an invoice of goods, we will sell it . . . with much advantage to both parties." More important, he asked Everett to help Leese assemble the *Eveline*'s cargo. "I depend on your giving your advice, assistance &c . . . to enable him to make purchases," wrote Larkin, "and should like to have you invest in the vessel."[22]

As the *Eveline* began her voyage to China, John Heard was traveling from Canton to Bombay. Although Kessressung Khooshalchund had continued to dispatch full cargoes of opium aboard the *Frolic*, they were consigning only a few chests to be sold by the Heards. Since the Heard firm earned more from commissions on sales than from freight fees, John wished to meet with Bombay exporters to solicit larger consignments. John also needed to determine how his firm could continue to obtain paying freights for the *Frolic* now that steamers were running from Bombay to China.

Heard "went to Kessressung's," finding the firm "in the Bazar in sort of a *den*." There he met Kavaldass Luxmichund, a Hindu who managed the firm for the heirs of the late Mr. Kessressung, and Tamooljee Rustomjee, the Parsee who handled the firm's English correspondence. John Heard stayed in Bombay for 24 days, establishing a warm relationship with Mr. Luxmichund. The Hindu manager promised to visit the owners in Ahmedabad and seek authority to use some of their capital to purchase opium for consignment to the Heards. Luxmichund saw no future for the *Frolic*, and like Heard he was personally in favor of replacing her with a larger clipper. Consequently, he promised to raise that matter again in Ahmedabad, advising Heard that if he could get authority to buy cotton, the vessel could be "made to pay," as he could "always have a cargo ready for her."

Mr. Luxmichund treated John Heard graciously and took him to call upon Sir Jamsetjee Jejeebhoy. "He is a fine looking old fellow," John wrote to Mr. Heard, "and affects the dignity of knighthood most amusingly." Sir Jamsetjee had surprised John by asking about specific members of the Heard firm, "particularly yourself," John informed his uncle, "what you were doing at home, if you were married &c. &c."[23] As he prepared to leave Bombay, John wrote: "The advantages of my trip have been in securing a small amount of consignments at the moment, and, I hope, producing such a favorable impression as shall lead to more extensive business here after. . . . [Luxmichund] has introduced me to several large Hindoo merchants who promise consignments, but you know how much Hindoo promises are worth."[24] However, John added, if he "gets the extension of powers from Ahmedabad, which he expects, I think we shall find our Bombay business increasing."[25]

John Heard visited once more with Kavaldass Luxmichund. "When I rose to go," he reported to old Mr. Heard, "he dipped his thumb into a dish of paint and gave me a mark on the forehead between the eyes, where . . . Hindoos wear the mark of their cast, so that I suppose I may now consider myself a baptized Hindoo. . . . He threw a heavy cashmere shawl over my shoulders, and put a diamond ring on my finger—truly Oriental liberality and magnificence." John descended from Luxmichund's office to his carriage and was greeted by the astonished stares of a "crowd of Hindoos" in the street. He "did not dare wipe off the smooch" until he "was out of sight." John Heard left Bombay aboard the steamer *Pekin*. During a layover in Ceylon, a native appraised the ring at two hundred rupees, but John observed, "I fancy tis worth something more as they probably thought I wished to sell it." As for the shawl, "What shall I do with it?" he asked his uncle. "Mother has the one which you gave her, and Aunt Mary always wears black."

Among other business, John had also discussed the future of the *Frolic* and Captain Faucon with Kavaldass Luxmichund. Although the vessel was obsolete and her captain disaffected, John Heard could neither sell her nor dismiss Faucon without the approval of both the Kessressung Khooshalchund firm and Faucon himself, since together they owned a controlling three-fifths interest in the clipper. When he returned to Canton in April 1849, Heard told his uncle that it would not be easy to dismiss Faucon. "I do not think we shall be able to part with him unless he *wishes* to go, as I find he is a favorite with K[essressung] K[hooshalchund]," but, John added, if Faucon "should wish to leave" the Indians had authorized a joint purchase of his one-fifth share. Meanwhile, Faucon was in India and would not return to China until July. John Heard, now attempting to minimize the damage Faucon's temperament might be doing to the firm, wrote, "It is not often that Faucon goes to the Coast and his brusque manners will not do much harm among the natives of Bombay."[26]

Back in China, Heard's attention turned to other business, and the California market appeared a good opportunity for large profits. "The country is populating so fast that 'ere long a direct trade of some consequence [will] spring up if they are rich enough to pay for the luxuries which China produces." The problem was that the Heards had no reliable contacts in California with whom to develop a venture. "I think," John added, "it would pay to send some one over if I had any one who would go."[27]

Unexpectedly, only a week after John wrote to old Mr. Heard suggesting why the firm might be slow in entering the California trade, the *Eveline* arrived in Canton. Larkin's relationship with Everett had brought the *Eveline* and her gold to the Heards—Jacob Leese, her supercargo, asked John Everett to help him purchase a cargo to sell in California. Suddenly, John Heard saw opportunity at the doorstep and sprang into action. As usual he reported everything to old Mr. Heard in Boston. "Shortly after the last mail left, a ship from California came in, the supercargo of which was an old friend of Everett, and for this reason consigned her to us." Full of excitement, John continued, "Now about California . . . this California ship . . . brings $60,000 worth of gold for investment, and [as] she is a small craft (the Eveline) not more than $30,000 will be used in filling her. The balance will be invested in another ship which the supercargo wishes to charter."[28]

Leese and Larkin intended to establish a commercial house with one branch in San Francisco operated by Leese, another in Monterey operated by Larkin, and a third "wherever trade might center," for which they were seeking a partner. Leese had offered to take the Heards' clerk, Brinley, "as a junior partner, giving him an interest equal to the proportion of the capital he could contribute." All this, John pointed out, would benefit Augustine Heard & Co., since Leese promised that the partners "would use their influence" to direct business to the Heards. John thought the arrangement a "capital one" and proposed to lend Brinley "$8 or $10,000 at 8 or 9% interest" to be paid back from his first profits. Advancing so much money would be inconvenient, but, John warned, "we cannot sit quietly by and see the California trade, which promises to be so important, slip through our fingers."

John estimated that hereafter the Heards would earn $3,000 to $4,000 per year in commissions on cargoes they purchased for Larkin and Leese. These cargoes would include such silks as they had formerly sold in Mexico "and a little of everything" that could "be had in China," known in the trade as "chow chow." "I consider it a great thing for us to start with the influence of old California residents, people who know the trade, and everybody in it," John concluded, noting wistfully, "I do wish we had a new Clipper such as I have so often described. I would then send the Frolic to California, and with Mr. Leese's help, we could keep her running with silk and chow chow cargoes for which she is just fitted." John recalled that he had exacted Kavaldass Luxmichund's promise to press the Kessressung Khooshalchund owners to invest in a new clipper: "I suppose we must wait until we see what K. K. says. I feel that bye and bye he will consent, but the sooner we have such a craft the better, so we can get the 'Frolic' into line for California."

Throughout May, June, and July 1849, the Heards purchased the *Eveline*'s cargo—their first foray into the California trade. If they had only known in advance that the vessel would be consigned to them, they could have placed orders with vendors and taken delivery of a cargo before she arrived. By the time they were authorized to place orders, local stocks of China goods were depleted, as four other vessels— the *Rhone*, the *Emmy*, the *Honolulu*, and the *Correo de Cobija*—had recently loaded large cargoes for California. In fact, when Leese had stopped in Honolulu in March on his way to China, he had worried that San Francisco might soon be glutted with China goods. Noting that at least three China cargoes would arrive before the *Eveline*, he had written Larkin asking whether he should bypass San Francisco on his return, and instead make a quick "run down the coast" to reach the more remote markets from Monterey to San Diego.[29]

With all these concerns in mind, John Everett, Jacob Leese, and the

Heard staff began to purchase the goods they anticipated would sell well in California. On August 3, when the *Eveline* was finally loaded for departure, her three bills of lading listed a total of 1,353 cases, packages, bales, rolls, and kegs, including the following:[30]

100 cases Sweetmeats	1 case Raisins
2 bales Blankets	1 case Silver Ware
25 cases Trunks	1 case Measuring Rods
100 rolls Matting	2 cases Scales & Weights
57 cases Furniture	7 cases Gutta Percha Buckets
1 case Pearl Buttons	689 packages China Ware
7 cases Clothing	6 packages Rattan Chairs
45 cases Lacquered Ware	12 packages Rattan Baskets
11 cases Sundries	3 packages Umbrellas
6 cases Boots & Shoes	92 packages Tea
14 cases Grass Cloth	55 kegs White Lead
8 cases Nankeens	2 cases Merchandise

Leese, Everett, and the Heards also made a number of special purchases for the personal use of the Larkin family. Thomas Larkin had given Leese 31¼ ounces of gold ($500) with a list of requests including "one set of drawers . . . 3 to 4 feet high having the top turn over for a writing desk," two portable writing desks, a set of chocolate-colored camphor wood trunks, fine matting for three rooms, shawls and clothing for his wife, Rachel, and daughter Caroline, a "full tea sett and dinner sett of best Chinaware [with] large pieces marked Rachel Larkin—small pieces marked R.L.," and finally "some few choice light filagree articles for table and sideboard display."[31]

Perhaps because the *Eveline* already carried 106 cases of silks, the Heards ignored Larkin's requests for specific clothes for Rachel and Caroline. But the items they did purchase clearly document the Larkins' transition to wealth and provide a vivid picture of export articles then available in China. The invoice included

2 writing desks	6 pearl seals
1 silver card case	1 tea & dinner sett (crockery)
1 silver card tray	1 ivory Mandarin boat
1 silver fan	1 ivory flower boat
1 silver cup	1 sett silver ware
1 gold watch chain	1 leather trunk

1 silver fan handle   1 silver basket
6 feather fans

These special purchases exceeded Larkin's $500 by $62.74, and Leese billed his rich partner for the balance.[32]

When the *Eveline* arrived in China, Captain Edward Faucon and the *Frolic* were on a voyage to Calcutta, and John Heard had not yet been able to discuss the *Frolic*'s future with her captain. By the time Faucon returned to Canton in July, Heard had come to the realization that the *Frolic* might be run profitably between China and California. Furthermore, with his years of experience on the California coast, Faucon was the best man for the trade.

Much of Faucon's unhappiness was apparently the consequence of his having so much of his own capital tied up in an obsolete vessel. John Heard was soon able to resolve this problem and informed his uncle, "as Faucon wished it, I took over his 1/5th of the Frolic, half on our own a/c and half on K.K.'s."[33] Faucon's outlook improved markedly once he was no longer burdened with a share in the *Frolic*, and so did his relationship with John Heard. By September 13 Heard had regained enough confidence in Faucon to dispatch him to Shanghai with a cargo of opium. The following day brought a serious setback.

"We had a very severe typhoon on the 14th," John Heard wrote a week later to his uncle. "The Frolic and the Antelope had gone to sea, bound for Shanghae on the day previous, but fortunately, both put back and came to anchor in Lymoon Passage, where they were totally dismasted. . . . Faucon cut away to prevent going ashore and the vessel is now repairing in H[ong] Kong." Other vessels had not weathered the storm so well, including one of John Heard's favorites. "The Coquette is much overdue from Shanghae, and great fears are entertained for her," he wrote. "There is a rumor that she was dismasted and then plundered by pirates."[34] In fact, the *Coquette* was totally lost and was never heard from again.

The morning after the typhoon, an unknown artist aboard the *Antelope* penciled the only picture we have of the *Frolic* (Figure 28).[35] It shows her from a great distance in silhouette on the horizon, stripped of her masts and rigging. Her hull, seen in profile, is heavily undercut at both stem and stern. A shattered mast, possibly belonging to the *Antelope*, floats in the foreground. Over-sparred, she had survived the

Figure 28. The *Frolic* dismasted in Hobe Bay, China, the morning after the typhoon of September 13, 1849. Enlarged from a pencil and ink sketch, artist unknown. Courtesy Peabody Essex Museum of Salem, Massachusetts.

storm only because her captain had ordered her masts and rigging cut away. Although there was no loss of life aboard the *Frolic*, she suffered extensive damage, and Captain Faucon spent $150 to charter the steamer *Canton* to tow the crippled vessel to Hong Kong. One Ching See was paid $20 for retrieving the *Frolic*'s masts and spars from the bay. These were scrapped, and the vessel was refurbished with all new materials.[36]

Damage not caused by the typhoon was also discovered while the *Frolic* was being repaired. Removing cast-iron ballast from deep in her hold, Faucon found that part of the *Frolic*'s keelson "was entirely gone with dry rot."[37] The *Frolic* was anchored off John Lamont's shipyard at East Point in Hong Kong while Faucon waited for Lamont to haul her out of the water. Faucon wanted to see if the vessel's copper sheathing had been battered by the masts and spars he had cut away during the typhoon. He saw no storm damage but found a problem far more severe: "On examining her bottom," Faucon reported to the Heards, "I found it very necessary to have the brig recoppered. The whole sheathing abt. the bows & along the bilges & bends was so far gone as to be filled with small holes."[38]

Repairs occupied much of November. The *Frolic*'s new standing rigging was "let go" and her masts lifted in order to replace the rotted keelson. Meanwhile, the worn copper sheathing was stripped and her bottom recaulked with 288 pounds of oakum and resheathed in new Dutch copper. The job was expensive. Insurance covered only two-thirds of the typhoon damage, leaving the *Frolic*'s owners responsible for the balance of nearly $1,800. The bill from John Lamont's shipyard came to $1,593.07.[39] We can imagine Faucon's relief that he had sold his one-fifth share of the *Frolic* in July, and that Kessressung Khooshalchund and the Heards would alone be responsible for these expenses.

As the *Frolic* lay idle in Hong Kong, the Heards received two offers to purchase her. The first came from Russell & Co., who wished to replace the *Coquette*, lost in the recent typhoon. The second offer came from a Mr. Parker, who wanted to run the *Frolic* between China and India. He wished to take delivery in seven months, when his charter on another vessel would expire. "He is willing to give all she is worth, say between $12000 & $15000," John informed Mr. Heard, adding, "I refused R[ussell] & Co. who want immediate delivery, but told Parker that *perhaps*, I would sell her, deliverable then, if in the meantime I could hear that a new vessel would be built for us."[40]

The proposed new clipper had become a sensitive subject for John Heard. Although he brought it up at every possible opportunity, he had been unable to convince either Mr. Heard or the Kessressung Khooshalchund firm to authorize building a new vessel. "You will think I am clipper mad," John wrote to his uncle, pointing out once again that a vessel of 400 to 450 tons could be built for $30,000. "All that is wanted is an out & out *clipper*," he noted, adding, "I think tis a pity to lose so good a chance to sell the Frolic, as she is entirely unfitted to our wants."[41]

John Heard worried for the *Frolic*'s short-term safety as well as her long-term future. Pirates had always preyed upon merchant vessels in the South China Sea. Now they were organized into well-armed fleets to attack opium clippers. "There is a fleet, under one man of over 100 junks," John wrote to his uncle on September 22, informing him that the well-known clipper *Sylph* was missing and believed captured. The steamer *Judea* had been sent to look for the *Sylph* but instead "fell in with a pirate fleet of over 50 sail," five of which she captured and burned.[42] A month later, English men-of-war were rendering a good account of pirates. "They destroyed a fleet of 23 Junks in a bay just to the Eastward of H[ong]. Kong, killing 400 men," wrote John, conceding that the remainder of the pirates—twelve thousand men—had escaped. Nonetheless, 57 junks had been destroyed since September 1— "each of them equal to a 10 gun brig of war."[43]

Captain Faucon was scheduled to sail the *Frolic* to Bombay as soon as she was repaired, and he too was concerned about the continuing depredations of the pirate fleets. Faucon knew the *Frolic*'s strength was her ability to outrun virtually any attacking vessel, and he had therefore armed her more for defense than offense. She carried antipersonnel weapons designed to maim and kill at close range, rather than heavier armaments to disable or sink another vessel. In 1847, Faucon had ordered twelve swivel-mounted, cap percussion blunderbusses from a Liverpool supplier, each designed to fire six musket balls per load.[44] He also purchased twelve tomahawks and six pairs of handcuffs.[45] Faucon could expect a barrage from the swivel guns to discourage any attacker who came within close range, while the tomahawks could be used to dispatch any who attempted to climb aboard. The handcuffs might have been intended for mutinous members of his own crew. As repairs of the *Frolic* neared completion and fears of piracy circulated through the shipping community, Faucon decided he needed additional weaponry. In November, he purchased six cutlasses, a dozen ship's muskets, and four pairs of pistols, along with six boxes of percussion caps and two dozen gun flints.[46]

In addition to small arms, the *Frolic* carried two cast-iron "six-pound" cannon, designed to fire an iron ball measuring 3.67 inches in diameter and weighing six pounds. The *Frolic* was originally equipped with two nine-pounders,[47] each weighing close to 1,700 pounds,[48] but Faucon had replaced these heavy guns with the much lighter six-pounders, weighing about 1,100 pounds each,[49] most likely to reduce weight near the bow. Like most Baltimore clippers, the *Frolic* was so over-sparred that with a light cargo and a full press of sail her bow was in danger of being driven under. A six-pound ball would do little structural damage to an attacking vessel, but if the gun were loaded with six or more pounds of musket balls and iron nails, it could rain indiscriminate death on the crew of any pirate vessel within range.

The *Frolic*, now completely repaired and fully armed, was dispatched to Bombay on December 5, 1849, for what would be her last cargo of opium. Just before her departure John Heard asked Captain Faucon to press the Indians for a final decision on the purchase of a new clipper. In February 1850 John received the awaited reply from Faucon and immediately reported it to old Mr. Heard. "The new clipper for the India trade must positively be given up. K.K. tells Faucon, 'no can,' & Faucon writes that there has been some split in the heirs of the property which K.K. manages, so that he is not able to do as he wishes." John had finally relinquished his obsession with a new clipper. "Steam is every day making such revolutions in trade, that I am not certain but we are better off without one, and am rather glad K.K. backed out." He noted that a steamer now ran directly from Bombay to Shanghai, and there was "talk of keeping one running" on the coast of China. "Please therefore consider the project of a clipper as dropped entirely," John concluded.[50]

The question of the *Frolic*'s future still remained. A month earlier, confident that Mr. Parker would buy the vessel, John had written to Mr. Heard that he expected to sell the *Frolic* when she returned to China, as she was "unfit for the [opium] Trade and not making any money in it."[51] Parker, however, had bought another vessel in the meantime. This forced John to formulate a new plan. "I have been thinking over the matter [of the *Frolic*] a good deal, and have pretty much made up my mind to send her to California when she returns from Bombay, and give Faucon a power of attorney to sell her there." John thought the *Frolic* would bring a higher selling price in California, for, as he put it, she was "just the craft to run up and down the coast there." John was unaware that San Francisco harbor was already clogged with scores of abandoned vessels whose crews had run off to the gold fields. John suggested that the Heard firm purchase a California-bound cargo for the *Frolic* on company account, drawing on their open credit with Barings. The cargo would be selected only after they had received "advices" concerning sale of the *Eveline*'s freight in San Francisco. This would determine which items they should "duplicate" and which they should avoid.[52]

When John Heard next wrote to his uncle a month later, he had worked out most of his plan for the *Frolic*'s voyage to California. "The cargo will be about $35,000 in silks and $15,000 in Chowchow," he wrote. "We [will] base our selections, by taking the articles which paid best in the Eveline's cargo—and send nothing but good staple articles, so there will be no danger of anything being broken or thrown away." In order to spread the risk, Heard decided to allow Faucon and Everett to invest $5,000 each in the venture. Another colleague, Mr. Moses, would be allowed a $10,000 interest "in order to avail of [his] knowledge of silks in selecting the cargo."

The supercargo would be J. C. Anthon, an experienced businessman who had been in San Francisco during the previous year and was "up to all the tricks and 'dodges' of the place." Anthon had agreed to manage and sell the cargo "without the intervention" of a San Francisco commission house. For his services he would take a 10 percent commission, returning 2 percent to Faucon "to assure his hearty cooperation" as assistant supercargo. Anthon's fee included all auction commissions, usually charged separately by San Francisco houses, which would save the Heards a hefty 5 percent.

Purchase of the *Frolic*'s cargo was already well under way when John reported, "we have not bought an article that did not pay 75% *clear profit* on the Eveline, while the average *profit* on the articles in her cargo which correspond to ours, was nearer 200%." John Heard could hardly contain his amazement at the profit the *Eveline* had realized. "Fancy selling a thing there for $7.75 which costs 75 cents. . . . Silk shawls costing $45 & 50 sold at $150 to 180. . . . I do not expect to make what the Eveline made, but surely you will own the chance is good for a profit of 20 to 30%."[53]

By April 17 most of the *Frolic*'s cargo had been purchased, and Mr. Anthon's passage to San Francisco had been booked aboard the *Stockholm*. "He will be there before the Frolic, and will make all arrangements for her," wrote John. This would include renting a building lot and supervising a crew of Chinese carpenters who would assemble the Chinese-manufactured, prefabricated house being shipped to San Francisco on the *Stockholm*, from which the *Frolic*'s cargo would be sold. "I expect to sell the house so that this important item will cost nothing," wrote John. "I expect also to save on labor as Anthon takes over cooleys, at high wages for China, but low wages for California." John's final instruction to Anthon regarding the *Frolic*'s cargo was to "sell only for cash" and to "give no credit." As for the *Frolic* herself, Anthon was authorized to sell her only if the voyage ended "indifferently." "If the voyage pays well," John considered, "it may be more for our interest to keep her in that line of business."[54]

When the *Frolic* finally returned from Bombay on May 21, 1850, she carried a full cargo of Malwa opium, but only a hundred chests were consigned to the Heards. This confirmed John Heard's long-festering suspicion that running the *Frolic* to India no longer guaranteed larger consignments of opium for his firm.[55] John also saw no future in continuing to run opium up the coast to Shanghai on the *Dart*. The day after the *Frolic* arrived, he wrote old Mr. Heard that the *Dart* had been sold for $7,500. "Less than she is worth," John conceded, but "she was loosing money, and would not have sold better six months hence—while she would have lost $500 to $1000 in the meantime."[56] By May 21, the Heards had assembled a full 135-ton cargo for the *Frolic*'s voyage to California. Her three bills of lading, dated May 30, 1850, listed a total of 1,602 cases, packages, rolls, and boxes:[57]

243 cases Silks	3 cases Silverware
18 cases Grass cloth	30 cases Camphor trunks
101 packages comprising 1 House	54 cases Furniture
4 cases Paintings	100 boxes Sweetmeats
30 cases Lacquered ware	174 packages Sundries
9 cases Scales & weights	84 cases Beer
676 rolls Chinaware	23 cases Merchandise
20 cases Chinaware	33 packages Merchandise

The silks shipped by the Heards included a range of items from uncut bolts of fabric to finished embroidered shawls. The silks alone had cost over $31,000. There was a prefabricated house, including carefully marked beams, boards, and planks, together with four exterior doors, eight columns and twenty "oyster windows," their individual panes fashioned from the translucent shells of giant Pacific mollusks. The sets of scales and weights each consisted of nine brass cups ranging from one dram to three pounds, with the cups designed to nest neatly, one inside the other. The camphor-wood trunks were nested, five trunks to each set. The four cases of paintings were from the workshop of Tinqua,[58] a well-known Chinese artist whose skilled assistants

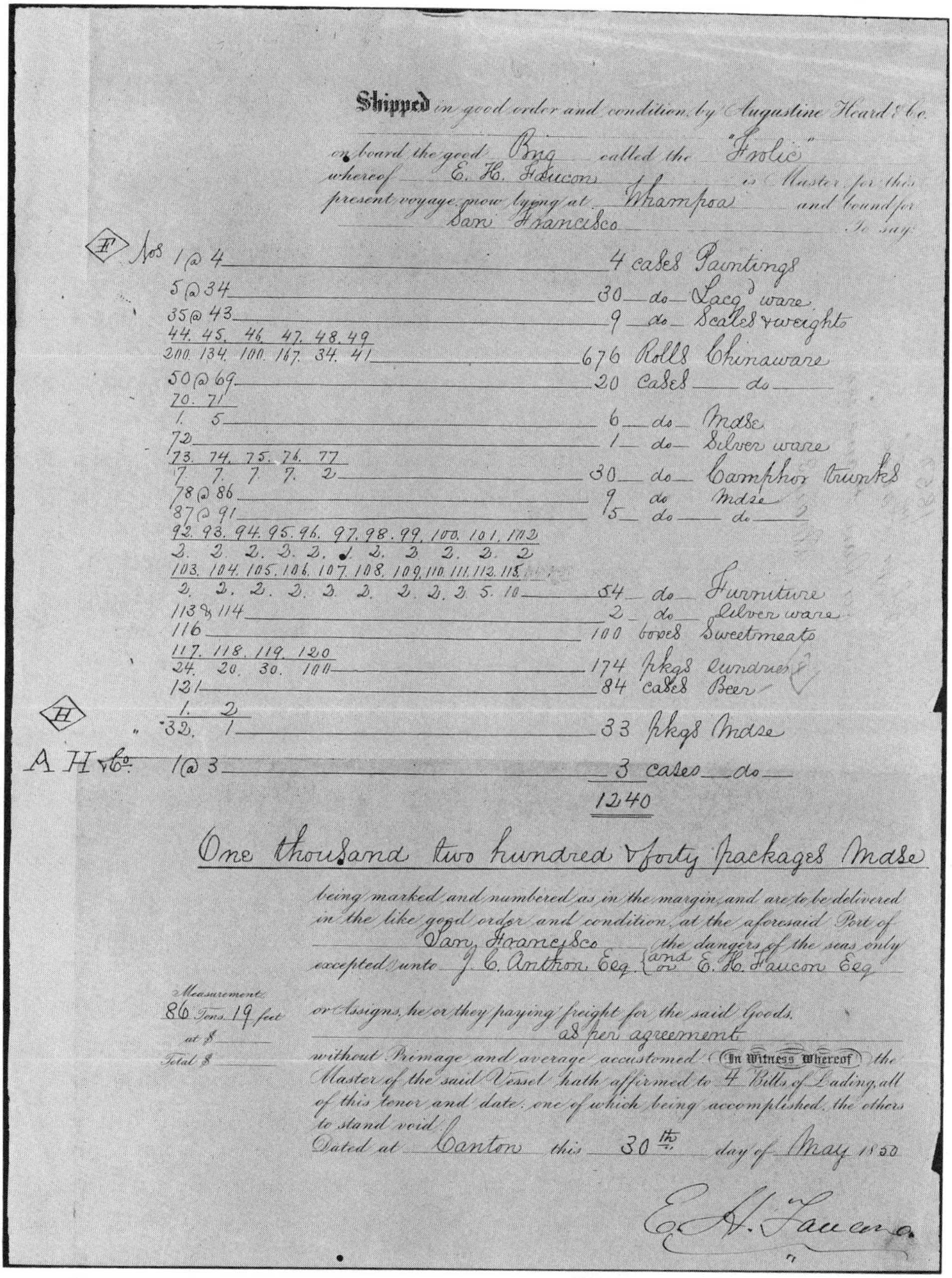

Shipped in good order and condition, by Augustine Heard & Co.

on board the good Brig called the "Frolic"
whereof E. H. Faucon is Master for this
present voyage now lying at Whampoa and bound for
San Francisco To say

F Nos 1 @ 4 — 4 cases Paintings
5 @ 34 — 30 do Lacq'd ware
35 @ 43 — 9 do Scales & weights
44. 45. 46. 47. 48. 49
200. 134. 100. 167. 34. 41 — 676 Rolls Chinaware
50 @ 69 — 20 cases do
70. 71
1. 5 — 6 do Mdse
72 — 1 do Silver ware
73. 74. 75. 76. 77
7. 7. 7. 7. 2 — 30 do Camphor trunks
78 @ 86 — 9 do Mdse
87 @ 91 — 5 do do
92. 93. 94. 95. 96. 97. 98. 99. 100. 101. 102.
3. 2. 2. 3. 3. 2. 2. 3. 2. 2. 2.
103. 104. 105. 106. 107. 108. 109. 110. 111. 112. 115.
2. 2. 2. 2. 3. 2. 2. 2. 3. 5. 10 — 54 do Furniture
113 & 114 — 2 do Silver ware
116 — 100 boxes Sweetmeats
117. 118. 119. 120
24. 20. 30. 100 — 174 pkgs Sundries
121 — 84 cases Beer
H 1. 2
32. 1 — 33 pkgs Mdse
A H & Co. 1 @ 3 — 3 cases do
1240

One thousand two hundred & forty packages Mdse

being marked and numbered as in the margin, and are to be delivered
in the like good order and condition, at the aforesaid Port of
San Francisco the dangers of the seas only
excepted unto J. C. Anthon Esq (and E. H. Faucon Esq

Measurement
86 Tons 19 feet
at $
Total $

or Assigns, he or they paying freight for the said Goods,
as per agreement
without Primage and average accustomed. In Witness whereof the
Master of the said Vessel hath affirmed to 4 Bills of Lading, all
of this tenor and date, one of which being accomplished, the others
to stand void.
Dated at Canton this 30th day of May 1850

E. H. Faucon

Figure 29. The first page of the *Frolic*'s three-page shipping manifest for her
final cargo, Canton, May 30, 1850. Courtesy Baker Library, Harvard Business
School.

painted mass-produced Chinese landscapes in India ink or water colors on pith paper for the export market.

The 676 rolls of chinaware contained inexpensive porcelaneous stoneware bowls and saucers of a suitable quality for miners in the California gold country. To reduce breakage during transport, these ceramic items were arranged in stacks, with wet clay placed between the individual pieces to prevent rattling. Each stack had a protective wrap of cheap matting or other padding material and probably was enclosed in an open-work, basket-like sheath of split bamboo. Because of their weight, these ceramic rolls were placed deep in the *Frolic*'s hold. Large jars and irregularly shaped items of chinaware that could not be stacked in rolls were packed in wooden cases and placed higher up in the hold.

The Chinese silverware shipped aboard the *Frolic* included egg spoons, suspender clasps, and tiny scallop-shaped tinder boxes designed to be worn as necklace ornaments, each enclosing a tuft of tinder and a flint. The 230 containers of unspecified merchandise and sundries contained such chow-chow items as ivory fans, flatware with ivory and mother-of-pearl handles, combs, umbrellas, measuring rods, games with engraved shell counters, and tens of thousands of porcelain beads, probably intended for trade to California Indians. There was even a small case of gold filigree jewelry containing earrings, brooches, bracelets, and stud-like buttons.[59] Possibly visualizing hordes of thirsty miners, their pockets filled with placer gold, the Heards completed their California cargo with 24 hogsheads of Edinburgh ale, purchased for $600. The ale was transferred into 509 dozen long-necked green bottles at 30 cents per dozen. The bottles were packed into ironbound cases, six dozen bottles of brew to a case.[60]

John Heard had secured insurance for his firm's $36,186 share of the *Frolic*'s cargo. Part came from the Western India Insurance Society and the remainder from the Imperial Marine Insurance Company. The other investors apparently arranged for their own insurance. The Heards' 2 percent premiums, covering one passage from Whampoa to San Francisco, totaled $723.72—with a half percent surcharge to be levied if the *Frolic* were to stop at the Sandwich Islands en route. Coverage was to terminate 24 hours after her arrival at San Francisco.[61] The *Frolic* herself was covered for damage or loss up to $12,500 under a long-standing policy with the Suffolk Insurance Company in Boston.[62]

Given favorable winds, Faucon's voyage to California would require a little under two months. A month's layover in San Francisco and the return voyage to China would bring its total duration to almost five months. It would be prohibitively expensive to re-provision the *Frolic* in San Francisco, so Faucon purchased enough bulk foods to feed his crew for the entire round-trip voyage. This included 9,310 pounds of rice, 3,990 pounds of potatoes, 683 pounds of bread, 200 pounds of sugar, 35 pounds of honey, and 34 gallons of vinegar, along with miscellaneous barrels of pork, dried fish, and flour.[63]

Captain Faucon also bought four hundred eggs, four dozen capons, four dozen fowls, four dozen geese, six dozen pigeons, and six pigs. To feed the 216 birds, he bought 1,330 pounds of paddy (unhusked rice). The pigs would be fed slop from the galley. Faucon took special care to ensure that he and his officers would not go thirsty, buying a barrel of wine, twelve dozen bottles of porter, eight dozen bottles of beer, four boxes of cider, several dozen bottles of brandy, and an unspecified number of bottles of gin. Additional supplies included firewood for the cook, wicks and tins of wood oil for lamps, and extra ballast. Finally, Faucon purchased a set of marine charts for the North Pacific. He paid $13.50 for these and $1.00 each for two bottles of Mr. Kidder's Cordials.

Faucon's departure for California was delayed by the need to replace part of his crew. Some of the *Frolic*'s opium had been pilfered on her return trip from Bombay. Faucon accused Fong Awai, the cook; Pow Akwai, the carpenter; and Kong Asg, the steward. Proclaiming their innocence and demanding payment of their salaries—which Faucon had withheld—these men hired a scribe to draft letters of complaint to Robert Bennet Forbes, the American consul in Canton. "We never stole any of the opium [and] we beg you will examine the matter and do justice in this case," they wrote.[64] No record survives of Forbes' action, if any, on the matter.

The *Frolic* departed Hong Kong for San Francisco at 8 A.M. on June 10, 1850, with 26 officers and men aboard. The first and second officers were Charles Deutcher and George Harrison. The crew included seventeen Lascars and Malays, supervised by a Serang (native) boatswain. There were also two Anglo seamen. The new cook, carpenter, and steward were probably Chinese.[65] Six weeks after the *Frolic* sailed, John Heard expressed his confidence in the voyage's financial success: "Advices received from California continue to be encouraging for the

Frolic. . . . The Eagle's cargo of similar goods has been sold at a good profit, and the Frolic will arrive there in good season, just as the miners are beginning to come down from the country and when gold ought to be plenty."[66]

The 6,000-mile passage from Hong Kong to the California coast was uneventful. Faucon made good time, averaging 5.4 statute miles per hour for the entire 46 days. On the afternoon of July 25, Faucon—as was his habit—calculated the *Frolic*'s longitude, employing each of his two chronometers. The two instruments gave measurements differing by sixteen miles, and Faucon, always prudent, took for the vessel's position the one farthest east. His intent was "to run in toward the land under snug sail, & as the weather appeared perfectly clear, & the coast a bold one," to sight land and then follow the southeast-tending coastline down to San Francisco.[67]

The chart that Faucon had purchased in Hong Kong was a Chinese copy of Norie's "North Pacific," based on George Vancouver's 1792–93 survey. Assuming this chart was accurate, and plotting his latitude and longitude, Faucon determined he was 60 miles from shore and about 100 miles north of San Francisco. He altered the *Frolic*'s course accordingly to east-southeast, so the vessel would gradually approach the coast.

Faucon was indeed 100 miles north of San Francisco. But on this section of coast, north of the missions, shipping traffic had been sparse and the shores poorly surveyed. Misled by Norie's chart, Faucon had drawn dangerously close to California's rock-strewn Mendocino coastline. That evening at sunset, 7:15 P.M., Faucon sighted the "faint outline of highland" apparently 50 to 60 miles to the east. Several hours earlier, anticipating sight of the coast and wishing to reduce the *Frolic*'s speed, he had "deemed it prudent to close reef [partially furl] the topsails & furl the jib, mainsail & t'g [topgallant] sail" in order "to be prepared to haul [turn the vessel] either way" should such a maneuver become necessary during the night.

By about 8 P.M. the wind, now from the north, had decreased markedly. Since the *Frolic* was now moving quite slowly, Faucon ordered the jib, mainsail, and topgallants reset and all of the reefs shaken out of the topsails. He could see the coastal mountains, apparently still at great distance, and Faucon felt all was well as he went below to do some writing. The moonlit night was deceptively clear, and while the

Frolic's first officer, Mr. Deutcher, studied the tops of the distant mountains, the clipper sailed ever closer to a mist-shrouded phalanx of surf-battered rocks fronting a low coastal terrace.

At 9:30 P.M., Mr. Deutcher finally lowered his gaze from the mountains to the surface of the ocean and spotted danger. Rushing below to Faucon's cabin he announced, "I see something to the windward which looks like breakers." "Breakers!" replied Faucon. "It's impossible. How do they bear?" "North, sir," answered Mr. Deutcher. "There can be no breakers in that direction," said Faucon as he followed Deutcher up the companionway to the deck.

On seeing the breakers for himself, Faucon ordered the helm turned hard to port. But even as he effected the turn, waves and a strong swell drove the vessel backwards. The *Frolic* struck stern first, snapping off her rudder and cracking her hull. As she filled with water, the swell drove her counterclockwise until, within moments, she lay alongside a large rock over which waves broke furiously. The situation was hopeless. Faucon ordered the *Frolic*'s two boats lowered, with one officer in charge of each. Most of the men climbed into the boats. Inexplicably, two Chinese, one Lascar, and three Malays refused to leave the sinking vessel. There was no time to save clothing or stores. Faucon carried two bottles of brandy, four of porter, and about a dozen "crackers" into one of the boats. Nothing else was saved.

Faucon ordered the boats to head south. During the night they followed an inhospitable coastline of 60-foot vertical cliffs, beneath which waves broke against jagged rocks. At daylight, Faucon finally landed on a beach where he had spotted fires, about seven miles, he estimated, from the wreck. This was almost certainly the broad, sandy bar at the mouth of Big River, which, if we trace Faucon's sinuous coastal course, is exactly six miles from the wreck. Faucon hiked two miles inland, looking for Indians who might provide some information. Finding no one, he returned to the beach.

As one of the boats was leaking and most of the crew wished to travel by land, Faucon ordered four oarsmen into the more seaworthy boat. With his two officers and a sick Lascar, they continued south. They made slow progress for the next three days, as they fought southerly winds and coastal fogs. They slept on beaches at night and ate mussels pulled from the rocks for sustenance. Finally, on July 29 at 5 P.M., they landed at a ranch where they were given beef and milk.

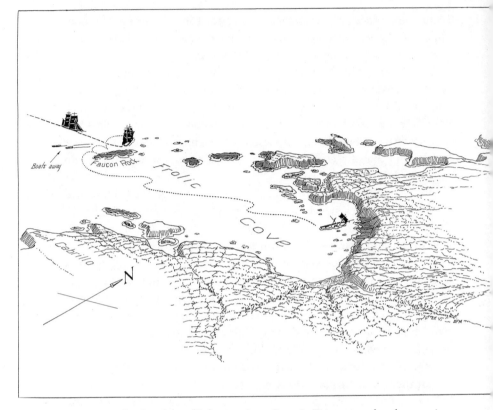

Figure 30. On the night of July 25, 1850, Captain Faucon saw breakers against offshore rocks and attempted to turn the *Frolic*. She struck stern-on and filled with water. Judging the vessel lost, Captain Faucon abandoned ship. The vessel later washed into an adjacent cove and lodged near shore, where she was pillaged. Original illustration by S. F. Manning.

This was probably the German rancho, about four miles north of Fort Ross, owned by Henry Hegeler and two partners. Here two of the oarsmen ran away. The next day Faucon reached Fort Ross, where he spent the night at the home of William Benitz, owner of the settlement. Faucon traveled on to Bodega the following morning and passed the night with Captain Stephen Smith, who operated a steam-powered sawmill there.

On Sunday, August 4, ten days after the wreck, Faucon arrived at San Francisco. Within hours he was interviewed by a reporter from the city's largest newspaper, the *Daily Alta California*. The following day an article appeared titled "Shipwreck and Loss of Life." Faucon, apparently estimating the *Frolic*'s cargo would have brought 200 percent over invoice, calculated the loss at $150,000.[68] That afternoon Faucon drafted a long report to the Heards in China. "It is my painful duty to communicate to you unwelcome news," he began, "as unwelcome for you to read as for me to write." He provided a detailed account of the wreck, ascribing the loss of his vessel to three causes. First, the coast was inaccurately charted north of San Francisco, "in some places to the extent of 35 miles." Second, there were unseasonably strong currents running north. Finally, although the weather appeared to be clear, there had been "a haze indistinguishable to the observer hanging over the coast."

Faucon suggested the Heards show his letter to the insurance underwriters in Canton. "The loss," he wrote, "must be classed as one of those ever likely to happen in the ordinary course of navigation & wh[ich] with all the vigilance, & prudence, & skill possible to be exercised, do & will continue to occur."[69] Four days later, wishing to protect themselves from future litigation, Faucon and his two officers signed an affidavit before Thomas Tilden, a notary public, once more describing the circumstances of the wreck and asserting that the loss was not due to any deficiency in the brig, her captain, his officers, or the crew.[70]

Having fulfilled his legal obligations, and shamed by the loss of his vessel, Faucon found solace in reflection on happier times. He wrote to his old friend Abel Stearns, a prominent businessman in Los Angeles. It had been thirteen years since Faucon's last visit to California, and he felt disoriented in the bustle of Gold Rush San Francisco. "Here evythg. is American & I must really say that I dont know the place," he wrote. "Except some old undisturbed land marks there is nothing to remind me of San Francisco as it used to be." Of their mutual friend John Everett, Faucon added whimsically, "I believe he is tired of waiting for Mrs. Stearns to become a widow. . . . Pray what chance shall I have if I wait!"[71]

Faucon had hoped to return to China immediately, but a few days later a rumor reached San Francisco that the *Frolic* "had been seen still hanging on the rocks." Concerned with protecting the Heards' interests, Faucon hurriedly arranged to be taken north aboard a "cutter" to see if anything could be saved.[72] As Edward Faucon sailed north in search of his wrecked clipper, John Heard in Canton, still confident the voyage would be profitable, was writing a letter to his uncle. John had just received a letter from old Mr. Heard, four months in transit, advising against sending the *Frolic* to California.

"I have felt badly . . . to find that you disapprove so decidedly of the *Frolic*'s voyage to California," John replied. "All the time the vessel was here I did not know what to do with her. Wherever I sent her, she must lose money except California." John told Mr. Heard that San Francisco prices were continuing high. Moreover, San Francisco had recently suffered an extensive fire that had destroyed large amounts of China goods similar to those aboard the *Frolic*. This, he noted, "should be *somewhat* in her favor." John predicted the *Frolic*'s voyage would make expenses plus 30 percent on the investment. Even so, he pointed out, "I should not be at all sorry to see the Frolic sailing under some other flag than the '*red white diamond.*'"[73]

Three weeks had passed since the wreck before Faucon returned to the Mendocino coast on about August 15. In those three weeks news of the wrecked vessel had rapidly spread along the coast and into the interior. There is no certain record that Faucon found the *Frolic*, but even if he had, it is unlikely that anything of value had been left by the hordes of looters that had descended upon her almost immediately.

Reconstruction of the events, aided by a modern marine chart,[74] suggests that the *Frolic* struck a rock about four hundred yards from shore, off a small unnamed cape half a mile north of Point Cabrillo. At the time of impact, a crewman had just counted eight fathoms (48 feet) on a hand-lead. Thus when Faucon abandoned ship the *Frolic* was being pounded by waves against a rock in relatively deep water. Responding to wave action, shifting tides, and winds against her sails, the *Frolic* bobbed, ground, and scraped her way around the rock over the next several days. Finally she was driven six hundred yards into a cove where she lodged, bow first, against a rocky bottom, only one hundred feet from shore. Lying in shallow water, the *Frolic* provided an easily accessible feast of riches.

Two Chinese crewmen, a Lascar, and three Malays had remained aboard the wrecked *Frolic* when Faucon abandoned her. The morning after, Faucon left eleven Lascars and Malays without provisions on the beach at Big River. The beached crew likely hiked the four miles (by

Figure 31. The *Frolic* wreck site, August 1850. Original illustration by S. F. Manning.

land) back across the headlands to view the wreck and to see if their comrades had survived. Meanwhile, the six sailors left on the *Frolic* probably spent a miserable night clinging to the foundering vessel's rigging, high above her wave-washed deck. We may assume that these men, shouting and waving to their comrades on shore, stayed with the vessel as she bumped her way into the calmer waters of the cove where she finally lodged. Here, fortified from the *Frolic*'s stock of porter, the seventeen crewmen probably scavenged all of the food and valuables they could carry before beginning their long walk.

Next came the Indians. Faucon had chosen to land on the beach at Big River because he saw campfires there, but the Indians had apparently retreated to their village, hidden in the nearby woods. Members of the Mitom band of Northern Pomo had established Buldam as a sum-

Figure 32. Pomo people camping at Buldam, near modern Mendocino, salvaged some of the *Frolic*'s cargo in 1850. This photograph by Carleton E. Watkins, taken around 1860, shows Buldam or a Pomo camp on the Mendocino Indian reservation near Fort Bragg. Courtesy California History Room, California State Library, Sacramento, California.

mer village on the north side of Big River. Their winter villages lay 25 miles east in Little Lake Valley, near the modern city of Willits.[75] The Mitom spent their summers along this section of the coast harvesting and drying shellfish. They would have watched with great interest as the *Frolic* washed toward shore and as her crew recovered food, clothing, and valuables. Once the sailors had departed, the Indians began their own salvage effort. Swimming out to the *Frolic,* the Indians descended through the open hatches into the vessel's water-filled hold. Here they found a chaotic jumble of packages, many buoyant enough to be floated ashore. During the next few weeks, joined by friends and neighbors from the interior, they carried away a considerable amount of cargo.

Meanwhile, word of the vessel and her cargo spread with the *Frolic*'s crew members to every ranch they passed. During the following months the *Frolic* was visited and plundered by unknown numbers of people from these ranches. By the spring of 1851, when Harry Meiggs, the San Francisco lumber dealer who had recently bought the mill at Bodega, sent his superintendent up the coast to see what might be retrieved, it was already too late. Although the superintendent, Jerome Ford, described Indian women of the vicinity wearing elegant silk shawls, he found nothing of value remaining at the wreck site.[76]

Numerous items from the *Frolic*'s cargo were seen in the northern Russian River valley near modern Ukiah in the summer of 1851. George Gibbs was an interpreter on a government expedition traveling through the area to make treaties with local Indian groups. In a journal entry dated August 23, 1851, Gibbs described reaching the northernmost house on the Russian River, owned by George Parker Armstrong (known locally as John Parker). "The house," wrote Gibbs, "was a small building . . . of poles filled in with clay, and thatched with tule." Gibbs was struck by the furniture inside the house, which he described as "incongruous . . . for upon the earthen floor and beside a bull's hide partition, stood huge china jars, camphor trunks, and lacquered ware in abundance, the relics of some vessel that had been wrecked on the coast during last spring."[77]

After searching for the *Frolic*—apparently unsuccessfully—Captain Faucon returned to San Francisco and sailed for China on September 16 as a passenger aboard the ship *T. W. Sears*.[78] A few days earlier J. C. Anthon, suffering severe dysentery, had sailed for Honolulu aboard another vessel, and died en route.[79] News of the wreck was finally announced in Hong Kong on October 3, when the *China Mail* published a short article excerpted from the *Daily Alta California* of August 5.[80]

John Heard shed no tears over the *Frolic*. "The vessel is splendidly sold," he gleefully informed his uncle, pointing out the clipper was insured for more than she was worth. John allowed that there would be a loss on the prefabricated house they had sent over with Anthon on the *Stockholm* to receive the *Frolic*'s cargo, but, he explained, "Taking this off, and also the deductions in settling the policy, we shall get 30% clear, which is good business without any risk. . . . I would rather the vessel had arrived, but we are saved the risk of fire in San Francisco."[81]

By the end of December, John Heard had closed the books on the wrecked clipper. He wrote to old Mr. Heard: "The *Frolic* is well rid of. She was always a bad vessel, cramped for room, & had got to be . . . six years old, and I *suspect*, would not have been found particularly sound, had she been opened a year hence." Captain Faucon arrived in China on November 6 and about a month later boarded the *Wisconsin* for New York.[82] Of him, John Heard reported that he had sailed for home, intending to buy into a ship he could command in the China trade. "I told him that I thought both you and Dixwell would aid him if in your power. I consider him a most economical, good man, and a very competent shipmaster," John wrote, "notwithstanding his ill luck."[83]

Although the active life of the *Frolic* ended on July 26, 1850, this story does not. The Heards and Dixwells continued in commerce. Captain Faucon, only 43 at the time of the wreck, lived another 44 years, and the Gardner brothers in Baltimore were just beginning some of their most productive years as shipbuilders. And even as the Mendocino surf battered the *Frolic* to pieces, she was already undergoing a transformation from oak frames and pine planks into the far more durable fabric of folklore.

Conclusion

The Passing of a Generation

WITHIN TWO DECADES of the loss of the *Frolic*, her nineteenth-century mercantile world had ceased to exist. The grand age of Baltimore shipbuilding and American commission houses in China ended with the Civil War, and the principals in the Heard firm had to adapt to an altered commercial reality.

When Captain Faucon returned to Boston in the summer of 1851, he planned to buy a share in another vessel and reenter the China trade. But he was soon distracted. Years earlier, John Everett had introduced him to the Weld family. Everett's sister Hannah was married to John Weld, who became a friend and business associate of Faucon's. John Weld managed Faucon's capital and in fact had loaned him $1,000 to help with the purchase of his one-fifth share in the *Frolic*.

Faucon had probably met Martha Weld, John's youngest sister, in 1837 when she was thirteen, just after he brought the hide-filled brig *Pilgrim* back from the California coast. Fourteen years had passed, and Martha Weld was now 27. Edward Faucon and Martha were married on May 20, 1852, exactly a year and a day after his return from China. Six weeks later her father, Daniel Weld, died at the age of 79. He left Martha a one-sixth share of his $158,708 estate, valued at $26,451.[1] By the mid-1850s, Faucon had successfully established himself in a new career—as a marine salvage specialist representing Boston insurance underwriters. Far from being sedentary, his new work required extensive travel, from St. Thomas in the West Indies to Nova Scotia.[2]

The new decade had brought change, too, to the Dixwell brothers. John Dixwell became a prominent figure in Boston commercial banking, with an appropriate standard of living, which included by 1849 a mansion on a large tract of land in Jamaica Plain, a suburb of Boston. George Dixwell remained a private speculator throughout the 1850s; one of his ventures brought him to San Francisco in 1854.[3] From 1857 to 1859 he served another term in China with the Heards. He lost much of his fortune in a bad investment in 1862 and returned to China to recoup his losses. He remained there ten years, directing the Heards' Shanghai office. During part of this time he also served as Russian vice-consul and as a municipal officer for the Shanghai foreign concession. George also became increasingly immersed in Chinese culture. He studied the Chinese language and entered into a relationship with Hoo Tsai-Shoon, the educated daughter of a Shanghai commercial family. On October 15, 1868, their son was born. They called him Teen Seng, or "Heaven Sent." Rather than suffer the social ostracism that would have resulted from giving his son his own surname, George named the boy Charles Sargent, using his mother's surname.[4]

Augustine Heard & Co. grew substantially during the 1850s. The firm opened offices in Hong Kong, Foochow, Amoy, and Ningpo.[5] John Heard was finally able to go home to Boston in 1852 when his younger brother, Augustine, took charge of the China operations. But only five years later the business climate in China changed again, requiring John's return. The Treaty of Tientsin, signed on July 3, 1858, legalized production and sale of opium in China. Although the Heards continued to import opium from India, legalization meant an end to the large profits derived from smuggling. John's task for the Heards between 1857 and 1862 was to diversify the firm to meet these new market conditions.

In 1859, John Heard accompanied the new American minister to Yokohama and became the first American civilian to enter Japan. Under John's direction, the Heards soon established agents at Yokohama, Nagasaki, and Kanegawa. The Treaty of Tientsin had also opened the interior of China to commerce, and in 1861 John Heard made the historic first trip up the Yangtze River to Nanking and Hankow on the firm's steamship *Fire Dart*, establishing a new and profitable transport business. In the same year, the Heards became the first commission house to represent American insurance companies in China.[6] By December 1862, when John retired from active business life in China, he could boast that he had left Augustine Heard & Co. "firmly established, rich, and second to none in China. . . . I doubt if many would not have called it the first."[7]

Although the Gardner shipbuilding firm had established its reputation constructing sleek, sharp Baltimore clippers, by 1850 the demand for such vessels had passed. The British navy had driven slavers from the ocean, and in peacetime there were no orders for privateers. The 290-ton brig *Ernani*, completed in 1848, was among the last traditional Baltimore clippers produced by the Gardners.[8]

The first half of the 1850s was the classic era of the mammoth clipper ships, which transported huge cargoes over long distances at record-breaking speeds. These vessels, at 1,000 to well over 2,000 tons burthen, were much larger than the traditional Baltimore clipper, which rarely exceeded 200 tons.[9] Although they were fast, the primary advantage of these massive ships was their ability to carry sizable cargoes at relatively cheap rates. The glorious reign of the large clippers lasted only eight years, from about 1850 to 1858. During this brief period the Gardner firm grew rapidly and then declined. Between 1851 and 1853 the Gardners completed four medium-sized clippers: the *Union*, the *Sirocco*, the *Atalanta*, and the *Euroclydon*, all ranging between 1,000 and 1,400 tons burthen. In 1854 and 1855 they launched the two largest vessels they were ever to build, the 1,811-ton *Napier* and the 1,800-ton *Whistling Wind*, both of which were over 215 feet in length.[10] With the demand for clippers already declining, the Gardners produced only two small barks in 1856 and 1857, neither exceeding 600 tons.

These were the last vessels built by the Gardner Brothers. After a period of poor health, George Gardner died at the age of 47 on August 24, 1857, "summoned," reported the *Baltimore Sun*, "most suddenly . . . by the grim messenger . . . to his last account."[11] Three years later, on December 2, 1860, the Gardner firm came to an end with the unexpected death of 57-year-old William Gardner, "stricken down by apoplexy."[12] The Gardner firm had been in business since 1813, but even if William and George Gardner had lived, the firm would probably not have remained in business for another five years. Maryland was a border state, and few Baltimore shipbuilding firms survived the port embargoes and disruptions of business that afflicted this region during the Civil War.

In December 1860, southern states began seceding from the Union, and on April 12, 1861, the Confederate attack on Fort Sumter began the Civil War. On April 15 President Lincoln called up 75,000 members of state militias. Two days later Jefferson Davis began licensing Confederate privateers, and on April 19 Lincoln ordered a blockade of all southern ports from Virginia to Texas.

The war was a time not only for acts of selfless patriotism but also for commercial opportunity. Robert Bennet Forbes and his brother, John Murray Forbes, both associated for years with Russell & Co., quickly saw a chance for financial gain through public service. On July 9, 1861, assisted by Richard Henry Dana, Jr. (then a prominent attorney), they drafted a bill to create a volunteer mercantile navy. The proposed bill empowered the U.S. government to purchase and arm merchant vessels and commission merchant captains. These vessels would be staffed by volunteer crews lured by prize money and would reinforce the Union blockade by preying on Confederate ships.[13]

The Forbes brothers and their associates purchased several ships, including the 1,012-ton *Fearnot*, intending to resell them to the government at a good profit. While the sale of the *Fearnot* was pending, they dispatched her to Liverpool, captained by their Milton friend and neighbor, Edward Horatio Faucon. Two months after Faucon brought her back to Boston, the Navy purchased the *Fearnot* for $40,000, and a few days later Faucon was offered a commission as acting master. He signed an oath of allegiance and on August 27, 1861, sailed the USS *Fearnot* out of Boston Harbor, armed with six 32-pounders and carrying supplies for the Union fleet on the Florida gulf coast.[14]

Faucon first joined a squadron blockading the mouth of the Mississippi River. In October 1862 he was promoted to acting volunteer lieutenant and given command of the 787-ton *Montgomery*, a screw-powered steamer blockading Wilmington, North Carolina. A few months later he was assigned to special duty commanding the chartered steamer *Ericsson*, towing rafts (designed to function as mine-sweeping devices) from New York for use in the blockade of South Carolina ports.

In the fall of 1863, Faucon returned to the *Montgomery*. By now the Confederate economy was suffering badly from the embargo. Blockade runners attempted to take cargo into and out of southern ports under cover of night, and there was prize money to be won for their capture. "Prize courts" determined the value of a captured vessel and her cargo, with a one-twentieth share going to the captain of the vessel apprehending her. Just after midnight on February 16, 1864, Faucon and his crew captured the British-registered steamer *Pet* as she attempted to leave Wilmington Harbor. The 233-ton iron vessel carried 450 bales of cotton and several barrels of liquor. Faucon placed his first officer and a prize crew aboard the *Pet* and dispatched her to Boston for adjudication.[15]

Seven months later Faucon captured the far more valuable steel-built, side-wheel steamer *Bat*. At 2:45 A.M. on October 10, he sighted the British-owned vessel and fired a single 30-pound round from his rifled Parrot gun. This hit the *Bat*'s deckhouse, severing a crewman's right leg. The *Bat* surrendered immediately, and by 3 A.M. Faucon had a surgeon aboard and a prize officer in command. Faucon submitted his official report of the capture for approval by his commander, D. L. Braine, and then sent it to Navy Secretary Gideon Welles.[16] But a month later, Lieutenant Commander Braine accused Faucon of tampering with the report, deleting a list of five other U.S. Navy steamers that had been within signaling distance of the *Bat* at the time of her capture, and asserting "the capture was known to no other vessel or vessels in the squadron until after sunrise." Braine charged that Faucon had altered the document to deprive the officers and crews on the "Maratanza, Victoria, Eolus, Emma and the Vicksburg in their just share of the proceeds of the prize . . . with the motive of benefiting himself pecuniarily."[17]

Edward Faucon was honorably discharged from the navy on September 4, 1865. In prize court proceedings in Boston on May 16, 1866, the *Bat* was valued at $155,645 and credited jointly to Faucon's *Montgomery* and the five other vessels. A month later the *Pet* was valued at $60,440 and wholly credited to Faucon's *Montgomery*. Faucon's personal share of the *Bat* amounted to $7,782, and he received $3,022 for the *Pet*.

By the time of the Civil War, many of those who had been associated with the *Frolic* as young men were nearing old age, and Augustine Heard, a full generation their senior, was well into his final decline. In September 1868 Edward Faucon attended Augustine Heard's funeral. Afterwards, he sent a reflective note to John Heard expressing the contemporary sentiment that New England merchants were representatives of God on earth. "He knew the true calling of a merchant," wrote Fau-

con, "one placed here by God to acquire in order that he may diffuse.
He never made the fatal mistake of making money as an end."

Another memorialist published a seven-stanza poem in a Boston
newspaper, titled "A Funeral at Ipswich." Employing the rich imagery
of manifest destiny, the anonymous author paid homage to Heard and
other Americans for their selfless labors in opening trade with China:

> Those noble merchants without steel or banners
> Carried truth East—and now the East is ours.
> Their trade was not in talk, but their words planted
> Faith between the oldest and youngest powers.[18]

The firm Augustine Heard established outlived him by only seven
years, declaring bankruptcy on April 19, 1875. The immediate cause
was misappropriation of funds by their Boston agent, but the underly-
ing cause was the firm's inability to adapt to the fundamental changes
in the China trade. In 1858, there had been only two banks in China,
but by 1865 there were a dozen.[19] The Heards and other commission
houses that had previously manipulated the exchange market to their
own advantage soon lost this lucrative business to the banks. Widespread use of the telegraph erased the supremacy they had once held
through their personal worldwide network of correspondents. Even the
extensive warehouses and specialized personnel that enabled houses
like the Heards to operate as self-sufficient entities became unnecessary,
expensive liabilities in the changing commercial climate of the 1860s.
Furthermore, as Chinese merchants learned Western business methods,
they no longer needed American commission merchants to serve as mid-
dlemen.

The old market in commodities that had once linked India, China,
Britain, and the United States also suffered disruption in the 1860s.
American cotton now had to compete with Indian cotton on the British
market. Opium was now grown and produced in China, and tea grown
in India and Ceylon competed with the Chinese product. By the end of
the 1860s it was no longer possible for a young man to go to China
and make a quick fortune in a commission house. The capital of the
American families who had grown rich in the China trade was now being used to finance the growth of industry in the United States.

Commerce had changed in Baltimore as well. By the beginning of the 1870s little was left at Fells Point to remind a visitor that only twenty years earlier it had been a major shipbuilding center. In July 1871 Frederick Douglass returned to Fells Point, where 35 years earlier he had caulked ships for the Gardner Brothers as a slave. In those 35 years, Douglass had become widely renowned as an author, editor, and spokesman for African Americans. In 1845, only seven years after his flight to freedom, he had received international acclaim for his autobiography, *Narrative of the Life of Frederick Douglass, an American Slave*. He founded the *North Star*, an abolitionist newspaper, in 1847 and edited it (through several name changes) until 1863. In 1864 he served as an advisor to Abraham Lincoln during his reelection campaign.[20]

The 53-year-old Douglass was now owner and editor of the Washington, D.C., newspaper *New National Era*. Douglass described his sentimental trip in a bittersweet article titled "The Editor's Visit to the Old Ship-yard in Baltimore."[21] Douglass wrote about his "education" there, and how he had taken his "first degrees in oakum spinning and tar boiling." He recalled the old shipyard as the "school-house" where he had "learned to write and to count." He remembered "its timber and boards" as his "first copy-books," and the "white carpenters"— his unwitting teachers—"writing 'larboard' and 'starboard' with chalk." He mused that during the three subsequent decades, every time he had "inhaled the pungent fragrance of boiling pitch" or "looked into the seams of a ship's deck," he had been "carried back in memory and emotion" to the scenes of "his youth and manhood in the ship-yards of Baltimore."

Douglass observed that the great days of the Baltimore shipyards were over, and the grand houses once occupied by the leading Fells Point shipbuilders were now mostly in the hands of German working people. The once numerous Irish whiskey shops had been replaced by lager beer saloons, and in place of the once flourishing shipyards he found processing plants for pickling and canning oysters. In the harbor, the ships and brigs that had once linked Fells Point with Liverpool, the West Indies, and South America were gone, supplanted by small schooners called "pungies" carrying oysters and vegetables.

As in everything he wrote, Douglass had a greater purpose and objective than mere nostalgia. He observed that Baltimore had for decades ignored the "vast and wealthy country to the north of her" which had stood "ready to pour its harvests of gold" into her commerce—all but for "the enslavement of a few negroes." He speculated that had not Baltimore traded in the "bodies and souls of men," her natural advantages—far superior to Boston and Philadelphia—would have made her the second most important commercial city on the eastern seaboard (after New York), through which the great wealth of America's interior would have been conducted to the outside world.

⁂

Richard Henry Dana, Jr., was busy during the Civil War and the years immediately following. During the war, as U.S. attorney for Massachusetts, he successfully convinced the predominantly democratic U.S. Supreme Court to sustain the Southern blockade by allowing capture of neutral vessels as prizes. In 1867 and 1868 he represented the United States in the treason trial of Jefferson Davis.[22] In November 1868 Dana ran unsuccessfully for Congress. To console himself on his loss, he turned his attention to a task he enjoyed completely, revision of *Two Years Before the Mast*.

In 1840, the 25-year-old Dana had sold the rights to his book for a paltry $250. Now, in 1868, when the copyright reverted to him, Dana decided to issue a revised "author's edition." This included a retrospective chapter describing his return in 1859 to the San Diego beach where, while scraping cowhides in July 1835, he had first met Captain Edward Horatio Faucon. Dana and Faucon had maintained their friendship over the years. Since Dana specialized in admiralty law and Faucon worked as a marine salvage consultant for insurance companies, they had many occasions to meet. For the new edition of *Two Years Before the Mast*, the two men "sat up together, in Cambridge, nearly the whole of a winter's night," going through the entire manuscript page by page, correcting errors and reminiscing about their youthful days aboard the *Pilgrim* and the *Alert*.[23]

John Everett, too, had served aboard the *Pilgrim* and the *Alert*, and it might have been his reading of the 1869 edition of *Two Years Before the Mast* that inspired him to make one last trip to California. Everett had remained with the Heards in Canton until 1852. He had returned to China for a final two-year tour of duty with the firm in 1858 before retiring to live on the income from his investments.

By 1895, all the principals in the *Frolic*'s saga were dead. John Dixwell, age 71 and suffering from heart disease, was the first to pass on in 1876. In 1882 Richard Henry Dana, Jr., succumbed to pneumonia while in Rome researching a book on international law. He was 66. George Basil Dixwell, the commercial genius who introduced the Heards to large-scale trade in Malwa opium, died in 1885 at the age of 71. He left an estate valued at $240,711, and his half-Chinese son, then a student at a Massachusetts prep school, received one-third. Dixwell's obituary noted that his works on the tariff would eventually "take a high rank as textbooks," adding, "his powers of illustration, analysis and repartee were unfailing sources of entertainment and instruction to his friends."[24]

John Everett, still a bachelor, was 79 when he died in 1889. John Heard died on February 20, 1894, at the age of 69. Three months later, on May 22, Edward Faucon died in his home on Milton Hill after a short illness. He was 87. "The deceased," wrote the *Milton News*, "for many years followed the seas, and was a prominent master in the palmy days of Boston's shipping."[25]

In 1880 the *Frolic* received her first mention by a "professional" historian, although not by name. Lyman Palmer's *History of Mendocino County* included this account: "During the winter of 1851–52, a vessel laden with silk and tea from China and Japan to San Francisco, was driven ashore at the mouth of the Noyo River."[26] Palmer was wrong about the date, wrong about the cargo of tea, wrong about Japan, and wrong in his location of the wreck near the mouth of the Noyo River, five miles north of the actual wreck site near Caspar. Indeed, Palmer's account was so distorted that later scholars wondered whether there might have been two different China trade vessels wrecked on the coast, as many Mendocino County residents believed.[27] By 1948, under the spell of local folklore, the *Frolic* had been further transformed into a "Chillean silk ship" in a local history by David Ryder.[28]

However, Palmer's 1880 account was correct in linking the unnamed wreck with the beginning of logging at Big River and the consequent establishment of the city of Mendocino. Palmer wrote that a group of men associated with a lumber mill at Bodega had traveled up the coast to see what might be salvaged from the wreck. "In passing up and down the coast," he reported, "the large and available redwood forests on Big River attracted attention, and wonderful reports concerning these woods, and their resources, were carried back to Bodega." As the Bodega woods were far inland, a large and expensive labor force was required to haul the lumber to the coast for shipping. When Henry Meiggs, the San Francisco lumber merchant associated with the Bodega mill, heard that there was easily accessible timber on Big River, he quickly established a mill there. Only two years after the loss of the *Frolic*, on July 19, 1852, the brig *Ontario* delivered Henry Meiggs's steam-powered sawmill to the mouth of Big River, establishing the first permanent white settlement on the Mendocino coast.[29]

Descendants of early families on the Mendocino coast have preserved several stories relating to the *Frolic* shipwreck. Jerome B. Ford, the Meiggs associate who led the unsuccessful 1851 expedition to salvage cargo from the vessel, noted Indian women wearing silk shawls from the wreck.[30] Although he reported that nothing of value was left on the *Frolic*, Ford did pick up one of her swords from the beach. Many years later, Ford's granddaughter, Alice Earl Wilder, remembered occasionally being allowed to play with the sword as a child in Mendocino. The Kelley family, too, had memories of the wreck of the "silk ship." Daisy Kelley McCallum often told how, during the early 1850s, her mother had fashioned dresses from three bolts of silk she had obtained from the Indians.

As the last surviving Faucon, Catherine Faucon inherited her father's effects. Over the years, she gradually donated her extensive and well-documented collection of heirlooms to museums and local archives. While these historic artifacts were easy to donate, written documents were different. The Faucon family would be remembered by what they left behind, and Catherine bore the heavy responsibility of deciding what should be preserved. Household items provided only mute testimony of good taste and respectability, but the written records that documented her father's employment in the opium trade were clearly an affront to twentieth-century morality.

In 1928 Catherine Faucon contacted the Massachusetts Historical Society, offering to donate a small packet of documents once belonging to her paternal grandfather, Nicolas Faucon. "As the last of my family," she wrote, "I feel it incumbent on me to find a home for—or else burn—papers which my father cared for."[31] During the next few years Catherine Faucon apparently destroyed almost all of the documents that had belonged to her father. She saved and later presented to the Massachusetts Historical Society her father's 1829–37 ships' logs from his days in the hide and tallow trade on the California coast. She also saved the log that recorded his movements during the first year of the Civil War. The only document saved concerning his employment in China was a small penciled portrait sketched there sometime during the late 1840s (see Figure 16).

Catherine Waters Faucon died on November 16, 1942. In memory of her father, she bequeathed $5,000 to Harvard College to be known as the Edward Horatio Faucon Fund. Perhaps thinking of her grandfather, Nicolas Michel Faucon, instructor of French at Harvard from 1806 to 1817, she asked that the money be invested and the income applied toward the salaries of instructors.[32] Catherine died secure in the knowledge that she had cleansed the record and that her father's reputation would stand unblemished. She could hardly have imagined that only 23 years after her death, sport divers would discover the wreck of her father's Baltimore-built opium clipper on the Mendocino coast of California.

Epilogue

Who Owns the Past?

It was on June 30, 1965, when I actually discovered it, but I didn't know it at the time. I was scuba diving and spear fishing with three other fellows when I got this strange, eerie feeling. I was about fifteen feet off the bottom, swimming slow and easy, looking for a big lingcod, and all of a sudden I had this funny feeling that something wasn't right. I did a 360-degree turn and surfaced to look around and everything seemed OK, but my buddy divers had disappeared and I couldn't see their bubbles anywhere. So I dived back down, but I still had this uncomfortable feeling that "something is wrong here." And as I swam along I began to notice there were objects on the bottom that didn't appear to be rocks. Some of them were round or cylindrical in shape, and others were square or rectangular. Then I began to realize what the problem was—the bottom looked man-made.

At first I didn't think much about it, but when I went home I got to wondering. "Well," I thought, "it could have been a barge that dropped a bunch of garbage on the bottom of the ocean, or it could have been a house that slipped off the cliff, or maybe it was a wrecked ship?"

During the next several days I kept going over it in my mind, and the more I thought about it the more I thought it might be a ship. I got out all my back issues of *Skin Diver* magazine and looked at pictures of shipwrecks underwater. I remember it was 3:30 A.M. when I finally knew it was a ship and I told my wife, "We're going back up to Fort Bragg." She thought I was crazy. Next morning I phoned Bill Kosonen, my diving buddy. "I'm pretty sure I've found an old ship," I said. "Let's go back over there, and if there's anything in it we'll go partners—fifty-fifty."

So the next weekend Bill and I swam

out from shore and got out to the location from dead reckoning, by lining ourselves up with objects I'd noted on shore. Then we dove down and hit right on top of the wreck site. We looked around for a little bit and saw lots of pieces of pottery and brass lying around on the bottom. There was a chain and an anchor. Nearby we noticed what looked like a pile of rocks with a hole about five feet wide going underneath, and when we stuck our heads and shoulders inside and looked up we could see the bottoms of dishes stuck to the roof.

Then we spotted this pile of bricks, maybe fifteen feet long, five feet wide, and three feet off the bottom. They were covered with some kind of growth and looked like they'd been there for many years. I pried one loose with my knife, chipped the encrustation off one of the corners—and it gleamed like silver.

I looked at Bill, and he looked at me, and boy, our eyes got big. We were giving the OK sign. "We've got it!" We thought, "Oh, boy, with all this stuff we've got a million dollars!" So up to our tubes we went, toting that brick, and we went for shore as fast as we could swim. Oh, were we excited! We jumped up and down on the beach hollering for our wives to come down from the bluff. "Look what we found!" we shouted. "And there's lots more of it out there!"

We were sure it was silver, so the next day we drove down to Sacramento to have it tested. When we laid the brick on the counter, the technician said, "I'll have to know exactly where you found it."

Well, I may look like a hick, but I don't think like a hick. I told him it came from the Pacific Ocean, and that was as close as he was going to get.

The assay came out 79 percent white cast iron. We'd found the ballast of the ship—and there went my million dollars!

—Jim Kennon, diver

Catherine Faucon had wanted her father remembered for his public life, as the dashing young captain portrayed by Richard Henry Dana, Jr., in *Two Years Before the Mast* and as a volunteer shipmaster in the Union navy during the Civil War. To accomplish this, she had destroyed her father's records of his career in China. She would have been horrified to learn that 23 years after her death Jim Kennon, a weekend scuba diver hoping to spear a lingcod, had discovered the wreck of the *Frolic*, her father's Baltimore-built opium clipper.

As a researcher, I was angry at Catherine Faucon for purging the historical record. Yet I couldn't really condemn her, for there is nothing unusual about her effort to present her family to history in the most favorable light. Indeed, all the historical record we possess might be said to be limited to what has been left us by armies of Catherine Faucons. Historians understand that most of the raw data from which they fashion the story of the past is a highly selective record, written mainly by a few upper-class white men, largely about themselves. The great majority of ordinary working people and their families have left us few written records of their own, and so are virtually invisible in the historical chronicle. Most people's lives are perceptible only in the peripheral vision of the elite; nonetheless, the professional historian attempts to draw a balanced view of the entire history from this incomplete and distorted data base.

Archaeology is different. Archaeologists do not focus on the written record that the elite have chosen to leave about themselves. Instead, they examine the unedited record that comprises what everyone has left behind—the material remains of how people actually lived and what they actually did. While the elite have produced most of the written record, ordinary people by their sheer numbers dominate the archaeological body of evidence. Both testimonies complement each other, and each contributes to a more balanced view of our past.

The written words of the historical record are explicit, and though they may distort the facts of the past, they nevertheless have the ring of truth. Archaeological data, on the other hand, are mute. Further, they are incomplete in their own way, "edited" by the vagaries of decomposition and preservation. Iron rusts; paper, cloth, and wood rot away; and bone dissolves in acid soil. As a consequence, the residuum of human occupation is often reduced to objects made of ceramics, glass, stone, and nonferrous metals. Like the historian, the archaeologist is issued a damaged deck of cards, but more of the cards are missing.

Archaeology has another special role to play in revealing and illuminating the past. Archaeology reveals solid objects that need to be explained—or explained away. Since explanation of a recovered object requires reconstructing the context of its use, the process requires a reexamination and often a rewrite of history. The *Frolic* shipwreck project illustrates this process. My attempt to explain the sherds of Chinese porcelain and green bottle glass that my students and I found at Three Chop Village during the summer of 1984 led me to trace a series of connections, eventually linking Boston merchants, Baltimore ship-builders, Bombay opium brokers, nouveaux riches entrepreneurs in Gold Rush California, and finally the Mitom Pomo of northern Mendocino County. Those interconnecting links, traced from a few pieces of porcelain and bottle glass, told a unique story of world commerce during the first half of the nineteenth century—a story of Americans engaged in the opium trade.

Telling that story enmeshed me in a web of competing interests. While it might seem that the archaeological record, buried beneath the ground or lying beneath the water, would be our national patrimony—the shared property of all—in reality it is not. The question "Who owns the past?" provokes a rancorous debate among property owners, government officials, museum directors, private collectors, wreck divers, Indians, historians, and archaeologists. This debate concerns not only the ownership of artifacts and the right to excavate them but the more subtle issue of who should tell their story.

For example, the Three Chop Village archaeological site is on public land in Jackson State Forest, and we were required to obtain permission from both state and county agencies to excavate there. The five-member Mendocino County Archaeological Commission, which has to approve all such "digs," was designed to represent the diverse views and interests of the county's population. It included a county government official, an archaeologist, a timber company executive, an Indian, and a community representative. I had to assure the commission that my interest in Three Chop Village was scholarly rather than commercial. Developers and property owners are often required to hire archaeologists to perform subsurface testing to certify that there is nothing of archaeological interest that a proposed development might destroy, and in such situations an Indian observer may be required to be present, to assure that no prehistoric graves are violated.

Ownership of the *Frolic* shipwreck site was another matter. Although the *Frolic* lies about 75 feet offshore and thus fell under the jurisdiction of the California State Lands Commission, the artifacts themselves were virtually all in the hands of the wreck divers who had found them. These were viewed as private property by the divers but as stolen antiquities by the state. This difference in viewpoints presented a problem for me. When I first began to contact the divers, they saw me as a representative of the state, inasmuch as I was a professor at San Jose

State University. They were afraid they would be prosecuted and their collections confiscated if their identities were revealed. Consequently, they were secretive about their collections and hesitant to mention the names of other divers. Their fear of prosecution was based on reality. Two of the divers, along with other members of their dive club, had recently been arrested for taking artifacts from another wreck.

As I contacted additional divers, I found that the issues of ownership were even more complicated than they first appeared. When the *Frolic* wreck site had been still relatively untouched, two divers—Louie Fratis and Jim Kennon—had independently informed state and federal agencies about it, but in both cases the agencies ignored them. It seemed that the government had no interest in the property it considered its own.

During the mid-1960s, while Fratis and Kennon were attempting to interest state and federal agencies in their discovery, the *Frolic* wreck site was essentially untouched. But during the fifteen years that followed, the site was badly damaged. In 1975 Dr. Robert Nash, a geographer associated with UCLA, heard about a wreck on the Mendocino coast with Chinese pottery. Nash was researching Chinese fishing junks that operated along the California coast during the late nineteenth century, and he asked two Southern California wreck divers to identify the vessel type. As Larry Pierson, one of the divers, tells the story:

Dr. Nash wanted it to be a Chinese junk, and I clearly remember his disappointment when we found the Rogers patent anchors and knew right away that it wasn't. Well, when we got back to Los Angeles, I typed up my notes and sent them to him, and we never again heard from him. I guess since it wasn't a junk he was no longer interested. So two years passed. Meanwhile Pat and I were getting bored diving the local wrecks around Los Angeles, so we decided it might be fun to dive the wreck up at Caspar.

One feature of the wreck was a large pile of cast-iron ballast bars, and we knew we would have a lot of trouble moving them by hand because they had corroded, swollen up, and solidified into a solid mass. Not only were they almost impossible to separate from one another, but they were quite heavy. Therefore, we brought explosives supplied by a friend. We set the explosives at strategic points and caused a small but sudden shock. We killed two or three fish, but we succeeded in jarring the ballast pile just enough to separate the bars from one another. The object was not to blow up the vessel but simply to nudge it just a little.

When we finally got to the bottom of the ballast pile there was a layer of sediment lying on the bedrock. That loose sediment contained beads and all kinds of small items. We bagged all that sediment, took it up to the boat, spread it out on the deck and went through it, picking out the obvious artifacts and throwing the rest overboard.

At the end of five days we had a substantial quantity of artifacts, including pistols, muskets, swords, coins, gold filigree jewelry, and beads. We brought it all back to Los Angeles and laid it out on Vic's driveway, arranging it into piles for division. We knew that each of us had a particular thing that we were rather fond of, so we made sure that person got that pile. It was a very amicable distribution.

—Larry Pierson, diver

I can appreciate the frustration the divers felt as they tried to involve the appropriate state and federal agencies in the study of the *Frolic*. I felt the same frustration two decades later when I was trying to convince the divers to return their collections to public ownership. Before I asked them, I needed to find a public agency willing to accept the artifacts.

When the higher administration of San Jose State University learned that I was about to receive "stolen property," I was forbidden to accept any *Frolic* artifacts in the name of the university. My argument that the artifacts were state property and that it was therefore proper for them to be returned to a state agency—the California State University—carried no weight. The California Department of Parks and Recreation, the agency responsible for receiving artifacts found on state lands, was facing budget cutbacks and preferred not to receive the collection. And the National Maritime Museum in San Francisco never responded to my proposal.

The reluctance of state and federal agencies to receive archaeological artifacts is not so much a function of bureaucratic indolence or ill will, but rather reflects a management problem. While the mandates of state agencies are statewide and the mandates of federal agencies are national, the archaeological resources themselves are local. Although state and federal agencies are well equipped to establish policy guidelines and maintain databases, they do not have the funding or staff to deal effectively with individual, local archaeological sites and artifacts.

Despite the lack of interest in the *Frolic* project from government agencies, there was an intense grassroots interest in Mendocino County.

Local newspapers wanted the story, local museums wanted to exhibit the artifacts, and the residents of houses overlooking the cove—once they knew the story—were eager to report any future pillaging of the *Frolic* site to the proper authorities. In 1989, I asked the Mendocino County Museum in Willits to establish a *Frolic* repository for artifacts returned by the wreck divers. My original motivation had been academic: I needed access to the *Frolic* artifacts in order to write a monograph describing her cargo of China trade goods. Still, there was a problem. Most of the divers wanted their treasures to be displayed and enjoyed by the public, and not left to languish in dead storage in a museum basement.

The divers cared about the things they had brought up from wrecks. As I visited them, from Chico to San Diego, I saw painstakingly restored *Frolic* portholes, brass gleaming, mounted on living room walls. I saw *Frolic* ceramics displayed on red velvet in glass cases, and gold filigree jewelry, Mexican dollars, and scores of other artifacts carefully wrapped and stored in dresser drawers. Each treasure was lovingly revealed to me by its collector with a story of how he had found it and how he planned to restore it. These were more than artifacts, they were the mnemonic tokens of the experiences that give lives meaning.

Asking the divers to donate these icons was not something I could do lightly. All transactions involve reciprocity, and these transactions required a special kind of compensation. Analyzing the artifacts in my monograph would not be enough. I had begun recording the stories of the wreck divers' forays on the *Frolic* in order to document the collections and record eyewitness accounts of the specific contexts from which the artifacts had been recovered. I eventually interviewed eight men—most of whom did not know one another—each of whom had dived and collected the *Frolic*. And as I conducted the interviews, I soon discovered that the stories of diving the *Frolic* were inseparable from the life stories of the divers.[1]

In these one- to five-hour interviews, not only did I obtain a detailed account of the plundering of the *Frolic*, but I heard the story of 40 years of wreck diving on the California coast—the development of technology, of information networks, and of research skills. These divers had touched history in the artifacts they had uncovered and collected, and they were part of the answer to the question, "Who owns the past?" Collecting these oral histories changed my relationship to the divers. I listened to their stories and faithfully edited them into narratives with all the verve, humor, and anger with which they were told. And in taking the divers seriously, as collaborators in the telling of the *Frolic*'s story, I discovered I had established a basis for reciprocity. As I began to write this book, I included the divers in my research loop. I shared with them my own joy of discovery, sending them drafts of chapters for comment and asking them to review drafts of the illustrations. As time passed, the divers came to feel a proprietary interest in my success, as it would be their success too.

It was in this improved environment that I began asking the divers to donate their collections to the *Frolic* Repository. Now that their stories were written down and a scientific monograph underway, the artifacts themselves had become more than sentimental talismans for the divers. They were now the evidence of their participation in a joint research effort. Twenty years earlier, Jim Kennon had loaned 150 pounds of *Frolic* artifacts to the Smithsonian for study, but the Smithsonian had lost them. He and the other divers wanted assurance that the artifacts they were donating now would be exhibited. That assurance came when Dan Taylor, director of the Mendocino County Museum, wrote a successful grant proposal, "The Journey of the *Frolic*," for the California Council for the Humanities. The grant would support linked exhibits at the three major museums in Mendocino County, each exhibit to focus on a different aspect of the *Frolic* story. Once we began to plan the exhibits, donation of artifacts swiftly followed.

Although we archaeologists are trained to recover things and to record the contexts in which they are found, our ultimate goal is to link those things to the behaviors of past people. But there is risk involved in bridging the chasm between mute artifacts and the actions and conduct of the people who used them. Many archaeologists play it safe, focusing more on the actual artifacts than on the broader cultural context in which those artifacts once functioned. I had taken that approach in *Western Pomo Prehistory*, where I had described our excavations at Three Chop Village, cataloging the flaked green bottle glass and blue-on-white porcelain sherds in all the deadly detail required of a scientific monograph. That monograph was destined for university libraries and the bookshelves of my professional colleagues, but it would never appear in a community bookstore. My initial pride in seeing the monograph published had been dampened by my realization that the infor-

mation in it was virtually inaccessible to the very people to whom it
might have been the most relevant—the people of Mendocino County.

As I gave talks about the *Frolic* to students and community groups,
I realized that they were far more interested in the story of the research
process and of the people whose lives had been touched by the *Frolic*
than they were by the bent and corroded artifacts I brought along to
illustrate my talks. I wanted to be sure that the story of these multiple
connections was included in the museum project. The local museums
in Mendocino County were eager to cooperate—after all, the *Frolic*
shipwreck was one of the earliest recorded events in the county. The
terms of the grant required that we form an advisory committee, and
the twenty people who eventually came together included historians,
educators, museum professionals, representatives of industry, a wreck
diver, a Mendocino Chinese American, and a Pomo Indian. Each of
them was provided with an early draft of this manuscript, and in the
summer of 1993 we met at the county library in Willits.

Coming to grips with the complex saga of the *Frolic* and the stories
of those connected with her proved a formidable task. Each advisor
seemed to focus on a particular part of the story, while ignoring the
connections among them. Only small portions of the *Frolic* story had
actually occurred in Mendocino County—the wreck of the vessel in
1850, the pillaging of the wreck between 1965 and 1982, and my excavations at Three Chop Village in 1984. There seemed no elegant way
to integrate Baltimore shipbuilding, Bombay-to-Canton opium commerce, the worldwide balance of trade in the early nineteenth century,
Pomo Indian lifeways, California wreck diving, and a profusion of
other complex topics.

By early afternoon, the discussion at our meeting had bogged down,
when Jim Delgado idly picked up a *Frolic* potsherd from the selection
of artifacts I had brought. Turning to face us, he assumed the character of Captain Faucon. Holding up the broken piece of porcelain, he
cursed the quality of the pottery while assuring us that his cargo would
have fetched a profit in San Francisco had the *Frolic* completed her voyage. Then, before our eyes, Jim sharply changed character and reflected
on the potsherd from the viewpoint of a Chinese merchant. Suddenly,
while Jim was still speaking, we realized that we could tell the whole
Frolic story in multiple voices pulled from original letters and docu-

ments, from the oral histories of wreck divers, and from my own words describing the excavations at Three Chop Village.

One of the community advisors sitting at the table that day was Kate Magruder, artistic director of the Ukiah Players Theatre. Jim's impromptu performance brought Kate to the edge of her seat, and two months later she submitted another proposal to the California Council for the Humanities, to research and stage a historical dramatization: *Voices from the 'Frolic' and Beyond*.

Each of the three museums now chose a portion of the *Frolic* story to tell. The Kelley House Museum in Mendocino began planning *Shipwreck! Impact of the Frolic*, to examine the effect of the wreck on the development of coastal communities. The Grace Hudson Museum, in *Wake of Change*, profiled the lasting consequences of the *Frolic* wreck for Indians and Asian Americans. The Mendocino County Museum would focus on the broader story of the vessel's commercial life in *From Canton to California*. Each museum independently employed the unique skills of the people in its local community to build models, assemble exhibits, and write scripts.

We had decided to credit each artifact in the museum exhibits to the wreck diver who had donated it, but the Mendocino County Museum went even further. It displayed photographic portraits of all participating divers, along with an exhibit of the diving outfit Jim Kennon had worn 30 years earlier when he first discovered the wreck. Passages from the wreck divers' oral histories were included in exhibit texts.

In January 1994, with the exhibit designs well under way, representatives of the three museums met to discuss which artifacts needed to be borrowed from other museums in order to establish the broader context of the *Frolic*'s story. Richard Everett, one of the curators involved, had joined the project through a strange coincidence. In my search for information documenting the lives of persons associated with the *Frolic* I had learned a great deal about the life of Captain Faucon. I had not been so successful tracing the life of his friend, John Hurd Everett, the young Boston merchant who had accompanied Faucon on most of his hide and tallow gathering trips to California. Everett had later followed Faucon to China, and as an employee of Augustine Heard & Co., had assembled the *Frolic*'s final cargo.

I knew that John Everett's brother, Oliver, had been a Harvard grad-

Figure 33. James Delgado (left) and Richard Everett (right) examine *Frolic* artifacts at an exhibit planning session in October 1993. Photo by Mark Rawitsch.

uate of the class of 1832, and a call to the Harvard Alumni Association led me through a 150-year chain of Everett descendants to Richard—John Everett's great-great-great nephew—who was, serendipitously, working as a designer constructing exhibits at the National Maritime Museum in San Francisco. Richard had never heard of John Everett before I contacted him, and he was thrilled to learn that he had a personal family connection to California's maritime history. His participation on the *Frolic* project advisory committee meant that at last we had the attention of the Maritime Museum. He was able to borrow family heirlooms from his New England relatives for our display, including the monogrammed laptop writing desk that John Everett had used during his years in China and a color portrait of him made on a thin slab of ivory by a Chinese artist. And Richard's casual visit to a local brewery eventually resulted in their agreement to produce a commemorative ale.[2]

Meanwhile, Kate Magruder was working with staff and students of Mendocino College and College of the Redwoods to develop characters and a script for the dramatization of the story *Voices from the 'Frolic' and Beyond*. The main characters—Captain Edward Horatio Faucon, a Pomo Indian, a Mendocino Chinese American, a wreck diver, and archaeologist Tom Layton—would address each other across space and time, each presenting a different perspective on the *Frolic*, each staking a personal claim to her history. Working with Kate on the script was Vicki Patterson, the multicultural specialist for the county schools, who also adapted parts of the *Frolic* story for elementary and secondary school curricula.

In order to be sure our publicity reached the whole county, we arranged for a series of seven feature articles to be published in four area newspapers. The articles—reissued as a booklet[3]—covered every aspect of our story, from the dig at Three Chop Village to the *Frolic*'s place in Gold Rush maritime history, the wreck divers' stories, the multicultural nature of the project and the contributions of community advisors, and the *Voices from the 'Frolic'* dramatization.

Voices from the 'Frolic' and Beyond was set to open on July 23,

Figure 34. Each year on July 25, the Mendocino Brewing Company issues 700 cases of Frolic Shipwreck Ale to commemorate the 6,108 bottles of Edinburgh ale lost in the *Frolic* shipwreck of July 25, 1850. Label design by S. F. Manning and Thomas Layton.

Figure 35. Wreck divers (from left to right) Larry Pierson, Vic LaFountaine, and Patrick Gibson join Thomas Layton (far right) in displaying the *Frolic* pennant at the *Frolic* exhibit opening in July 1994 at the Grace Hudson Museum in Ukiah, California. Photo courtesy Larry Pierson.

1994, simultaneously with the exhibit at the Grace Hudson Museum. As I entered the museum that opening night, I saw the *Frolic* pennant— an eight-foot splash of red, white, and blue emblazoned with the black and gold emblem of Maryland—hanging in the entrance, flanked by the Augustine Heard Company's red and white diamond flag and the Bear Flag of the state of California. In the gallery next to the main exhibit hall, the reception was in full swing. The staff of the Mendocino Brewing Company poured rich, amber samples of Frolic Shipwreck Ale. Three wreck divers, clutching exhibit posters and empty ale bottles, hailed me as I came in. One handed me an 1823 Dutch East India Company copper cent, his last treasure from the *Frolic*, and together we crossed the street to the County Auditorium for the premiere performance of *Voices from the 'Frolic.'* Not only was every seat filled, but people stood along the walls and even crept into the aisles. Vicki Patterson explained the Chautauqua format. Following the performance, the players would return to the stage—still "in character"—to take questions from the audience.

The performance began with the archaeologist addressing the audience from Three Chop Village as the excavation progressed, a student by his side working a sifting screen. It was unnerving to see an actor portraying a character who was supposed to be me, even using the words of my monograph, *Western Pomo Prehistory*, to describe "his" research design. He described the heat and the mosquitoes and—as he bent down to pick up a large potsherd—his concern that the site seemed contaminated with historic bottle glass and porcelain. Just as Jim Delgado's impromptu performance with a potsherd had inspired our stalled committee meeting one year earlier, that same potsherd was now the hub of the *Voices* dramatization. As each character held the piece of porcelain, it became the catalyst for him or her to expose a different perspective on the *Frolic*'s story.

Captain Faucon described the course of his business career, from

Figure 36. Michael Oakes as Captain Edward Horatio Faucon in *Voices from the 'Frolic.'* Photo by Larry Melious, Willits, California.

hauling hides and tallow on the California coast to transporting opium from Bombay to Canton and participating in the China trade. Holding the potsherd high, he declared it "cheap utility ware—but it would have turned a profit had it reached San Francisco." Yip Lee, a Mendocino Chinese woman, saw it differently. Gently cradling the shard, she told us, "This bowl is made of China. The earth of China. Here is China in my hand." Then she spoke of the lives of Chinese in "Gold Mountain"—the place we call California. The wreck diver added the collector's viewpoint, describing how he had found pieces of pottery on the ocean floor: "It was almost like following a trail of bread crumbs someone had left to bring you into the site."

But for me, the most powerful parts of the performance were the dialogues between the Indian and the archaeologist. Linda Noel, a gifted poet and a full-blooded Konkow Maidu, had agreed to write and act the part of the Pomo Indian. Early in the performance, just as the archaeologist had finished describing his research design and the questions he intended to answer, Linda took the potsherd from his hand and addressed the audience:

> I have my own questions.
> Do you realize what you hold in your hand?
> Can you feel the thousands of years you hold in the chips you find,
> the echoing shadow of the hands that shaped them,
> that worked those pieces, that placed those points?
> Can you feel their power?
> The archaeologist need not dig us up to observe and preserve us,
>   catalog us, categorize us, and mythologize us.
> We have our own names and our own myths.
> Do you know my name?
>
> What you call artifacts are in fact the parts of my life shape,
> the broken willow worn by water,
> part of the weave of who I am.
> You call my history 'artifact' and name my species
> but you live to see only dead Indians.
> You are lost in history.
> You hold my bone/flesh in your hands.
> Even in death you take from us
> but we are not all dead.

My research might have been well intended—to advance knowledge of our human past—but there was truth in Linda Noel's words. She was

Figure 37. Linda Noel, who wrote and acted the part of the Pomo elder in *Voices from the 'Frolic.'* Photo by Larry Melious, Willits, California.

describing the very real status of archaeology in the eyes of many California Indians.

Later in the performance, the archaeologist criticized the wreck diver for having built his collection of *Frolic* artifacts "in either utter ignorance or total disregard of laws protecting antiquities in the coastal waters of California." Linda returned to the stage to express the Indian point of view. "Collections?" she said, addressing the archaeologist. "You've violated more than any Antiquities Act. Consider the violation of my bloodline, my history. The Antiquities Act cannot compare with the acts of unearthing sacred objects that are the seeds of my breathing today—right here, right now."

And as Linda stood there, trembling, the archaeologist—my character—gave the perfunctory answer of a bureaucrat. "That's very interesting," he said. "I'd like to have one of my grad students record your views on tape at some point."

I had known that the *Voices* project would need to employ literary devices to dramatize the message. But it was hard for me not to take personally the archaeologist character's insensitivity—perhaps because I felt vulnerable on a number of different levels. Early drafts of this book barely mentioned the Pomo Indians whose village I had excavated. I had provided rich biographical background for the other characters in the story, but the Indians had been introduced only through their artifacts at Three Chop Village and hardly mentioned after that. Yet how could I personalize the story of Pomo people whose richly textured lives at the time of the *Frolic* shipwreck were being lived outside of recorded history? Linda Noel's resonating indictment of archaeology in the *Voices* dramatization was largely correct. "You call my history 'artifact' and name my species." But what is the archaeologist to do? We are trained to infer generalized prehistoric cultural systems from artifacts and their contexts. True, I had minimized the role of the very people whose village on Three Chop Ridge had inspired the whole research saga. Yet it seemed a breach of etiquette—if not an act of outright arrogance—for me to imagine that I could describe the Indians' encounter with the *Frolic* from their point of view.

To describe the thoughts and feelings of Mitom Pomo people in 1850 seemed more in the realm of literature than social science. Perhaps the solution would be to fashion an ethnographically based account of the *Frolic* wreck's discovery by the Pomo from the point of view of a Pomo person at the scene. I asked Vicki Patterson for help, and after searching through the ethnographies, she found the name "Keetana," a compound of the Northern Pomo words for "top notch" and "hand." As Vicki explained it, Pomo people liked to pun between Pomo and English, and "top notch," referring to a quail's top feather, combined with the word for "hand," would result in an English slang term for a Pomo headman—a top-notch hand. Keetana's story, as I told it, became the prologue for this book, and his figure—wearing the otter-skin cape of a headman—would be drawn into Sam Manning's illustration of the Indians discovering the wreck site. Using Keetana's voice, I was able to introduce meaningful ethnographic information about the Mitom Pomo into the story of the *Frolic*.

So the loop was closed and the book written. Standing on Three Chop Ridge in 1984 holding a few pieces of porcelain and green bottle glass, I had no idea that eleven years later I would still be researching their meaning. Nor could I have realized into what unfamiliar realms that research would draw me. I began the project as an artifact-based materialist, but by slow increments I learned to do more. And I have come to believe that we archaeologists must deal far more creatively with our data if we are to return it to the public—to whom history belongs—in a meaningful form.

This book was inspired by artifacts, and it bears the imprint of my materialist training—nuts and bolts descriptions of how to build a boat, grow opium, assemble a cargo, and run a business—but in the end, it is a story of connections. It is those personal connections, and not the dry descriptions of artifacts, that have brought this story to life and made it accessible. Perhaps that is only a small epiphany, but I will carry it with me for the remainder of my career.

Appendixes

Inventory of George Gardner's Shipyard

The Baltimore City Registry of Wills contains this inventory of George Gardner's shipyard, dated March 17, 1834, "a true and perfect Inventory of all and singular the goods chattels, and personal estate of George Gardner late of Baltimore County deceased appraised by the subscribers William Davy and John A. Robb."

105 Cedar posts	@50¢	52.50
72 Locust ditto	@25	18.
8 White oak	@3.	24.
28 Small floors	@2.	56.
15 Large ditto	@6.	90.
35 White oak knees	@1.50	35.
2178 Feet yellow pine plank	@2½¢	54.35
51 Spruce spars 357 inches	@.10	35.70
9 White pine masts	@8.	72.
8 fld masts pine logs &c	@3.	24.
Old moulds		8.
914 feet oak timber	@1.75	16.
Launching ways & hauling up ways		125.
Ribbands, shours, standards, prows, stage plank & blocks		73.
2 Large Locus timbers		7.
219 lbs copper bolts	@.25	54.75
Scrap copper		19.40
350 lbs Scrap iron	@1½¢	4.25
500 lbs iron bolts	@4¢	20.

½ Bbl tar $1.25 - 1 Bbl rosin	3.	4.25
844 feet 5 inch live oak timber	@1.	844.
Oakum $1. - Birch brooms	37½¢	1.37½
4 Plugging bitts $4. 1 pitch ladle @2.		6.
1 Stove & pipe $5. 1 hauling chair 3.50		8.50
7 Punches 3.50 - 2 pr timber hooks 3.		6.50
31 Augers & shanks 7.75 - 2 Chains 69 lb	@12½¢ - 8.62½	16.37½
39 Timber clamps 204 lb	@4¢	8.16
11 Reaming irons		1.50
6 Cant hooks	@75¢	4.50
2 Crabs $5. - 5 Cross cut saws $8.		13.
1 Ladder 4. - 2 Tackle falls & blocks 10.		14.
1 Grind stone $1. - 1 gin fall & blocks 13.		14.
10 Old blocks 1.50 - 3 Gins $24.		25.50
10 Saw benches $12. 1 pair wheels 10.		22.
1 Copper pitch boiler $40. 1 steam stove 20.		60.
2 Pitch pots & stands 6. 2 old pots $2.		8.
4 Jack screws $40. - 5 slice irons 1.50		41.50
3 Crow bars 2.50 126 ribband screws	@37½¢	49.12½
1 Pair chain clamps 2.50 - 4 Screw clamps $20		22.50
4 Creening clamps 68 lbs	@4¢	2.72
4 Horsing irons $2. 2 windlass cranks $1.		3.
2 Grind stone cranks $1. 74 rings & plates @ 2¢		2.48
1 Old anvil 50¢ 1 mould loft $75.		75.50
1 Stabl $2. - 1 Tool shop $6.		8.
2 Card tables 8. - 1 side board 15.		23.
12 Windsor chairs 3. 2 pictures 1.		4.
1 Ingrain carpet 6. - 2 plated candlesticks 50¢		6.50
1 Cherry table 2. - 15 common chairs @ 25¢		5.75
1 Mahogany table 4. 1 small looking glass 1.		5.
1 Pr Andirons & fender 3. - 1 high post bedstead 5.		8.
1 Low post bedstead 3. - 1 small mahogany buraw 4.		7.
1 Walnut writing desk 3. - 1 Bed & bedding 15.		18.
5 Pictures @ 25¢ - 1 writing desk & table in office $5.		6.25
1 Long chest in Office		3.
1 Blackman named Robert Frisby slave for life aged 25 to 30 years old		200.

	$2337.93
Ballance remaining in Marine Bank	20.00
Mechanic "	.87
	$2358.80

Laying Out and Building the 'Frolic'

Once John Dixwell had approved the half-model of the *Frolic*, known as the lift model, the actual building could begin.* Before shaping, each lift of the model was carefully divided into equal increments in both directions from the midpoint, toward both stem and stern. The *Frolic*'s hull, at 97 feet, may have been divided into sixteen such increments, or stations, each equivalent to a six-foot interval, thus accounting for 96 feet of her length. The remaining foot would have been divided between stem and stern.

As a first step, the boards (lifts) of the model were separated. Then the widths of the hull at each station were carefully measured, a process known as "taking offsets." Since the lift model had been fashioned at a 1-to-48 scale ($^1/_4$ inch equal to one foot), these measurements, or offsets, could later be converted to full size using a special ruler on which each quarter inch of the drawing was multiplied by 48.

The next step was to lay down, in full size, the lines of the hull taken from the lift model. Stations were marked as parallel vertical lines, six feet apart, on the light-painted floor of the mould loft. The *Frolic*'s water lines (horizontal slices) were then drawn at increments representing the upper edge of each lift, and into this grid were drawn the profile (elevation view), the slope and shape of the stem and stern posts, and the ends of the keel, comprising the vessel's backbone.

In this abbreviated full-size drawing, a "body plan" was then drawn between the ends of the vessel. This was composed of cross-sectional curves taken at

* This description of traditional Baltimore shipbuilding has benefited from extended discussions with marine architect John G. Earle of Easton, Maryland. Mr. Earle, however, should not be held responsible for the way I have structured the information provided by him.

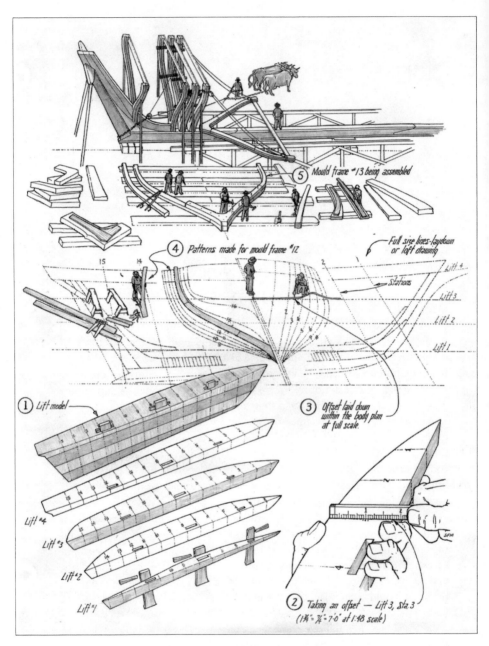

Figure 38. Building the *Frolic*: the lift model; separating the lifts; taking off-sets; laying down the plan; shaping frame moulds; and assembling frames. Original illustration by S. F. Manning.

each station of the hull by transverse measurement of the lifts. These curves represented the outboard edges of ribs, or mould frames, set to each station. Together, the backbone profile and the body plan determined the sizes and shapes of the timbers that became the ship's frame, around which planking would be bent for a watertight skin.[1]

When Mr. Gardner felt the lines had reached an optimal configuration, ship-wrights could make the moulds, thin wooden templates serving as full-size patterns for the frames (or ribs) of the vessel. Moulds were prepared for frames representing each station, and occasionally for "intermediate frames" between stations. The few Baltimore clippers for which measurements are known had frames spaced about eighteen inches on center.[2] If, as seems likely, this was true for the *Frolic*, there would have been three intermediate frames between each pair of station frames, for a total of 57 frames (see Figure 14).

Insurance inspections performed at Whampoa, China, in 1847 and 1849 reveal that the *Frolic* was constructed, in typical Baltimore fashion, from white oak, pine, and locust.[3] Frames, keel, and knees were fashioned from white oak, hull and deck planking from yellow pine. Locust was used for the treenails (pronounced "trunnels"), long dowel-like pegs for fastening hull planking to frames.

While the loftsman made the *Frolic*'s frame moulds, heavy timbers were selected for her keel. By 1844, eastern forests were too depleted for a 75-to-80-foot keel to be taken in one piece from a single white oak trunk. The *Frolic*'s keel, roughly a foot wide and two feet deep, was probably formed from three or more timbers, each overlapping in long beveled joints called scarfs. Another oak timber, the false keel, was lightly fastened to its bottom side to provide a measure of protection if the vessel should run aground or scrape over a reef. The keel was laid on wooden support blocks evenly spaced along its length and inclining up from the water's edge, so that gravity could assist when it was time to launch the vessel.

As the *Frolic*'s frame moulds were completed, they were taken one at a time from the loft to the yard where her massive ribs were pieced together from curved sections ("futtocks") of white oak. The specialized woodsmen who supplied shipbuilders scoured eastern forests for oaks with natural curves where limbs or roots angled to meet trunks or where main trunks forked apart. Because sap was believed to induce rot, these short, awkwardly bent sections of timber were harvested in winter, when "the sap was down," and stockpiled by shipbuilders in anticipation of each new vessel. The builders made the frames in two laminations, joining curved sections end to end and then fastening a second thickness spanning every joint.

The *Frolic*'s frames amidships were large and unwieldy, each over 10 feet tall and spanning almost 24 feet. As each frame was finished a temporary beam was nailed across its open end to prevent it from spreading, and a gang of car-

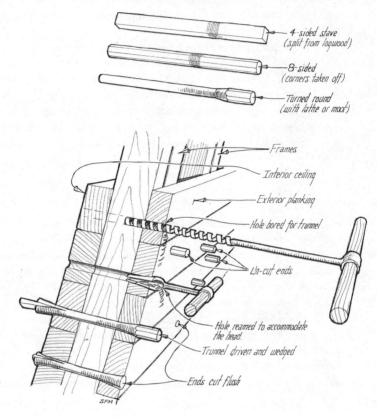

Treenails, trenels, or trunnels —

4-sided stave
(split from logwood)

8-sided
(corners taken off)

Turned round
(with lathe or moot)

Frames

Interior ceiling

Exterior planking

Hole bored for trunnel

Un-cut ends

Hole reamed to accommodate
the head

Trunnel driven and wedged

Ends cut flush

Figure 39. Locust treenails were used to fasten pine planking to the *Frolic*'s oak frames. Original illustration by S. F. Manning.

penters and apprentices dragged it into position on the keel and tilted it upright. Each frame was initially propped up with shores set in the ground and held a proper distance from adjacent frames with temporary horizontal timbers, called ribbands, nailed to the outside.

The aft portion of the *Frolic*'s hull was framed to form a rounded tuck below the waterline, while the overhang above was framed to make a square, flat transom.[4] When the notched floors of the frames had been properly placed on the keel, a heavy oak timber called the keelson was laid over them, sandwiching the frames between. Holes were bored three feet or more through the keelson, through the frame, and deep into the keel with ship augers. Inch-thick copper rods were driven into the holes to fasten all of these layers together. The *Frolic*'s frames were also held in place just below deck level by a horizontal band of heavy oak timbers extending from stem to stern. This assembly, termed the "clamp," provided a foundation for deck beams traversing the hull.

The *Frolic* was planked in yellow pine, brought north to Baltimore in lumber schooners from the forests of Georgia and South Carolina. These trees, often called pitch pines, grew straight and tall to reach sunlight high above the forest floor. Their lower limbs, starved for light, tended to fall away, leaving only small knots. For generations this straight, hard, resinous wood had been preferred by Baltimore shipbuilders for planking. Each course of pine planking was initially held against the *Frolic*'s frames with large shores or wedges. If the bend seemed too great, the plank spent hours in a steambox. When the plank was in place, one-inch holes were bored through it and through the frame behind it (see Figure 15).

Locust treenails were then driven in to hold the plank tightly. The locust was native to Maryland, and skilled woodturners using foot-powered lathes kept Baltimore shipyards supplied with thousands of these wooden bolts. Exposed to seawater once the vessel was launched, the treenails would swell to produce a watertight seal. During the installation of the *Frolic*'s exterior planking, she would often have looked like a large, fat porcupine with the treenails protruding like hundreds of stubby spines from her flanks. As planking progressed, these would be cut flush with the planking's surface.

The vessel's interior planking (or ceiling) was spiked or treenailed into place after stops were placed horizontally between each pair of frames, well above the floor, to support a filling of rock salt. This was a traditional technique for preventing decay. Moisture that seeped through the planking would dissolve some of the salt, and the wood below would be pickled in the resulting brine.

Unfortunately for the *Frolic*, salt proved an ineffective fungicide in the tropics. Only a year after her launching, Captain Faucon discovered rot deep in the *Frolic*'s hold, eliciting a swift letter of concern from John Dixwell to the Heard firm in China. "Captain F. complains of some appearance of rot in his vessel. Her timber was selected with great care, and there should be nothing of this kind, if she is kept full of salt. We do not expect a vessel to last here [Boston] without this, and it is of vastly more importance in the hot climate of China and with so drying a cargo as opium. If she is not screened by an awning, kept well wet & full of salt she will inevitably decay."[5] Despite Dixwell's warnings, rot continued to trouble the *Frolic*. Three years later, during the repairs that followed her dismasting in the 1849 typhoon, Captain Faucon reported to the Heard firm, "Yesterday, after removing a portion of the kentledge [cast iron ballast blocks] along the keelson, I discovered a place where it was entirely gone with dry rot. . . . It will be necessary to remove nearly the whole of the keel-son, & to do so we shall have to lift up both lower masts."[6]

When the *Frolic*'s hull, ceiling, and deck had been planked, carpenters could begin building bulkheads to separate her cargo hold from the crew's quarters "before the mast" and from the officers' quarters near the stern. Meanwhile, bales of oakum (shredded hemp soaked in pine tar) were being purchased for caulking. Caulkers picked apart these masses of sticky fiber, twisting them into rope-like lengths. These were driven into the seams between the planks with a short, dull, wide-bladed chisel-like tool called a caulking iron. The outside edge of each pine plank had a $3/8$-inch bevel to admit these driven strands of oakum.

When the *Frolic*'s hull caulking was completed and all the treenails sawn off, the hull was planed and tarred, and the underbody sheathed with overlapping two-by-four-foot brass-composition sheets (termed yellow metal), nailed over a backing of tarred felt. Sheathing thickness was rated in ounces per square foot, and the *Frolic* was sheathed with 24-ounce, 26-ounce, and 28-ounce sheets.[7] The heaviest, at 28 ounces, was probably nailed to her bow and along her load-water line, the 26-ounce sheets along her bilges and bottom, and the thin 24-ounce material to her keel.[8] The *Frolic*'s sheathing and nails cost $1,392.51, compared to $5,016 for her hull. Clearly the salvage value of metal sheathing and nails was an important concern for a shipowner. Three years later, in China, when the *Frolic*'s worn-out yellow metal was replaced with copper, the Dixwells found it was worthless as scrap because in the Far East there were no facilities to melt it down and roll out new sheets.

Outfitting the 'Frolic'

The following is a transcription of John Dixwell's itemized account for building and outfitting the *Frolic*. It shows the items Dixwell purchased and the
amounts paid, as well as commissions taken.[1]

Brig *Frolic* Outfits

To Building the hull of Brig Frolic, measuring 209 Tons @ $24.	5016.
Extra work on Hull, Spars, Yards, Oakum & Caulking	
altering spars &c	581.95
Copper & nails 24 26 28 23¢ per lb	1392.51
Duck for Sails #s 2, 3, 4, 5, 7, 8, 9 = 897.59 Lead &	
Sheath'g. paper 25.80	923.39
Cordage for standing & running rigging, Bolt rope, Spunyarn &c	1311.69
Sail making: 27 Sails cont'g. 101½ Bolts Duck, Fitting sails,	
Parsline &c	528.48
Blocks & block work, Dead eyes, Steering apparatus. Sheaves &c	441.37
Chains for rigging, bowsprit shrouds, sheets &c Ensign & pennant	198.61
Coppering Brig, and Spars, sheets copper & metal utensils, pantry	256.46
Long Boat, 2 Yawls, Oars, Gratings, Boat Hooks, and Plank	324.62
Blacksmith's work on Brig, Rowlocks, Thimbles, Bolts Screws &c	927.70
Joiner's work on Brig, Sky lights, Companion, Coops, hog house &c	494.13
Windlass work, patent lights, Hoisting machine, Brass work	
& blocks	381.16
Water Casks, Harness Casks, Breakers, Bucklers, Kids,	
& mast hoops	145.83

Painting Brig 236.25 extra work glass, and glazing Putty & oil 38.98 275.23
Rigging Brig complete including all extra work on rigg'g & fitting   250.
Anchors & exp's w'g 943, 824, 275, ea 135.80 2 Iron St.
    anch. & stock'g 140.03   275.83
Cables &ex. 90 fath's 1 inch, 90 fath. 15/16, 90 fath. 3/4
    Tools, pins shack & hooks   740.88
Carving Trailboards 43.20 Carnboose 20.66 Deck Plugs 15.60
    Scraping 15.   94.46
Guns 2 9lb. Cannon with carriages & gear 100.- Small arms
    & Shot 162.60   262.60
Compasses, Lamp for do. & retouching do 46.50 Binnacle
    Timep'e 13.50   60.
Cabin Furniture 41.25 Upholstery, damask Curtains &
    drawer knobs 66.48   107.73
Salt, Tar & Varnish 51.40 Extra paints & labor on board 184.12
    Tools 8.50   244.02
Towels, Linen & Table cloths 23.07 Lamps & glass 26.-
    Deck Lights 4.25   53.32
Hide Wheel rope 6.80 Small Ensign 7. Cost of models
    transhipped 3.54   17.34
Capt. Fitzgerald overseer's bill 180.83 Birckhead & Pearce
    age'ts. com. 341.57   522.40
My Commission on Cost Brig Frolic $15,827.71 @ 2½ %   395.69
    16,223.40

Outfits

To Chandlery 786.28, Hardware 138.94, Stationary 12.50
    Medic. ch. 55.-   992.72
Crockery & Glassware 70.31 Duck for spare sails 121.45
    G. Powder 28.50   220.26
Wood 87.69 18 Tons Iron Kentledge & 60 Tons Stone Ballast,
    Junk &c 453.56   541.25
Candles 10.33 Bread 2510 lbs at 3 1/8¢ 1996 lbs @ 2½ 139.75
    Lemon Syrup 6.   156.08
water 4.30 Beef 30 Bbls & Pork 15 Bbls & exp's 369.75,
    Butter 31.57 Cheese 4.23   409.85
water filterer 5. wine, Cider, & Ale 60.26 Kegs 7.70 Brand for
    name 2.25   75.21
Fresh meat & sausages 36. Pigs 19.- Fowls 30.- Preserved
    meats 60.50   145.50

wharfage & drayage 42.25 Flour 64.- 150 Ball Cartridges 4.50
    Postage 14.86   125.61
advertizing in Baltimore & Boston 6.75 Sea letter & articles 4.50
    Clear'e 9.60   20.85
Shipp'g crew & adv. wages 379.25 Mates & Stew'd. board 63.
    Capt. F. board & exp. 154.   596.25
Pilotage to sea 35.75 Fire Insurance on rigging while in stow 1.20   36.95
Specie on board 89.94 Fire Ins. on vessel while building 12000 16.-   105.94
Ins. 20,000 on vessel & 5000 on frt on board or not, 1 year fr
    Dec. 8 3½ % p. 876.   876.
Birckhead & Pearce, agents in Baltimore commission on outfits   72.49
My Commission on Outfits Brig Frolic amt'g to 4374.96
    @ 2½ % 109.36   4484.32
                                                    $20,707.72

Boston
Jany. 11. 1845
J.J. Dixwell

Reference Matter

Notes

Abbreviations

Heard 1   Heard Collection, Part One
Heard 2   Heard Collection, Part Two
MHS   Massachusetts Historical Society

Heard 1 and Heard 2 are archived at Baker Library, Harvard University Graduate School of Business Administration.

Introduction

1. For a discussion of the "direct historical approach" in archaeology, see Strong. Also see Heizer, "Direct Historical Approach."

2. The site record for CA-MEN-790 is on file at the Northwest Information Center of the California Archaeological Inventory, Department of Anthropology, Sonoma State University, Rohnert Park, Calif.

3. Shangraw and Von der Porten.

4. Lubbock, p. 384.

5. Fairburn, *Merchant Sail*, p. 2584.

6. The Jerome B. Ford diary is now lost. These details come to us as remembered by his son Jerome Chester Ford in 1933 and quoted in Bear and Stebbins, p. 9.

7. Gwenlian MacCallum Yonce, unpublished oral history transcript, Kelley House Museum Archive, Mendocino, Calif., n.d.

8. Layton, chap. 4.

9. Lubbock, p. 384.

10. Forbes, *Personal Reminiscences.*

11. See Works Progress Administration.

12. "Local Matters," *Baltimore Sun,* Dec. 7, 1844.

13. Port of Baltimore Federal Register of Ships or Vessels, National Archives, Record Group 41, Washington, D.C.

14. Layton, pp. 173–208.

Chapter 1

1. Much of the Augustine Heard biographical material in this chapter is derived from Waters. For his essay Waters drew heavily from the Augustine Heard papers, now held by the Baker Library of the Harvard University Graduate School of Business Administration.

2. Morison, p. 29.

3. Ibid., p. 52.

4. Ibid.

5. Beeching, p. 20.

6. Morison, p. 67.

7. Hao, p. 29.

8. Ibid., p. 28.

9. Beeching, p. 22.

10. Ibid., p. 26.

11. Ibid., p. 31.

12. Ibid., p. 33.

13. Ibid., p. 42.

14. Hao, p. 30.

15. Heard became quite fond of Coolidge, and in grandfatherly fashion he looked after the young man's family of five children in Boston. The relationship with Green, however, had soured before Heard left China, and by the spring of 1838 Coolidge likewise found himself in conflict with Green. Anticipating dissolution of the partnership, Coolidge returned to Boston to see his family and to confer with Heard. When Coolidge sailed for China that summer, he carried Heard's authorization to establish a new firm in the event of an emergency. In early December, shortly after his return to Canton, Coolidge was forced out of Russell & Co.

16. Chesneaux et al., p. 55.

17. Beeching, p. 43.

18. Chesneaux et al., pp. 56–57.

19. Beeching, p. 77.

20. Chesneaux et al., p. 65.

21. Hao, p. 31.

22. Augustine Heard (Boston) to Joseph Coolidge (Canton), May 7, 1841, quoted by Waters, p. 37.

23. Epes Dixwell (Boston) to John Dixwell (Calcutta), May 13, 1833, Wigglesworth Family Papers, Ms. N-114, MHS. Frederick Tudor of Boston had pioneered shipping ice to the West Indies before the War of 1812 and by 1820 had established icehouses in Savannah, Charleston, and New Orleans. The *Tuscany*'s ice cargo for India posed a far greater challenge, as the vessel would cross the equator twice during a four-month voyage. A fifty-foot section of the *Tuscany*'s interior, between the forward and after hatch, was converted to an ice

hold, and the ship's mast and pump were well boxed and insulated. The ice blocks were packed tightly in a solid mass over two plank floors, with a foot of dried tanbark sandwiched between. The tanbark came from Boston's tanning vats, where thousands of hides from California were soaked and cured into supple leather. The tanbark was stuffed between plank walls to insulate the cargo from the sides of the ship. A foot of hay with a plank roof was laid on top, and the remaining space beneath the deck, out to the sides of the vessel, was stuffed with yet more tanbark. Not surprisingly, Tudor's agreement stipulated that the *Tuscany*'s sealed hatches were never to be opened during transit.

When the ice arrived at Calcutta and had been unloaded into a specially insulated warehouse, a full 100 tons of the original 180 had survived the voyage (Fairburn, pp. 571–72). Dixwell's experiences in marketing the first cargo of ice to reach Calcutta are remembered in numerous anecdotes. One Parsee wondered what sort of tree the ice had grown on, and some indignant customers demanded their money back after leaving a purchase in the sun (Morison, p. 282).

24. Although Wigglesworth specialized in "West Indian" goods from tropical lands encircling the Caribbean, he also traded in products from India, China, and the East Indian archipelago (modern Indonesia). Prices for these commodities were subject to sudden change, and fortunes could be won or lost on the strength of current market information. Hence it was common practice for businessmen to maintain active international correspondence with distant associates to keep apprised of market conditions.

As John assembled a return cargo for the *Tuscany*, he received a note from his brother Epes, also working for Mr. Wigglesworth (Epes Dixwell [Boston] to John Dixwell [Calcutta], Aug. 8, 1833, Wigglesworth Family Papers, Ms. N-114, MHS). Epes listed current Boston prices of fifteen relevant commodities. Among these were myrrh, gum arabic, gum cophal, gunnybags, Manila hemp, hides, horn tips, indigo, Sumatra pepper, saltpeter, shellac, turmeric, yellow berries, and ginger, as well as four kinds of coffee: Sumatra, Porto Rico, Porto Cabella, and Santo Domingo. Epes Dixwell enclosed with his note a contract signed by John Titus of Augustine Titus & Co., stipulating: "Whereas John J. Dixwell of Boston, merchant, has agreed to import, at his own risk, from Calcutta, one hundred male monkeys of the light faced species common in Bengal . . . [Augustine Titus & Co.] agree[s] to pay $10 for each monkey delivered alive to Boston : . . [where] we have depos. $200 w/ Thomas Wigglesworth" (John Titus [Boston] to John Dixwell [Calcutta], Aug. 8, 1833, ibid.). We can only imagine the shipboard ambience of the homeward-bound *Tuscany*!

25. Epes Dixwell (Boston) to John Dixwell (London), Apr. 22, 1838, Wigglesworth Family Papers, Ms. N-114, MHS.

26. Genealogical notes on the Dixwells, Wigglesworth Family Papers, Ms. N-114, MHS.

27. Morison, pp. 114–16.

28. *Boston City Directory* (1839).

29. *Boston City Directory* (1841).

30. Henrietta Sargent (Boston) to George Dixwell (Canton), Aug. 29, 1841, Wigglesworth Family Papers, Ms. N-114, MHS.

31. Fay, p. 289.   32. Ibid.

33. Ibid., p. 290.   34. Ibid., p. 291.

35. John Heard, Diary (autobiography written in 1891), Heard 1, FP 4, pp. 31–32.

36. John Heard had spent a disappointing three years at Phillips Academy, Andover, dropping out at thirteen to sail with his uncle, Captain Joseph Farley, to Havana. This voyage had been followed by two years of uninspired performance as a clerk (Waters, p. 39). John's concerned parents hoped a term in China with "Uncle Augustine" would reform the boy.

37. Classified advertisement, *Canton Register*, Jan. 11, 1842.

38. John Heard, Diary, p. 37.

39. John Heard's Dec. 13, 1842, letter to his parents is quoted at length by Waters, pp. 40–44.

40. John Heard, Diary, p. 50.   41. Hao, pp. 114–15.

42. LeFevour, p. 13.   43. Greenberg, p. 222, app. 2.

44. Beeching, p. 82.   45. Lubbock, pp. 382–83, app. B.

46. Fairburn, p. 3019.   47. Dulles, p. 202.

48. John Dixwell (Boston) to Augustine Heard (Canton), Feb. 5, 1844, Heard 1, EM 3-1.

49. John Heard, Diary, p. 52.

50. John Heard (Canton) to Augustine Heard (Boston), Sept. 1, 1844, Heard 1, EM 4.

51. George Dixwell (Canton) to Augustine Heard (Boston), Dec. 10, 1844, Heard 1, EM 3-2.

52. John Dixwell (Boston) to Baring Bros. & Co. (London), July 15, 1844, Heard Collection, as cited in an unpublished manuscript on the China trade authored and generously supplied by Jacques Downs, Ph.D.

53. George Dixwell (Canton) to Augustine Heard (aboard the *Sappho* for Boston), Aug. 6, 1844, Heard 1, EM 3-2.

Chapter 2

1. *Baltimore American*, July 4, 1838.

2. "The Mexican Sloop of War," *Baltimore Sun*, July 12, 1838, p. 2.

3. "The Ship Venus," *Baltimore Sun*, July 14, 1838.

4. U.S. House of Representatives, p. 474.

5. Spear.

6. U.S. House of Representatives, p. 661.

7. Ibid., p. 21.   8. Ibid., p. 106.

9. Ibid., p. 110.   10. Spear.

11. U.S. House of Representatives, p. 110.

12. Spear.

13. U.S. House of Representatives, p.106.

14. Ibid., p. 21.

15. Spear.

16. U.S. House of Representatives, pp. 124, 106.

17. Bourne, p. 274.

18. Chapelle, *Baltimore Clipper*, p. 64.

19. Scharf, pp. 100–103.

20. Chapelle, *Search for Speed*, p. 142.

21. Scharf, p. 104.

22. Chapelle, *Search for Speed*, p. 146.

23. Chapelle, *Baltimore Clipper*, p. 64.

24. Cranwell and Crane, pp. 34, 41.

25. Ibid., p. 266.   26. Scharf, p. 111.

27. Ruckert, p. 36.   28. Bourne, p. 275.

29. Griffin, p. 3.   30. Ibid., p. 5.

31. Robinson, p. 39. Most of these Baltimore-built privateer clippers operated under aliases, so it is impossible to trace any particular vessel to the yards of Gardner and Robson. For example, the privateer *Orb*, owned by Archibald Kerr during the War of 1812 (Cranwell and Crane, p. 410), reappeared in South America from 1817 to 1819 variously as the *Congresso*, the *Tyger*, and the *Pueyrredon* (Griffin, p. 9), while in the spirit of the times her Baltimore captain, Joseph Almieda, became Don Jose Almieda (Cranwell and Crane, p. 10).

32. Robinson, p. 54.

33. George Gardner, Last Will and Testament, Dec. 16, 1830, Baltimore Registry of Wills, Court House East, Baltimore.

34. At the time of his death, George Gardner was owed money by the Citizen Line of Steamboats and four other private customers for repairs completed. There were also claims from 22 general creditors, including bills for timber; handling and inspecting live oak; supplying knees, masts, spars, and augers; and eight hundred pounds of oakum. There were additional bills for timber used in building a floating stage, for towing stages, and for recovery of a drifting stage. When the estate was finally settled in 1835, a balance of $2,785.62 was divided equally among Gardner's eight children. This small residual reveals

that Gardner had relatively little capital tied up in property and equipment. The shipyard's inventory (see Appendix A) provides a unique view of the tools and supplies used by the Gardners to build and repair vessels. George Gardner's inventory, Mar. 17, 1834; George Gardner's additional inventory, Nov. 23, 1835; George Gardner's first administration account, Nov. 23, 1835; Baltimore Registry of Wills, Court House East, Baltimore.

35. *Matchett's Baltimore City Directory*, 1833.

36. Preston.

37. Douglass, *Narrative*.

38. Thomas Kemp had purchased his retirement estate, near St. Michaels, from Hugh Auld's father, Col. Hugh Auld, and Hugh Jr. had been trained as a shipwright in St. Michaels under Thomas Kemp's brother, Joseph. In the early nineteenth century family ties ran deep, and it was only natural to place Fred Bailey (later Frederick Douglass) with the Gardners, who were the successors to Thomas Kemp in Baltimore.

39. Douglass, *Narrative*, pp. 127–28.

40. Olson, p. 90.

41. Douglass, *Narrative*, p. 129.

42. Olson, p. 91.

43. Douglass, *Life and Times*, pp. 182–84.

44. Preston, p. 146.

Chapter 3

1. John Dixwell, quoted in John Heard (Canton) to Augustine Heard (London), Aug. 24, 1844, Heard 1, EM 4-1.

2. The *Dart* was completed and dispatched by Sept. 14, almost three months before the *Frolic*, indicating that George Dixwell considered establishing the coastal delivery system a higher priority.

3. John Dixwell's detailed account of the expenditures for the *Frolic* can be found in Appendix C.

4. W. and G. Gardner, Master Carpenter's Certificate, District of Baltimore, Dec. 1, 1844, National Archives, Record Group 41, Washington, D.C.

5. Smith, p. 17.

6. Edward Faucon (Bombay) to Augustine Heard & Co. (Canton), Apr. 5, 1845, Heard 2, S18, F14.

7. Chapelle, *Baltimore Clipper*, p. 103.

8. Ibid., pp. 170–71.

9. Edward Faucon (Bombay) to Augustine Heard & Co. (Canton), Apr. 5, 1845, Heard 2, S18, F14.

10. Chapelle, p. 105.

11. John Dixwell (Boston) account, Jan. 1, 1845, Heard 2, Case 28, F25.

12. Esther Dixwell (Boston) to George Dixwell (Canton), Sept. 2, 1844, Wigglesworth Family Papers, Ms. N-114, MHS.

13. John Dixwell (Baltimore) to Augustine Heard & Co. (Canton), Sept. 9, 1844, Heard 2, LV12, F32.

14. John Dixwell (Boston) to Augustine Heard & Co. (Canton), Sept. 14, 1844, Heard 2, LV12, F32.

15. Obituary of Mrs. Martha Weld Faucon, *Milton (Mass.) Record*, May 30, 1913.

16. Catherine Waters Faucon, "Record of the life of Nicolas Michel Faucon, 1773–1817, being extracts from the few papers he left and other sources." Ms., May 24, 1928, Harvard University Archives, Cambridge, Mass.

17. For the period 1818 to 1839, issues of the *Boston City Directory* list John Waters as secretary of the New England Marine Insurance Company.

18. Edward H. Faucon, Journal of Voyages, MHS. This journal includes ships' logs of Faucon's voyages to California aboard the *Plant*, the *Chalcedony*, the *Alert*, and the *Pilgrim*.

19. Morison, p. 290. 20. Ogden, p. 290.
21. Dana, p. 206. 22. Ibid.
23. Ibid., p. 237.

24. Gorham Palfrey Faucon, autobiographical essay, Harvard College Class Book of 1875, pp. 261–63. Ms., Harvard University Archives, Cambridge, Mass.

25. Fritzsche.

26. Morison, p. 269.

27. Dana, p. 233.

28. Our knowledge of the items built or purchased for the *Frolic* comes from John Dixwell's itemized accounting of the costs for building and outfitting the *Frolic*. Heard 2, S18, F16, Jan. 11, 1845.

29. "Local Matters," *Baltimore Sun*, Dec. 7, 1844.

30. Faucon's description of the passage from Baltimore to Bombay and his critique of the vessel are found in Edward Faucon (Bombay) to Augustine Heard & Co. (Canton), Apr. 5, 1845, Heard 2, S18, F14.

31. Edward Faucon (Anjer Roads) to Augustine Heard & Co. (Canton), Apr. 27, 1846, Heard 2, S18, F14.

Chapter 4

1. The other two large opium exporters were the firm of B. & A. Hormujee, also Parsee, who consigned to Dent & Co.; and Kessressung Khooshalchund, a firm owned by Hindus, who were opportunistic in their consignments.

2. Downs, p. 437.

3. George Dixwell (Canton) to Augustine Heard (in transit to New York), Nov. 17, 1844, Heard 1, EM 3-2.

4. Ibid., Dec. 10, 1844.

5. John Heard (Canton) to Augustine Heard (in transit to New York), Oct. 20, 1844, Heard 1, EM 4-1.

6. Martin Murray & Co. (Bombay) to Augustine Heard & Co. (Canton), Feb. 5, 1845, Heard 2, LV11, F16.

7. John Heard (Canton) to Augustine Heard (in transit to New York), Oct. 20, 1844, Heard 1, EM 4-1.

8. John Heard (Bombay) to Augustine Heard (Boston), Mar. 1, 1849, Heard 1, EM 5-2.

9. George Dixwell (Canton) to Augustine Heard (in transit to New York), Mar. 4, 1844, Heard 1, EM 3-2.

10. George Dixwell (Canton) to Augustine Heard (in transit to New York), Dec. 10, 1844, Heard 1, EM 3-2.

11. George Dixwell (Shanghai) to Augustine Heard (Boston), May 9, 1845, Heard 1, EM 3-2.

12. Kessressung Khooshalchund & Co. (Bombay) to Augustine Heard & Co. (Canton), July 4, 1845, Heard 2, LV11, F18.

13. Kessressung Khooshalchund Co. (Bombay) to Augustine Heard & Co. (Canton), July 25, 1845, Heard 2, LV11, F18.

14. Jehangeer Cursetjee (Bombay) to Augustine Heard & Co. (Canton), July 26, 1845, Heard 2, LV12, F1.

15. The following discussion of Malwa opium production is derived from Impey. The only known copy of this publication in the United States is in the Yale University Library. For an additional description of Malwa opium production see Aberigh-Mackay.

16. Greenberg, pp. 126–29.

17. Ibid., p. 131.

18. Owen, p. 101.

19. Elliot, pp. 30–31. The only known copy of this volume in the United States is in the library of the Peabody Essex Museum at Salem.

20. Edward Faucon (Bombay) to Augustine Heard & Co. (Canton), Apr. 5, 1845, Heard 2, S18, F14.

21. Martin Murray & Co. (Bombay) to Augustine Heard & Co. (Canton), Apr. 9, 1845, Heard 2, LV11, F16.

22. Martin Murray & Co. (Bombay) to Augustine Heard & Co. (Canton), Apr. 24, 1845, Heard 2, LV11, F16.

23. Martin Murray & Co. (Bombay), List of Freight Outward of Brig *Frolic* . . . for Macao, May 8, 1845, Heard 2, S18, F13.

24. Kessressung Khooshalchund Co. (Bombay) to Augustine Heard & Co. (Canton), May 5, 1845, Heard 2, LV11, F18.

25. Martin Murray & Co. (Bombay) to Augustine Heard & Co. (Canton), May 8, 1845, Heard 2, LV11, F16.

26. Kessressung Khooshalchund Co. (Bombay) to Augustine Heard & Co. (Canton), May 5, 1845, Heard 2, LV11, F18.

27. Kessressung Khooshalchund Co. (Bombay) to Augustine Heard & Co. (Canton), May 3, 1845, Heard 2, LV11, F18.

28. Ibid.

29. Lubbock, p. 267.

30. John Heard (Canton) to Augustine Heard (Boston), June 8, 1845, Heard 1, EM 4-2.

31. John Heard (Canton) to Augustine Heard (Boston), Apr. 20, 1845, Heard 1, EM 4-2.

32. George Dixwell (Macao) to Augustine Heard (New York), May 30, 1845, Heard 1, EM 3-2.

33. John Heard (Canton) to Augustine Heard (Boston), June 20, 1845, Heard 1, EM 4-2.

34. George Dixwell (Canton) to Augustine Heard (in transit to New York), Nov. 8, 1844, Heard 1, EM 3-2.

35. John Heard (Canton) to Augustine Heard (Boston), Apr. 20, 1845, Heard 1, EM 4-2.

36. John Heard (Canton) to Augustine Heard (Boston), June 20, 1845, Heard 1, EM 4-2.

37. The treasure cargo included 183,037 taels of Sycee silver in addition to $11,995 and 5,000 Cowchin dollars. A Canton tael was equal to $1.39 American. Augustine Heard & Co. (Canton and Macao), Bills of Lading, June 22, 23, 26, 1845, Heard 2, S18, F12.

38. Edward Faucon (Java Sea) to Augustine Heard & Co. (Canton), July 23, 1845, Heard 2, S18, F14.

39. Edward Faucon (Singapore) to Augustine Heard & Co. (Canton), Oct. 7, 1845, Heard 2, S18, F14.

40. John Heard (Canton) to Augustine Heard (Boston), June 22, 1845, Heard 1, EM 4-2.

41. George Dixwell (Macao) to Augustine Heard (Boston), July 27, 1845, Heard 1, EM 3-2.

42. Jehangeer Cursetjee's last letter to the Heards (July 26, 1845, Heard 2, S18, F14) had been upbeat and cheerful: "After the 15 August (Coconut Day)," he had written, "it is my intention to go to some of the opium growing districts of Malwa to visit my old and intimate friend Huttesung Kessrisung Esq." Cursetjee had then described Mr. Kessressung's construction of a religious temple at Ahmedabad around which poor people could live without paying rent. The temple had cost "a full 6 lac Rupees," and Kessressung "had invited all his old friends of different sects" to attend the dedication ceremony in February.

43. On Sept. 5, 1845, the firm addressed three letters to the Heards, all of which are designated Kessressung Khooshalchund Co. (Bombay) to Augustine Heard & Co. (Canton), Sept. 5, 1845, Heard 2, LV11, F18.

44. Ibid.

45. Edward Faucon (Singapore) to Augustine Heard & Co. (Canton), Oct. 7, 1845, Heard 2, S18, F14.

46. Kessressung Khooshalchund Co. (Bombay) to Augustine Heard & Co. (Canton), Sept. 5, 1845, Heard 2, LV11, F18.

47. Kessressung Khooshalchund Co. (Bombay) to Augustine Heard & Co. (Canton), Nov. 10, 1845, Heard 2, LV11, F18.

48. Ibid.

Chapter 5

1. Lockwood, p. 7.

2. Ibid., p. 9.

3. I thank Jacques M. Downs for explaining these relationships to me.

4. George Dixwell (Canton) to Augustine Heard (Boston), Feb. 5, 1845, Heard 1, EM 3-2.

5. Hidy, p. 135.

6. R. G. Dun & Co. Credit Ledger, Baltimore, Md., vol. 7, p. 231. R. G. Dun & Co. Collection, Baker Library, Harvard University Graduate School of Business Administration.

7. John Dixwell (Baltimore) to Augustine Heard & Co. (Canton), Sept. 9, 1844, Heard 2, LV12, F32.

8. George Dixwell (Canton) to Augustine Heard (Boston), Jan. 19, 1845, Heard 1, EM 3-2.

9. Ibid.

10. George Dixwell (Shanghai) to Augustine Heard (Boston), May 9, 1845, Heard 1, EM 3-2.

11. George Dixwell (Canton) to Augustine Heard (New York), May 30, 1845, Heard 1, EM 3-2.

12. John Heard (Canton) to Augustine Heard (Boston), June 8, 1845, Heard 1, EM 4-2.

13. John Heard (Canton) to Augustine Heard (Boston), Nov. 25, 1846, Heard 1, EM 4-4.

14. Ibid.

15. John Heard (Canton) to Augustine Heard (Boston), Nov. 13, 1845, Heard 1, EM 4-1.

16. R. Forbes, *Remarks on China*, p. 46.

17. Ibid.

18. Kessressung Khooshalchund Co. (Bombay) to Augustine Heard & Co. (Canton), Sept. 11, 1845, Heard 2, LV11, F18.

19. Kessressung Khooshalchund Co. (Bombay) to Augustine Heard & Co. (Canton), Sept. 11, 1845, Heard 2, LV11, F18.

20. William Endicott (Cumsingmoon) to Augustine Heard & Co. (Canton), Nov. 3, 1845, Heard 2, S23, F5.

21. Edward Faucon (Bombay) to Augustine Heard & Co. (Canton), Jan. 10, 1846, Heard 2, S18, F14.

22. N. Baylies, *Snipe*, Cumsingmoon. Comments on Malwa opium excerpted from several 1846 inventories, Heard 2, S24, F3.

23. Edward Faucon (Singapore) to Augustine Heard & Co. (Canton), Mar. 2, 1846, Heard 2, S18, F14.

24. John Heard (Canton) to Augustine Heard (Boston), Aug. 23, 1846, Heard 1, EM 4-3.

25. C. F. Harding (Chusan) to Augustine Heard & Co. (Canton), Feb. 2, 1845, Heard 2, S3 (*Don Juan*, Chusan).

26. John Heard (Canton) to Augustine Heard (Boston), Sept. 27, 1846, Heard 1, EM 4-3.

27. Opium Examiner's Certificate, signatures illegible, *Snipe*, Woosung, Aug. 21, 1846, Heard 2, S24, F2.

28. Charles A. Fearon (Shanghai) to Bush & Co. (Hong Kong), Sept. 11, 1846, Heard 2, LV10, F8.

29. John Heard (Canton) to Augustine Heard (Boston), Nov. 25, 1846, Heard 1, EM 4-4.

30. Hao, pp. 36–37.

31. Impey, p. 11.

32. Kessressung Khooshalchund Co. (Bombay) to Augustine Heard & Co. (Canton), Jan. 19, 1846, Heard 2, LV11, F18.

33. John Heard (Canton) to Augustine Heard (Boston), June 8, 1845, Heard 1, EM 4-2.

34. Augustine Heard & Co. (Canton) to J. Porter, Esq., June 26, 1846, Heard 2, S17, F18.

35. Kessressung Khooshalchund Co. (Bombay) to Augustine Heard & Co. (Canton), invoice for opium shipped on Captain Faucon's account, Jan. 18, 1846, Heard 2, S18, F9.

36. Edward Faucon (Cumsingmoon) to Augustine Heard & Co. (Canton), July 24, 1846, Heard 2, S23, F8.

37. John Heard (Canton) to Augustine Heard (Boston), Jan. 10, 1846, Heard 1, EM 4-3.

38. Edward Faucon (Cumsingmoon) to Augustine Heard & Co. (Canton), Mar. 28, 1846, Heard 2, S23, F8.

39. Kessressung Khooshalchund Co. (Bombay) to Augustine Heard & Co. (Canton), Oct. 6, 1846, Heard 2, LV11, F18.

40. Kessressung Khooshalchund Co. (Bombay) to Augustine Heard & Co. (Canton), Jan. 12, 1847, Heard 2, LV11, F19.

41. Epes Dixwell (Cambridge) to George Dixwell (en route from Canton to Boston), May 8, 1847, Wigglesworth Family Papers, Ms. N-114, MHS.

42. Edward Faucon (Bombay) to Augustine Heard & Co. (Canton), Jan. 26, 1847, Heard 2, S18, F14.

43. B. & A. Hormujee (Bombay) to Augustine Heard & Co. (Canton), June 4, 1847, Heard 2, LV12, F2.

44. Kessressung Khooshalchund Co. (Bombay) to Augustine Heard & Co. (Canton), June 12, 1847, Heard 2, LV11, F19.

45. Kessressung Khooshalchund Co. (Bombay) to Augustine Heard & Co. (Canton), Oct. 18, 1847, Heard 2, LV11, F19.

46. John Heard (Canton) to Augustine Heard (Boston), Oct. 25, 1847, Heard 1, EM 4-4.

47. Ibid.

48. John Heard (Canton) to Augustine Heard (Boston), Apr. 19, 1848, Heard 1, EM 5-1.

49. John Heard (Canton) to Augustine Heard (Boston), July 13, 1848, Heard 1, EM 5-1.

50. Kessressung Khooshalchund Co. (Bombay) to Augustine Heard & Co. (Canton), Sept. 18, 1848, Heard 2, LV11, F19.

51. Kessressung Khooshalchund Co. (Bombay) to Augustine Heard & Co. (Canton), Oct. 1848, Heard 2, LV11, F19.

52. Edward Faucon (Hong Kong), advanced wages for *Frolic* crews paid in 1848, Aug. 10, 1848, Heard 2, S18, F10.

53. John Heard (Canton) to Augustine Heard (Boston), Oct. 27, 1848, Heard 1, EM 5-1.

Chapter 6

1. John Dixwell (Boston) to Augustine Heard & Co. (Canton), Dec. 5, 1848, Heard 2, LV12, F35.

2. John Dixwell (Boston) to Augustine Heard & Co. (Canton), Jan. 6, 1849, Heard 2, LV12, F35.

3. Hawgood, p. xxiii.

4. John Everett (Boston) to Thomas Larkin (Monterey), Mar. 23, 1845, in Hammond, vol. 3, pp. 88–90.

5. Ibid.

6. John Everett (Boston) to Thomas Larkin (Monterey), Sept. 1, 1845, in Hammond, vol. 3, pp. 333–34.

7. Hawgood, p. 17.

8. Hicks et al., p. 550.

9. John Everett (Boston) to Thomas Larkin (Monterey), Dec. 12, 1845, in Hammond, vol. 4, pp. 118–21.

10. John Dixwell (Boston) to Augustine Heard & Co. (Canton), Apr. 30, 1845, Heard 2, LV12, F32.

11. John Dixwell (Boston) to Augustine Heard & Co. (Canton), May 6, 1845, Heard 2, LV12, F32.

12. Thomas Larkin (Monterey) to John Everett (Boston), June 18, 1846, in Hammond, vol. 5, pp. 47–49.

13. Thomas Larkin (Monterey) to Rev. William M. Rogers (Boston), June 18, 1846, in Hammond, vol. 5, pp. 44–47.

14. John Everett (Boston) to Thomas Larkin (Monterey), Mar. 26, 1846, in Hammond, vol. 4, pp. 266–68.

15. John Everett (Boston) to Thomas Larkin (Monterey), Apr. 26, 1846, in Hammond, vol. 4, pp. 349–51.

16. John Heard (Canton) to Augustine Heard (Boston), Nov. 25, 1846, Heard 1, EM 5-1.

17. John Heard (Canton) to Augustine Heard (Boston), Feb. 23, 1847, Heard 1, EM 5-1.

18. John Everett (Canton) to Thomas Larkin (Monterey), Sept. 6, 1847, in Hammond, vol. 6, pp. 319–20.

19. Nunis, p. 181, note 66. See also Hammond, vol. 4, p. 331.

20. Bethuel Phelps (San Francisco) to Thomas Larkin (Monterey), bill of sale for *Eveline*, Jan. 16, 1849, in Hammond, vol. 8, pp. 96–97.

21. Thomas Larkin (Monterey), contract with Jacob Leese, Feb. 12, 1849, in Hammond, vol. 8, pp. 138–39.

22. Thomas Larkin (Monterey) to John Everett (Canton), Feb. 14, 1849, in Hammond, vol. 8, pp. 147–48.

23. John Heard (Bombay) to Augustine Heard (Boston), Mar. 1, 1849, Heard 1, EM 5-2.

24. John Heard (Steamer *Pekin*) to Augustine Heard (Boston), Apr. 3, 1849, Heard 1, EM 5-2.

25. John Heard (Bombay) to Augustine Heard (Boston), Mar. 14, 1849, Heard 1, EM 5-2.

26. John Heard (Canton) to Augustine Heard (Boston), Apr. 22, 1849, Heard 1, EM 5-2.

27. Ibid.

28. John Heard (Canton) to Augustine Heard (Boston), May 20, 1849, Heard 1, EM 5-2.

29. Jacob Leese (Honolulu) to Thomas Larkin (Monterey), Mar. 20, 1849, in Hammond, vol. 8, pp. 181–82.

30. Augustine Heard & Co., bills of lading for *Eveline* (Hong Kong), Aug. 3, 1849, Heard 2, S5.

31. Thomas Larkin (Monterey) to Jacob Leese, Feb. 15, 1849, in Hammond, vol. 8, pp. 149–50.

32. Jacob Leese (Hong Kong) to Thomas Larkin (Monterey), Aug. 4, 1849, in Hammond, vol. 8, p. 253.

33. John Heard (Canton) to Augustine Heard (Boston), Aug. 15, 1849, Heard 1, EM 5-2.

34. John Heard (Canton) to Augustine Heard (Boston), Sept. 22, 1849, Heard 1, EM 5-2.

35. "China Hobe Bay—The morning after the Typhoon of 13 Sept. 1849—the Clipper 'Frolic' dismasted—taken from the deck of the 'Antelope,' also dismasted—," unsigned pencil and ink, M12470-25, Peabody Essex Museum of Salem, Mass.

36. Repairs to the *Frolic* began immediately and took five weeks (Edward Faucon [Hong Kong] to Augustine Heard & Co. [Canton], Oct. 22, 1849, Heard 2, S18, F14). The bill for masts, yards, booms, 42 blocks, canvas for new sails, towing, and a multitude of ancillary supplies and services came to $5,342.40. The *Frolic*'s insurance policy covered two-thirds of these charges, while her owners were obliged to pay the balance of $1,775.46 (Statement of General Average pr Brig *Frolic* . . . for losses sustained . . . during the Typhoon in September 1849 [Hong Kong], Jan. 19, 1850, Heard 2, S18, F16).

37. Edward Faucon (Hong Kong) to Augustine Heard & Co. (Canton), Oct. 22, 1849, Heard 2, S18, F14.

38. Edward Faucon (Hong Kong) to Augustine Heard & Co. (Canton), Nov. 8, 1849, Heard 2, S18, F14.

39. In addition to charging for supplies and supervisory services, Lamont also billed the Heards for 910 man-days of labor at 60 cents per day—the equivalent of 40 workmen laboring for 20 days (Invoice, "The brig *Frolic*, Captain Faucon on owners account, to John Lamont, East Point, Hong Kong," Nov. 23, 1849, Heard 2, S18, F16).

40. John Heard (Canton) to Augustine Heard (Boston), Oct. 23, 1849, Heard 1, EM 5-2.

41. Ibid.

42. John Heard (Canton) to Augustine Heard (Boston), Sept. 22, 1849, Heard 1, EM 5-2.

43. John Heard (Canton) to Augustine Heard (Boston), Oct. 23, 1849, Heard 1, EM 5-2.

44. Invoice, Williams & Powell (Liverpool) to Augustine Heard & Co. (Canton), Nov. 2, 1847, Heard 2, S18, F16.

45. John Dixwell (Boston) to Augustine Heard & Co. (Canton), June 3, 1847, Heard 2, LV12, F34.

46. Invoice, Bowra, Humphreys & Co. (Victoria, Hong Kong) to Owners of the *Frolic*, Nov. 23, 1849, Heard 2, S18, F6.

47. John Dixwell (Boston), Brig *Frolic* and Outfits, Jan. 11, 1845, Heard 2, S18, F16.

48. I thank ordnance manufacturer Paul Barnett of South Bend Replicas, South Bend, Ind., for providing this average weight for iron nine-pounders.

49. I thank Oliver Seeler of Albion, Calif., for measuring the cannon raised from the *Frolic* shipwreck.

50. John Heard (Canton) to Augustine Heard (Boston), Feb. 20, 1850, Heard 1, EM 5-3.

51. John Heard (Canton) to Augustine Heard (Boston), Jan. 26, 1850, Heard 1, EM 5-3.

52. John Heard (Canton) to Augustine Heard (Boston), Feb. 20, 1850, Heard 1, EM 5-3.

53. John Heard (Canton) to Augustine Heard (Boston), Mar. 23, 1850, Heard 1, EM 5-3.

54. John Heard (Canton) to Augustine Heard (Boston), Apr. 17, 1850, Heard 1, EM 5-3.

55. John Heard (Canton) to Augustine Heard (Boston), Jan. 26, 1850, Heard 1, EM 5-3.

56. John Heard (Canton) to Augustine Heard (Boston), May 17, 1850, Heard 1, EM 5-3.

57. Augustine Heard & Co., bills of lading for *Frolic* (Canton), May 30, 1850, Heard 2, S18, F12.

58. John Everett (Canton), order for comprador to pay Tinqua $87.50 for pictures a/c *Frolic*, Apr. 9, 1850, Heard 2, S18, F9.

59. All of the items listed here are present in collections recovered from the *Frolic* shipwreck. Most have been donated to the *Frolic* Shipwreck Repository at the Mendocino County Museum in Willits, Calif.

60. Invoice, N. Gilbert (Canton) to Augustine Heard & Co. (Canton), for Edinburgh ale, for bottling, and for packing cases, May 23, 1850, Heard 2, S18, F6.

61. Macvicar & Co. (Canton), agents for Asiatic Marine Insurance Office, to Augustine Heard & Co. (Canton), May 21, 1850, Heard 2, S18, F14. See also Western India Insurance Society, policy no. 221, June 19, 1850, Heard 2, S18, F3; Imperial Marine Insurance Co., policy no. 668, June 19, 1850, Heard 2, S18, F3.

62. Suffolk Insurance Company (Boston), policy no. 10453, Jan. 6, 1849, Heard 2, S18, F3. The annual premium on this policy, calculated at 4.5 percent of insured value, was $562.50.

63. Edward Faucon (Canton) to Augustine Heard & Co. (Canton), portage and disbursement a/c of the *Frolic* 1850, Nov. 11, 1850, Heard 2, S18, F10.

Also see Edward Faucon, request for Augustine Heard & Co. (Canton) to pay Thomas Hunt for supplies, May 31, 1850, Heard 2, S18, F2.

64. Fong Awai (Canton) to R. B. Forbes, Esq., American consul (Canton), May 25, 1850; also Pow Akwai and Kong Asg (Canton) to R. B. Forbes, Esq., American consul (Canton), May 27, 1850, American Consular Records, National Archives, Washington, D.C.

65. Edward Faucon (Canton) to Augustine Heard & Co. (Canton), portage and disbursement a/c of the *Frolic* 1850, Nov. 11, 1850, Heard 2, S18, F10.

66. John Heard (Canton) to Augustine Heard (Boston), July 18, 1850, Heard 2, EM 5-3.

67. Edward Faucon (San Francisco) to Augustine Heard & Co. (Canton), Aug. 5, 1850, Heard 2, S18, F14. This important letter, describing the loss of the *Frolic*, covers the period from July 25 until Faucon's arrival in San Francisco on Aug. 4, 1850.

68. "Shipwreck and Loss of Life," *Daily Alta California* (San Francisco), Aug. 5, 1850.

69. Edward Faucon (San Francisco) to Augustine Heard & Co. (Canton), Aug. 5, 1850, Heard 2, S18, F14.

70. Edward Faucon, Charles Deutcher, and George Harrison (San Francisco), sworn statement describing the loss of the *Frolic*, notarized by Thomas Tilden, Aug. 9, 1850, Heard 2, S18, F16.

71. Edward Faucon (San Francisco) to Don Abel Stearns (Pueblo de los Angeles), Aug. 9, 1850, Stearns Collection, Huntington Library, San Marino, Calif.

72. John Dixwell (Boston) to Augustine Heard & Co. (Canton), Oct. 7, 1850, Heard 2, LV 12, F36. Dixwell notes having received a letter from J. C. Anthon dated Aug. 14, 1850, mentioning Faucon's departure to search for the *Frolic*.

73. John Heard (Canton) to Augustine Heard (Boston), Aug. 17, 1850, Heard 1, EM 5-3.

74. Nautical chart, West Coast, Albion, Calif., to Caspar, Calif. Scale 1:10,000. Catalog no. 2, panel N, 6th ed., Nov. 12, 1983, National Oceanic and Atmospheric Administration, Washington, D.C.

75. Stewart, p. 37.

76. Jerome B. Ford's diary of the trip is now lost. The details come to us as remembered by his son, Jerome Chester Ford, in 1933. See Bear and Stebbins, p. 9.

77. Heizer, *George Gibb's Journal*, p. 15.

78. Edward H. Faucon, "Journals of Voyages: 1850–1863," handwritten notebook, MHS.

79. John Dixwell (Boston) to Augustine Heard & Co. (Canton), Nov. 4, 1850, and Dec. 10, 1850, Heard 2, LV12, F36.

80. *China Mail* (Hong Kong), Oct. 3, 1850.

81. John Heard (Canton) to Augustine Heard (Boston), Oct. 25, 1850, Heard 1, EM 5-3.

82. Edward Faucon, "Journals of Voyages: 1850–1863," handwritten notebook, MHS.

83. John Heard (Canton) to Augustine Heard (Boston), Dec. 21, 1850, Heard 1, EM 5-3.

Conclusion

1. Inventory of the Estate of Daniel Weld, Probate Court of the County of Suffolk, July 20, 1852, Boston.

2. Dana, p. 508.

3. George Dixwell (New York) to John Heard (Boston?), extracts from a letter of July 22, 1855, Heard 1, EM 3-2.

4. George's brother Epes Dixwell was enjoying considerable success as headmaster of the Boston Latin School. In 1849, 25 of the 27-member graduating class were accepted to college; the new president of the school called it "an unprecedented event." Epes lived a comfortable life. In 1848, with financial help from George, he purchased a large house in Cambridge. In July 1849 he informed George—the recently retired opium merchant—"I am enjoying my vacation in my own house with all its conveniences . . . which I owe in great part to you" (Epes Dixwell [Cambridge] to George Dixwell [London?], July 30, 1849, Wigglesworth Family Papers, Ms. N-114, MHS).

Epes's comfort was threatened in 1851, when the city of Boston passed an ordinance requiring that all teachers in its public schools reside within the city limits. As Epes preferred Cambridge, he was obliged to resign after fifteen years as headmaster at Boston Latin. That same year, probably with financial assistance from John and George, Epes Dixwell had his own schoolhouse built in Boston on Boylston Street. He limited enrollment to 50 boys and charged an annual fee of $250 for each student. For twenty years, until his retirement in 1871, Dixwell's School remained among the best known and most successful college preparatory schools in New England. The first class to enter Dixwell's School included ten-year-old Oliver Wendell Holmes, Jr. Twenty-one years later, after surviving the Civil War and a bullet through his neck at Antietam, Holmes married Dixwell's eldest daughter, Fanny. For a discussion of Dixwell's School, Fanny Dixwell, and Oliver Wendell Holmes, Jr., see Bowen. For biographical information on Epes Dixwell see Sargent and Sargent.

5. Lockwood, pp. 5, 63.

6. Ibid., pp. 107–9. See also Edward W. Hanson, *The Heards of Ipswich, Massachusetts*, 1986, p. 153. This manuscript is on file at the New England Historical Genealogical Society Library in Boston.

7. Waters, p. 47.

8. Ironically, it had been the *Ernani*'s arrival in China that effectively ended the *Frolic*'s career as an opium clipper. In 1849, while John Heard had been considering a Mr. Parker's offer to buy the *Frolic*, Parker had purchased the *Ernani* instead—a newer, sleeker, and much larger vessel. John Heard responded to the canceled order by dispatching the aging *Frolic* to California, on what was to be her final voyage.

9. Until 1850 the Gardners had built at least three vessels per year, mostly small brigs, barks, and schooners, as well as the occasional steamer. After that year, the Gardners rarely produced more than one vessel annually, but most of these were larger than 1,000 tons.

10. For a discussion of the rise and decline of the "clipper era" in Baltimore, and a partial listing of the Gardner Brothers' vessels, see Fairburn, pp. 2750–52.

11. Notice of death of George W. Gardner, *Baltimore Sun*, Aug. 25, 1857, p. 1.

12. Notice of death of William Gardner, *Baltimore Sun*, Dec. 3, 1860, p. 1.

13. For a discussion of the Forbes brothers' role in establishing a "volunteer navy" and mention of Captain Faucon commanding the *Fearnot*, see S. Forbes, pp. 227–28.

14. For the *Fearnot*'s log, see Edward H. Faucon, "Journals of Voyages: 1850–1863," handwritten notebook, MHS. For Faucon's naval record see National Archives, Record Group 24, Washington, D.C. See also Callahan, p. 190.

15. Acting Volunteer Lieutenant E. H. Faucon (USS *Montgomery*) to Acting Rear Admiral S. P. Lee, Feb. 16, 1864, *Official Records of the Union and Confederate Navies in the War of the Rebellion* (hereafter referred to as *ORN*), U.S. Printing Office, Washington, D.C., 1894–1927, series 1, vol. 9, pp. 486–87.

16. Acting Volunteer Lieutenant E. H. Faucon (USS *Montgomery*) to Navy Secretary Gideon Welles (Washington, D.C.), Oct. 10, 1864, *ORN*, series 1, vol. 10, pp. 548–49.

17. Lieutenant Commander D. L. Braine (USS *Pequot*) to Navy Secretary Gideon Welles (Washington, D.C.), Nov. 9, 1864, *ORN*, series 1, vol. 10, pp. 550–51.

18. Waters, p. 51.

19. The following analysis of the decline of Augustine Heard & Co. is taken from Lockwood, pp. 108–9.

20. Preston, pp. 201–2.

21. Frederick Douglass, "The Editor's Visit to the Old Ship-yard in Baltimore," *New National Era* (Washington, D.C.), July 6, 1871.

22. *Dictionary of American Biography* (New York: Scribner's, 1959), vol. 3, pp. 60–61.

23. Letter of sympathy from Edward H. Faucon (Milton, Mass.) to Rich-

ard H. Dana III, following the death of his father, Jan. 9, 1882, Dana Family Papers, MHS.

24. Obituary of George B. Dixwell, *Boston Transcript*, Apr. 11, 1885.

25. Obituary of Captain Edward H. Faucon, *Milton (Mass.) News*, May 26, 1894.

26. Palmer, p. 398.

27. By the early 1930s, Jerome Chester Ford had come to believe that both the sword found by his father and the Kelley family's bolts of silk had come not from the wreck at Caspar visited by his father in 1851 but from the mysterious "other" vessel. In fact, he believed that the sword had been shipped by a theatrical company as a prop! (Alice Earl Wilder, Apr. 15, 1963, notes on file at the Kelley House Museum, Mendocino, Calif.) In 1933, when his niece, Alice Earl Wilder, asked the old man about Daisy Kelley McCallum's story that her family's silks had come from the wreck at Caspar, Ford dismissed it as wrong. "Why say anything about it," he remarked; "she has just mixed up the wrecks." (Alice Earl Wilder to Otis R. Johnson [San Francisco], Feb. 24, 1949, letter on file at the Kelley House Museum, Mendocino, Calif.)

28. Ryder, p. 52.

29. Palmer, pp. 398–99.

30. Bear and Stebbins, p. 9.

31. Catherine W. Faucon (Milton, Mass.) to Julius H. Tuttle, librarian, Massachusetts Historical Society (Boston), Oct. 5, 1928, MHS.

32. Catherine W. Faucon, Last Will and Testament, Apr. 16, 1941, Suffolk County Probate Court, Boston. See also the inventory and appraisal of Catherine Faucon's estate, filed Apr. 2, 1943, at the Suffolk County Probate Court. See also a newspaper article, "The Will of Miss C. W. Faucon," *Milton (Mass.) Record*, Dec. 12, 1942.

Epilogue

1. The taped interviews were open-ended. I explained to the divers that their stories were an integral part of the *Frolic* project and their opinions regarding the management of offshore cultural resources needed to be expressed. I asked each diver to tell his life story, leading up to his diving the *Frolic*. Next, I asked each for a detailed description of his exploits on the *Frolic*. Finally, I asked each man to suggest ways that professional archaeologists and wreck divers could work together.

2. The local microbrewery Everett visited was Hopland's Mendocino Brewing Company. Sitting at the bar over a Red Tail Ale, he related the entire story of the *Frolic*—complete with the 6,108 bottles of Edinburgh ale she had been carrying when she was wrecked. Richard's audience included the brewmaster's

assistant, who countered with a story of his own. A sealed bottle of beer over a hundred years old had been brought up from a wreck at the bottom of the English Channel, and a fellow brewmaster had salvaged enough yeast from it to reconstruct a seemingly extinct species of beer. Hopefully, he asked Richard if any intact bottles had been brought up from the *Frolic*.

To everyone's regret, all of the long-necked green bottles that had held the *Frolic*'s cargo of Edinburgh ale had been broken on the rocks off Caspar along with the *Frolic* herself. But once they heard the *Frolic*'s story, the staff of the Mendocino Brewing Company were delighted to set about producing an approximate replica. They agreed to release at least 700 cases of Scotch ale annually on the July 25 anniversary of the *Frolic* shipwreck. The label featured a drawing of the *Frolic* herself sailing across a map of the Pacific Rim. One dollar for each bottle of Frolic Shipwreck Ale sold would be contributed to a fund to support the study, curation, and exhibition of the growing collection in the *Frolic* Repository.

3. Mark Howland Rawitsch, "Journey of the *Frolic*: The Story of the Story," Mendocino County Museum Grassroots History Publication No. 10. Published in cooperation with the Mendocino College Community Extension.

Appendix B

1. Wood, pp. 89–90.

2. Chapelle, *Baltimore Clipper*, pp. 114–16.

3. N. de la Croix, Surveyor of Shipping (Whampoa), Sept. 10, 1847, and March 16, 1849, Heard 2, S18, F1.

4. The *Frolic*'s "round tuck" is noted on the master carpenter's certificate, whereas her "square stern" is listed on her federal registry, both in the National Archives, Record Group 41, Washington, D.C.

5. John Dixwell (Boston) to Augustine Heard & Co. (Canton), Apr. 20, 1846, Heard 2, LV12, F34.

6. Edward Faucon (Hong Kong) to Augustine Heard & Co. (Canton), Oct. 22, 1849, Heard 2, S18, F14.

7. John Dixwell, account of costs for building and outfitting the *Frolic*, Heard 2, S18, F16, Jan. 11, 1845.

8. Campbell, pp. 43–44.

Appendix C

1. John Dixwell, account of costs for building and outfitting the *Frolic*, Heard 2, S18, F16, Jan. 11, 1845.

Bibliography

Aberigh-Mackay, G. R. *The Chiefs of Central India,* vol. 1. Calcutta: Thacker, Spink, 1878.

Bear, Dorothy, and Beth Stebbins. *Mendocino: Book Two.* Mendocino, Calif.: Gull Press, 1977.

Beeching, Jack. *The Chinese Opium Wars.* London: Hutchinson, 1975.

Bourne, M. Florence. "Thomas Kemp, Shipbuilder, and His Home, Wades Point." *Maryland Historical Magazine* 49 (1954): 271–89.

Bowen, Catherine Drinker. *Yankee from Olympus: Justice Holmes and His Family.* Boston: Little, Brown, 1944.

Callahan, Edward W., ed. *List of Officers of the Navy of the United States and of the Marine Corps from 1775–1900.* New York: L. R. Hamersly, 1901.

Campbell, George F. *China Tea Clippers.* New York: David McKay, 1974.

Chapelle, Howard I. *The Baltimore Clipper: Its Origin and Development.* 1930. Reprint, New York: Dover Publications, 1988.

———. *The Search for Speed Under Sail, 1700–1855.* London: George Allen & Unwin, 1968.

Chesneaux, Jean, Marianne Bastid, and Marie-Claire Bergere. *China: From the Opium Wars to the 1911 Revolution.* New York: Pantheon, 1976.

Cranwell, John, and William Crane. *Men of Marque: A History of Private Armed Vessels out of Baltimore During the War of 1812.* New York: Norton, 1940.

Dana, Richard Henry, Jr. *Two Years Before the Mast: A Personal Narrative.* 1840. Reprint, Cambridge, Mass.: Riverside Press, 1911.

Douglass, Frederick. *Life and Times of Frederick Douglass.* Rev. ed., 1892. Reprint, London: Collier-Macmillan, 1962.

————. *Narrative of the Life of an American Slave*, ed. Benjamin Quarles. Cambridge, Mass.: Harvard University Press, 1967.

Downs, Jacques M. "American Merchants in the China Opium Trade, 1800–1840." *Business History Review* 42, no. 4 (1968): 418–42.

Dulles, Foster Rhea. *The Old China Trade*. Cambridge, Mass.: Riverside Press, 1930.

Elliot, A. W. *The Rules and Practice of the Bombay Custom House*. Bombay: American Mission Press, 1843.

Everett, Edward F. *Genealogy of the Everett Family*. Boston: Henry W. Dutton, 1860.

Fairburn, William A. *Merchant Sail*. Center Lovell, Maine: Fairburn Marine Educational Foundation, 1945–55.

Fay, Peter Ward. *The Opium War: 1840–1842*. New York: Norton, 1976.

Forbes, Robert Bennet. *Personal Reminiscences*. Boston, 1882.

————. *Remarks on China and the China Trade*. Boston: Samuel N. Dickinson, 1844.

Forbes, Sarah Hughes, ed. *Letters and Recollections of John Murray Forbes*. Boston: Houghton Mifflin, 1900.

Fritzsche, Bruno. "On Liberal Terms: The Boston Hide Merchants of California." *Business History Review* 42, no. 4 (1968): 467–81.

Greenberg, Michael. *British Trade and the Opening of China, 1800–1842*. Cambridge: Cambridge University Press, 1951.

Griffin, Charles C. "Privateering from Baltimore During the Spanish American Wars of Independence." *Maryland Historical Magazine* 35 (1940): 1–25.

Hammond, George P., ed. *The Larkin Papers: Personal, Business, and Official Correspondence of Thomas Oliver Larkin, Merchant and United States Consul in California*. 10 vols. Berkeley: University of California Press, 1951–68.

Hao Yen-p'ing. *The Commercial Revolution in Nineteenth Century China: The Rise of Sino-Western Mercantile Capitalism*. Berkeley: University of California Press, 1986.

Hawgood, John A., ed. *First and Last Consul: Thomas Oliver Larkin and the Americanization of California*. San Marino, Calif: Huntington Library, 1962.

Heizer, Robert F. "The Direct Historical Approach in California Archaeology." *American Antiquity* 7, no. 2 (1941): 98–122.

————, ed. *George Gibb's Journal of Redick McKee's Expedition Through Northwestern California in 1851*. Archaeological Research Facility, Department of Anthropology. Berkeley: University of California, 1972.

Hicks, John, George Mowry, and Robert Burke. *The Federal Union: A History of the United States to 1877*. Boston: Houghton Mifflin, 1964.

Hidy, Ralph W. *The House of Baring in American Trade and Finance: English*

Merchant Bankers at Work, 1763–1861. Cambridge: Harvard University Press, 1949.

Impey, Elijah. *A Report on the Cultivation, Preparation, and Adulteration of Malwa Opium*. Bombay, 1848.

Keith, Robert C. *Baltimore Harbor: A Picture History*. Rev. ed. Baltimore: Ocean World Publishing Co., 1988.

Layton, Thomas N. *Western Pomo Prehistory: Excavations at Albion Head, Nightbirds' Retreat, and Three Chop Village, Mendocino County, California*. Institute of Archaeology, Monograph 32. Los Angeles: University of California, 1991.

LeFevour, Edward. *Western Enterprise in Late Ch'ing China: A Selective Survey of Jardine, Matheson & Company's Operations, 1842–1895*. Harvard University East Asian Monograph No. 26. Cambridge, 1970.

Lockwood, Stephen C. *Augustine Heard and Company, 1858–1862, American Merchants in China*. Cambridge: Harvard University Press, 1971.

Lubbock, Basil. *The Opium Clippers*. Glasgow: Brown, Son & Ferguson, 1933.

Morison, Samuel Eliot. *The Maritime History of Massachusetts: 1783–1860*. Boston: Houghton Mifflin, 1961.

Nunis, Doyce B., ed. *The California Diary of Faxon Dean Atherton: 1836–1839*. San Francisco: California Historical Society, 1964.

Ogden, Adele. "Boston Hide Droghers Along California Shores." *Quarterly of the California Historical Society* 8, no. 4 (1929): 289–305.

Olson, Sherry H. *Baltimore: The Building of an American City*. Baltimore: Johns Hopkins University Press, 1980.

Owen, David E. *British Opium Policy in China and India*. New Haven: Yale University Press, 1934.

Palmer, Lyman L. *History of Mendocino County, California*. San Francisco: Alley, Bowen, 1880.

Preston, Dickson J. *Young Frederick Douglass: The Maryland Years*. Baltimore: Johns Hopkins University Press, 1980.

Robinson, Ralph J. "The Baltimore Clipper Story, part 3, The Spanish American Wars of Liberation." *Baltimore Magazine* (July 1956).

Ruckert, Norman G. *The Fells Point Story*. Baltimore: Bodine, 1976.

Ryder, David Warren. *Memories of the Mendocino Coast*. San Francisco, 1948.

Sargent, Emma W., and Charles S. Sargent. *Epes Dixwell of Gloucester and His Descendants*. Boston: Houghton Mifflin, 1923.

Scharf, J. Thomas. *History of Baltimore City and County*. 1887. Reprint, Baltimore: Regional Publishing, 1971.

———. *History of Maryland*. 1879. Reprint, Hatboro, Pa.: Tradition Press, 1967.

Shangraw, Clarence, and Edward P. Von der Porten. *The Drake and Cermeño Expeditions' Chinese Porcelains at Drakes Bay, California, 1579 and 1595.* Santa Rosa, Calif: Santa Rosa Junior College and the Drake Navigators Guild, 1981.

Smith, Melbourne. "A Distinctive American Creation . . . The Baltimore Clipper." *Sea History Magazine* (Summer 1979): 16–18.

Spear, John R. "Tales of Forgotten Slavers," *Public Ledger* (Baltimore), Jan. 1903.

Stewart, Omer C. *Notes on Pomo Ethnogeography.* University of California Publications in American Archaeology and Ethnology, vol. 40, no. 2. Berkeley, 1943.

Strong, William Duncan. "From History to Prehistory in the Northern Great Plains." *Smithsonian Miscellaneous Collections*, vol. 100, pp. 353–94. Washington, D.C., 1940.

U.S. House of Representatives. *Search and Seizure of American Vessels on Coast of Africa, &c.*, Message from the President of the United States, M. Van Buren, 26th Congress, 2d session, Mar. 3, 1841, H. Doc. 115.

Waters, Thomas Franklin. *Augustine Heard and His Friends.* Ipswich, Mass.: Ipswich Historical Society, 1916.

Wood, Virginia S. *Live Oaking: Southern Timber for Tall Ships.* Boston: Northeastern University Press, 1981.

Works Progress Administration. *Alphabetical List of Ship Registers, District of Boston, Massachusetts: Compiled by the National Archive Project and Division of Women's and Professional Projects.* Boston, 1939.

Index

In this index an "f" after a number indicates a separate reference on the next page, and an "ff" indicates separate references on the next two pages. A continuous discussion over two or more pages is indicated by a span of page numbers, e.g., "57–59." *Passim* is used for a cluster of references in close but not consecutive sequence.

Library of Congress Cataloging-in-Publication Data

Layton, Thomas N.
  The voyage of the 'Frolic' : New England merchants and the opium
trade / Thomas N. Layton.
     p.   cm.
  Includes bibliographical references and index.
  ISBN 0-8047-2909-3 (cl.) : ISBN 0-8047-3849-1 (pbk.)
    1. Shipwreck—California—Mendocino County—History—19th
century.   2. Frolic (Brig)   3. Mendocino County (Calif.)—
Antiquities.   4. Excavations (Archaeology)—California—Mendocino
County.   5. United States—Commerce—China.   6. China—Commerce—
United States.   7. Pomo Indians—California—Mendocino County—
History—19th century.   8. Opium trade—United States—
History—19th century.   I. Title.
F868.M5L39   1997
979.4'1501—dc21   96-44320
                                                                    CIP

(∞) This book is printed on acid-free, recycled paper.

Original printing 1997
Last figure below indicates year of this printing:
06   05   04   03   02   01   00   99